Hal Painter's heartbreaking fight to regain custody of his little boy, Mark, has been reported in *Life, McCall's* and other national magazines. Thousands of sympathetic parents have written him to express their outrage and dismay at a court ruling that has become a *cause celebre* in domestic law.

In that ruling, an Iowa court declared Hal Painter an unfit guardian for his own son because he was "unconventional, arty, bohemian and probably intellectually stimulating," "an agnostic if not an atheist," and a man who "read a lot of Zen Buddhism."

Now Hal Painter tells of the tragic accident that took the life of his wife and little girl, of his attempt to rebuild a shattered life, and of the frustrating and seemingly endless struggle to win back his own boy. *Mark, I Love You* is the book he wrote when all hope seemed gone. It is a truly disturbing account of the blindness of the law, and a deeply moving story of a father's love.

> "A human tragedy out of Dickens, Dreiser and our own nineteen-sixties . . . the implications of this single human encounter with respectable America are frightening."—*New York Times*

Mark, I Love You

Hal Painter

BALLANTINE BOOKS • NEW YORK

Epilogue reprinted by permission from the March 1969 issue of *Good Housekeeping* magazine.

Library of Congress Catalog Card Number: 67-20797

This edition published by arrangement with Simon and Schuster.

First Printing: April, 1969

Printed in the United States of America

BALLANTINE BOOKS, INC.
101 Fifth Avenue, New York, N. Y. 10003

To Mark
To Jeanne,
To Janet,
And to my wife, Marylyn.

CONTENTS

PART ONE

Four Beans in the Walden Pot

1

IN THE BEGINNING there was Mark and Jeanne and Janet. And in the beginning, as in all beginnings, was written the end—not the end of all things for all time but an end nonetheless to a family of four. There were my son and daughter and wife and I, and then two of these were one day suddenly gone, leaving two. With these who remained, my son and I, I sought a new beginning.

Jeanne, twenty-nine; Janet, almost three; Mark, well over four; myself, thirty. The four of us lived in a white house on the side of a hill so steep that the student apartment house a few doors down—with its stained and weathered shingles, rattan furniture, books, pennants and tennis rackets—sagged in back and threatened to become an unexpected oddity in the city park of Pullman below.

On any weekday morning, at about eight o'clock, the narrow street in front of our house proved conclusively what all the neighbors said about it: it was much too narrow for the hundreds of cars bound that hour for the university at the top of the hill. Several of our neighbors —not the younger but the older, more practical ones—had suggested that the city cut down the big maples and add another lane.

When I worked at the university as an editor in one of the publishing departments, I usually walked to work. It was about a half mile, uphill most of the way, to my office, and I enjoyed the long walk under the big maples. Often I looked forward to the few seconds it took to pass the tiny Chinese grocery about half a block above our house. I would look at its locked front door, with a cardboard sign that said OPEN AT 11 (it really didn't open till 11:15 or 11:30), and somehow delight in the thought that the proprietor—a roly-poly, good-humored Chinese with a handsome family—was sound asleep in the big apartment under the store, in this cool hour of the morning when almost everyone else in town was trudging to work, by foot or by car, to the university.

His business, like most others in town, owed its modest existence to the "university people," as most of the population was called by those who owned the dozens of small shops, none of them very big, along the main street that skirted the seven hills over which the town unrolled like a Flemish village by Brueghel.

A small pamphlet issued to newcomers by the local chamber of commerce made note that Rome too was a city of seven hills, but there was little that was Rome-like in our town, nothing splendid, nothing grand.

On the highest hill, rearing hardly five hundred feet into the eastern Washington sky, sat The University, a curiously Gothic assemblage in red brick and stone, with a few modern, squarish dormitories that seemed to intrude. At the foot of the hill, on the town side, was a big heating plant that spewed smoke through a huge chimney and gave you the feeling that the university was a factory.

When the university was founded in the 1890s, in the heart of the great wheat belt that brought eastern Washington most of its fame and fortune, its purpose was to produce farmers first and then civil engineers. In recent years the university has taken on the coloration of a liberal-arts school, and part of my job as editor and writer was to help change the image from farm school to sophisticated university, to convince prospective students that the university had entered the new era of science and the arts and that the sowing of seed was now to be a thing of the mind. It was a task I found difficult.

When the university-bound traffic subsided, about nine o'clock, the street in front of our house became a place of quiet charm and quaint old houses. A perennial housing shortage made the price of these old houses, with their ancient plumbing, sagging floors, cubicle rooms and sometimes precipitate shingles, seem outrageously high; but it was their charm and age you were willing to pay for, and you could make do with the rest.

Jeanne and I settled for a two-story duplex that fell somewhere between the ancient and the modern. It was to be both home and enterprise, though more home than business endeavor. As for the business end, we were fortunate in having been found by a young college professor and his pregnant wife, who were desperate for a place to live. Jeanne and I were at the time desperate for new friends. In the months to come, there would be no business like this business; our clients became our best friends, and it was to be a profound and lasting relationship.

It was a home and enterprise that we had launched with a gift to Jeanne of $3,000 in stocks from her father. I had known nothing about the stocks until one day Jeanne and I were sitting in our tiny rented apartment and speculating on all the splendid possibilities of home ownership: romping room for Mark and Janet, a place to pound nails and rearrange walls whenever the spirit moved us, a certain pride, a feeling of independence, and the knowledge that we might be creating an estate, whatever that is.

Jeanne told me that all this was possible: her father had a few months before given her enough for a sizable down payment. She had wanted it to be a surprise, she explained. Besides, she liked the new town; it appealed to her so much more than the other towns we had lived in, with the exception of Anchorage, which, it seemed, we had left eons ago.

It puzzled me that she had not told me about the stock until now, and I wondered why her father and mother had not mentioned it to me. But I accepted Jeanne's explanation. After all, it was a boon and a pleasant surprise, and it came at a time when it could be put to pleasant use. Years later I would learn why Jeanne's parents had kept the gift a secret, as well as the answers to so many puzzling things about the relationship between Jeanne's parents and me. They too would be a surprise; but they would not be a boon, and they would not be pleasant.

But none of this was on Jeanne's and my mind when we decided to invest her father's gift in the duplex. In the intangible matters of mind and spirit Jeanne and I occupied the same ground. But in her ideal world she included the moneyed, practical world—a world I often ignore, in hope that there is at least a village somewhere where things are altogether different.

In the keystone-shaped back yard of our new house, that village had its beginnings.

The village began with Mark and Janet; a few locust trees that made for too much sweeping but kept the house reasonably cool in the long, hot summer; a wooden bench; a fire ring—Wagnerian in the spring—of flag lilies; a pile of wood to split in the winter; a rusty tricycle; Mark's rubber ball-peen hammer, which had made its modest dent on almost everything; and such assorted possessions as Mark and Janet could scatter as quickly as they could muster and which made for a lawn-sung discord of tin cans, broken wooden ducks, pieces of string, a pink stuffed elephant that badly needed a bath, and a little wooden man who hammered on a drum when you pulled him by a string, except that one of his wheels was missing.

This was the fragment of the village which I had dreamed of years ago: a wooded place by the sea, with paths leading from the backs of the rustic houses to steep mountains of tall trees, rock and snow, where wild animals—bear, caribou, sheep and goat—were both seen and unseen, and where, farther back, there were mysterious mountains peopled by snow-country nomads about whom were heard strange tales of pagan rites in caves of ice, witchcraft, and unreasonable powers over nature.

The village people were like the Danes I had read about who had settled in Iceland in the early part of the century. And it was not without some imagination on my part that they became earnest, perpetually happy people, with a keen sense of humor, who spent long hours reading Shakespeare, Ibsen, Strindberg and, since, Camus, Nabokov, Thurber, Dickens, and even Henry Miller—in front of the winter fire. They raised happy children with the sense of freedom afforded by wide spaces and understanding parents, who managed to find dignity in working the land and fishing the sea, wrote poems, books and music, and painted pictures a bit like Paul Klee, Miro, Max Ernst and Andrew Wyeth. They laughed a lot at big parties, drank some, spoke uninhibitedly, relished the marriage bed, had few taboos, thumbed their noses at anything resembling bureaucracy and repression, ate well, and maintained an amazing anarchy, a loose but efficient government founded on compassion. They had all the human faults and foibles but doted not too long on them and had within a realistic melancholy, knowing that it would all end when there would be too many of them, when the physical compression of too many bodies would rob them of space and its freedoms and force the turning in of the mind, into the microcosm, for new but uneasy freedoms.

The half-parcel village of my backyard was a small

start, more of the microcosm than of that expansive place by the sea, but for the time it did nicely. It had two happy children, my wife and me, and privacy.

The one path led down the hill, to the city swimming pool and a small park full of tall trees, swings and slides, and lots of grass. The only nomads within its depths were the neighborhood children who played hide-and-seek behind the trees; the only wild animals were the barking dogs which drove Janet into my arms and sent Mark running at them with glorious shouts.

Pagan rites were conducted over portable barbecues in the summer, and no one had any power over the weather, especially in the winter when the snow indelibly asserted its blanket authority over all.

The sea and its fish were sadly missing, but the swimming pool, when it was open, had a certain air about it. The only mountain was the one I trudged to work each morning, and that was a bore; but it was said that the university's steep hills made for shapely legs on the coeds, and so there was some solace in hiking up the hill behind a girl in her senior year of climbing.

Upstairs were John and Carol and the baby, Sean—yet to be born but very much in front of his time and kicking hard at his mother's ribs. John had just got his Ph.D. from the University of California at Berkeley and had come north for his first teaching job. His degree was in thermodynamics, and his specialty was the mystique of bubbles and the strange way they have of disrupting the cooling systems of such things as atomic reactors. His was a very serious and complex pursuit, but he wore his doctor's robes casually. Tall, nervous, full of the devil, brilliant, witty and of immense compassion, he became a delightful and frequent companion.

I first became acquainted with Carol when one afternoon I went upstairs to help in some small matter about the apartment. She sat in a rattan chair, reading a book of ancient music and wearing a plastic hair drier bellowed with air pushed through a plastic pipe. Though normally slim and nicely figured, she was now bulging in front and looked like a Turkish sultan having a recording of *Scheherazade* piped into his turban. She was a little embarrassed by my intrusion but overcame it with sparkling good humor and the offer of a glass of sherry in exchange for whatever it was I had to do about the living-room heating vent. John was in the next room making pleasant tinkling sounds with medieval finger cymbals.

My asking about the sound in the next room brought a pleasant dissertation by Carol on Renaissance music, in which both she and John were expert. In Berkeley they had sung with a madrigal choir of some professional status and had cut a couple of records. Within the next few minutes I was introduced to the recorder, an ancient cross between flute and clarinet. They had three and I was invited to play one.

Carol and I started with something easy. My childhood training in the clarinet enabled me to finger at least half the notes, while Carol played harmony to my stuttering melody.

Entranced by the noise, John came in and accompanied us with the cymbals. All the toodle-oo and ting-ting must have carried to the basement by way of the heating vent, where Jeanne, Mark and Janet were engrossed in sorting laundry—Mark and Janet peripherally. Jeanne came upstairs, knocked on the screen door, was invited in, and found John standing on a chair in order to see the music stand otherwise obscured by Carol's Turkish-sultan's hat with its side-pack blower, while all of us made music that even in Renaissance times might have sounded Stone Age—mostly because of me.

Jeanne was followed by Janet and Mark, who didn't bother to knock and came running into the living room. Janet stopped short at the door, full of surprise and wonder, and stood transfixed and making little mouths. To Mark the scene was an invitation. He put both hands on the floor and did some sort of dance with his legs. One leg went up and then the other. Then both went up, and his dance turned into a somersault. His next dance was with his head wedged safely in one corner of the room.

Jeanne laughed, and she laughed until there were tears

in her eyes. It was a funny and wonderful scene and it meant a great deal to her. It meant a great deal to both of us, for it was the discovery of new friends, in a new house, in a new town.

The outlook was splendid, but it hadn't always been this way. It seemed that now we had arrived at a high point in our lives. The adventures, the near tragedies, the uncertainties and the wanderings of the years past seemed gone and done with.

In the next few months it was to be even better: all the things we had hoped for would seem to come true. Life-long ambitions would seem to be fulfilled, Mark and Janet's future would seem sound and secure, and there seemed to be little more that we could ask for, other than for the small things we could surely do without. It wouldn't be perfect; it wouldn't be complete. It wouldn't be and it couldn't be. But we would be somewhere along the way.

But before the year was out I would look back in disbelief. Jeanne and Janet would die in a car crash, and our life here would end as simply and swiftly as that, without notice, without warning, leaving just Mark and me. And not long after that Jeanne's parents would, in an Iowa court, try to take my son from me.

None of these things seemed possible now. Nor did they ever seem possible, not now, not from the beginning, not ever.

2

JEANNE'S ARRIVAL in Anchorage was inconspicuously heralded in the managing editor's daily assignment book. He matter-of-factly noted that a new girl would be arriving in a week to take over the society desk —and he further noted, somewhat wryly, that her father was the well-to-do owner of an Iowa country newspaper, no doubt to tantalize some of us bachelors.

Myself, I couldn't have cared less that the daughter of a well-to-do Iowa newspaper owner was coming. Though it might offer the possibility of fulfilling the dream of at least a couple of the aspiring young would-be newspaper owners I had come across in my short newspaper career, the thought of one day falling heir to an Iowa country weekly was the antithesis of all I had come to Alaska for.

I had never been there, but I pictured Iowa as a flat, stolid expanse inhabited by Grant Wood farmers and their wives—a picture I was to retain, if updated a bit, the few times I would visit the state. I wondered what the new girl would be like. Would she be attractive, would she like me, would I like her? Or would she be an Iowa plod's plodding daughter come to Alaska on a lark, by special arrangement by her father?

I didn't give the matter much thought and stuck more or less to my own plans of breaking away from the newspaper and going north to live with the Eskimos. I was living in a surplus Army tent at the time, at the edge of the city, with a packing-crate desk and a Yukon stove. When I could stand the loneliness, I sat at my desk writing a fantasy titled "Babes in Boobyland," a veiled, indefinite critique of the civilization I fancied I had left behind.

My own trek north to Alaska had been the culmination of a slow-burning dream that perhaps began in my childhood with Jack London's tales of the wild North, which I had sustained during four years in the Navy and which came to a roaring Sam Magee flame when I became bored and disenchanted with my third year of college in San Francisco.

I had answered a trade-journal ad for a reporter in Anchorage, padded my credentials with more experience than I had (six months' reporting on a small daily in Washington State was the best I could offer, had I told the truth), reconvinced myself that I had left college and pursued a newspaper job to learn to write and break away from a poke-along and effete academia, and talked a journeyman newspaper friend into telling my prospective Alaska editor I was "one hell of a good feature writer." The Alaska newspaper job, to my surprise, came through. I sold everything I had to get there, including my camera and typewriter. I arrived with $50, an Army ski parka I had bought in Hawaii, and a double-barreled shotgun. In a few months, I imagined, I would use this steppingstone for a grand leap into the Artic and a life of hunting, exploring, and writing among the natives.

My meeting Jeanne changed all this. It was perhaps the meeting of two half-baked primitives, though Jeanne's half-baked side had a finer finish than mine.

I was pleased to discover that Jeanne was apparently not the plodding daughter. There was something enigmatic, charming, Pan-like in her manner, though it took me awhile to see through the veil of reserve she wore. Some of my newspaper friends seemed to think that she worked too diligently at being a proper society editor, not knowing that she thought society writing was a tedious bore but stuck to it out of a sense of duty. It wasn't like her to be cute and chatty in the office. She didn't flirt and tease but stuck doggedly to her work, of which there was more than an abundance.

Her would-be office romancers found her too earnest and businesslike and soon turned their attentions to the new girl in advertising, a giddy redhead who answered every flirtation. This pleased me, for being a bit reserved myself, I was afraid Jeanne would take a shine to someone before I had a chance.

Her eyes intrigued me, and so did her somewhat aloof manner. She wore glasses, but they failed to conceal eyes that were extraordinarily large and liquid and overwhelmingly brown. Something warm, mysterious, romantic and slightly wild lay within. I fancied I had discovered an interesting and unusual girl who led a secret and adventurous life. It took me a week to overcome my shyness, but I finally asked her for a date.

Our first date was to have a drink at the Malemute Saloon, of Robert W. Service fame, though neither Robert

W. Service nor Dangerous Dan Magrew had ever been there. Jeanne didn't like whiskey, had gagged on her first taste of it, but drank a strong Bourbon and water, her second taste of it, with a smile that concealed a queasy stomach. She drank it all.

We sat in a dark corner, in cane-back chairs with red plush bottoms, under a Victorian kerosene lamp fitted with an amber light bulb and a red glass shade. Jeanne said she had seen the same lamp for sale at one of the local department stores.

I asked her if she'd read the poems of Robert W. Service, and was she familiar with his Dangerous Dan Magrew. She told me she had read it and wasn't much impressed, that she really preferred reading history, because there was more truth to it and, in the end, more romance.

So we talked about Alaska and what it meant to her. She wasn't quite sure, she said; she found it exciting but puzzling.

What had brought her to Alaska? She wasn't quite sure, except that on the night of her graduation from Grinnell College, deep in the heart of Iowa, she had got a phone call from Juneau offering her a job—one of the many she had applied for. She wanted to be a reporter, but the thrill of flying three thousand miles to Alaska overcame the thought that a clerking job in a newspaper advertising department was less than her calling.

Previously she had given some thought to going to Greece, though God knew how in the world she would arrange it. The idea had been inspired by her studies of the classical world in her last semester at Grinnell. Her last year of college had bored her to the point of wanting to give up and strike out on her own.

For a time she held a job on an Iowa newspaper, with the thought of becoming a female Bruce Catton and "doing for the Army of the West"—so she wrote in her diary—"what Catton did for the Army of the Potomac." Strangely, it was the history of Civil War naval operations on the Mississippi that most intrigued her.

But at this point other things came into her life. Men,

for instance. There was a "golden voiced" young man from New Zealand who inspired her with thoughts of going to Australia. And there were a couple of fresh-out-of-college boys whom she found nice but a bit too giddy to take seriously, despite their flattering attentions. Only once did thoughts of marriage come so close as to trouble her.

She became infatuated with a man thirteen years her senior, whom she found balding, unattractive but full of wonderfully wild schemes and an immense imagination, and supposed it was the attraction of an opposite. Had she known him longer, she decided in the end, she might have "learned to gamble without being nervous." But as it was, she was glad he didn't propose—sorry, too—and thus was both relieved and disappointed when she returned to school. She had been chaste but romantically adventurous, kept her head but lost her emotions to thoughts of love, sex, and what it was to be a woman.

When she returned to Grinnell, it was the future that possessed most of her thoughts. She was indifferent to high grades, but never let them fall low enough to lose her scholarship. She worried that her father and mother expected more of her.

Studies of the Far East, Greece and Old England held her attention, and she decided that the history of her own times did not because "it lacked the romance of old." And then she was taken with a marvelous realization: her favorite subjects were the "wild Welsh and the Scots. I must be a primitive myself," she decided, "for I most enjoy thinking about savages."

Her romantic attachment to the Welsh and the Scots was a bit odd, considering that she had grown up in Iowa, where she had been taught, by her parents and by tradition, to think of Iowa's contingent of Celts as "those shanty Irish," who lived on the other side of the ruts in the road, as it were, and showed little consideration for Iowa respectability by farming in the most unlikely places, caring little that their front porches sagged, that their houses went unpainted, and not particularly caring what other Iowans thought.

As if to prove her affinity, Jeanne dressed as a boy and broke into an exclusively men's dinner and observed a collegiate ritual that since time and Grinnell began was performed for and by men, for men and men only. She called it the most entertaining act of her college career and was quite pleased with herself.

This was the woman, girl, and Pan I met in Anchorage, who had become disgusted with mere clerking on a Juneau newspaper and trekked farther north to fake it as a society editor but did such a good job the editor had to hire two girls to replace her when she left.

After our first date at the Malemute Saloon, we started going to dinner often. I began to feel I was getting to know her, and it made me all the more intrigued.

When we got better acquainted, Jeanne introduced me to her square-dance friends. The dances were at the YMCA, where Jeanne had gone to meet friends when she had first come to town. I didn't like square dancing, but I went anyway. It gave me a chance to spend more time with Jeanne.

I took her on long rides in a Ford pickup truck that often had to be pushed to get it started when the weather turned cold, and most of our dates were in the winter. The right window was missing and I had replaced it with cardboard and tape that did little to keep out the cold. Sometimes it was ten below when we would take a leisurely drive down Turnagain Arm; it had to be leisurely, to keep the truck from skidding on the ice and plunging over the cliff and into the ice-choked sea. Jeanne, in mittens, parka and snowboots, never complained. She even helped me push the truck to get it started.

We went snowshoeing on winter evenings when the setting sun turned the snow red. I taught Jeanne to shoot a pistol, and we would drive down Cook Inlet and shoot at tin cans and bottles in the water. We went ice skating on Spenard Lake and at the city ice rink. We had steak dinners, after a day of hiking, in Jeanne's basement apartment, sat on the couch and talked about Alaska. More and more we began to talk about what Alaska meant to *us,* abstractly at first, as though not to make it *too* apparent we were talking about the two of us when one of us would say, "Do you suppose two people could . . ."

So we wondered what it would be like if two people homesteaded 160 acres, built a huge log house and had four or five children. Or what if two people, if they didn't have money to homestead, just got a log cabin and had two kids. Or what if two people went north, to the Arctic, and wrote books and stories about the Indians and the Eskimos. Or what if two people just got an apartment on L Street for the time being, and . . . And so it finally boiled down to what if two people, the two of us, for instance, got married.

We talked about it in earnest at three in the morning of February 9, 1957, after the annual Anchorage Valentine ball and after four months of a sometimes puzzling, frustrating, exhilarating, painful and joyful courtship. We had sized each other up, wondered and searched, each wondering who and what the other was, deciding at last that we were in love, though what kind of pioneers we didn't know, but willing to risk and gamble on the future, in love, and not *really* caring what kind of pioneers we were or whether we were pioneers at all, or whatever.

It was at Jeanne's insistence that on the agreed date of April 7, 1957—two months after our engagement—we have a church wedding, but we would keep it simple, as both of us wanted. I had wanted a civil wedding, with readings from The Kasidah of Jaji Abdu El-Yezdi, Kahlil Gibran, and Dylan Thomas. Jeanne liked the idea, but she felt a church wedding would at least in part mollify her parents, who she thought were upset at our quick courtship and our sudden wedding announcement.

Her parents, Dwight and Margaret Bannister, came to Anchorage from their farm in Ames about a week before the wedding. I knew little about them and didn't know what to expect.

Jeanne had told me that her father owned a farm of eighty acres, most of which he leased to a neighboring corn farmer; that he was part owner of a country newspaper and had sold another; that he was a farm extension editor at Iowa State University in Ames.

And that was about all I knew about him, except that Jeanne had told me he was upset because I had sent him a biographical sketch he had asked for—for the wedding announcement in the Ames paper—in a plain brown envelope. Jeanne told me he had written to her to ask what kind of man it was who didn't use formal white stationery. He had doubts, he had said, about my suitability as a husband. I thought it a small matter, but it concerned me that her father had already formed an opinion.

What's more, Jeanne said her father wasn't laughing at the imaginary adventure I had included in my biographical sketch, something about my having once crossed the Atlantic in a balloon.

About this time I received a letter from one of Jeanne's sisters in Ames. I was told "not to worry about my father," that "Jeanne's the only one who understands him." It was the first letter I had received from any of Jeanne's relatives—my first real contact with the Bannister family—and it came like a message from another planet.

I pressed Jeanne. What was her father like, and was he coming to try to stop the marriage? I didn't show her her sister's letter. Jeanne laughed at me; there was no reason to be concerned, she said. They had run the wedding announcement in the Ames paper, and so what was there to worry about?

I had mixed feelings as Jeanne and I waited at the Anchorage airport for her parents to arrive. The sky was low and gray, not much different from any other spring day in Anchorage, except that the sky gave forth a brilliant white light. There were still patches of snow along each side of the runway, but the grass was bright green, almost luminous.

My plaid wool shirt was open at the collar and I was wearing my suede sport jacket. I had debated about wearing a necktie but had thought, the hell with it: there was no point in pretending to be something I was not. Besides, I felt at least a little defiant toward my father-in-law-to-be. Nonetheless, I wanted to make a good impression. Mostly I wanted our wedding plans to go smoothly, but I wanted also to be genuinely liked by and to like her father.

The plane was a few minutes late. Only a few people—a family of four, several young couples—were waiting. Jeanne and I were the only ones who seemed eager for the plane to arrive. We stood at the runway gate watching the sky. The others stood talking near the double glass doors that kept the cold air from penetrating the airport lounge, seemingly unmindful that the plane was overdue.

Jeanne and I were the first to see it. The plane dropped down from the clouds, circled at the far end of the runway, and seemed to take forever to touch the ground. At last the big silver liner, perched on black rubber tires that seemed ludicrous on such a birdlike machine, stopped a few yards from the gate. Four big propellers fanned the cold, moist air and blew dust from the asphalt runway. Jeanne pulled her coat collar around her neck and squinted, standing on her toes to catch a glimpse of her parents.

The engines stopped, and for a moment this winged transcontinental bird, ship and bus sat transfixed and seemingly empty in its own imposing silence. Four men in blue jackets and flyer's caps pushed the gangway against the plane's side with a muted metallic thud. I felt uneasy and nervous.

I watched as the thick hatch was pushed open and tried to see into the darkness inside. At last, several beyond-middle-age couples started down the gangway. They walked slowly, behind an elderly woman who cautiously picked her way down each step. I wondered which were Jeanne's parents. None of the couples looked our way; they seemed to be concentrating on getting safely down the steep gangway.

"There they are," said Jeanne.

I searched each face, each pair of eyes. None of the eyes caught mine.

"Where are they?"

Jeanne pointed to a short man in a cattleman's short-brimmed Stetson. The Stetson took me by surprise. I knew her father wasn't a cattleman—rather, he edited university farm bulletins. Maybe he's a would-be rancher, a Western type, I thought; this would be good.

Jeanne's mother must be the tall, thin woman in back of him. For a moment I wondered if Jeanne would be as thin when she got beyond middle age. Neither of her parents seemed to see us.

Her father walked toward our gate with a long stride—a little bit like Jeanne's walk. Despite a bulky sheepskin coat that fell below his knees, he seemed small and lean. The coat too was like one of Jeanne's: dark-brown fleece collar, dirty-gray gabardine, big round buttons. It fit him well in the shoulders but hung loose below the waist, like a woman's dress. The bottom of his coat flew up with each step.

Nervous but smiling, I held out my hand to him as he approached. I wondered what he would say, how he would greet me. I tried to catch his eye, but he seemed to be looking directly over my shoulder. His eyes were dark and deep-set in a lean, craggy face. He looked stern, and I wondered if he would stare me in the eye and ask point-blank what made me think I should marry his daughter. I kept smiling, my hand still outstretched.

But his hand didn't take mine. He brushed past without looking at me and walked directly to Jeanne.

I let my hand drop as Jeanne's mother walked past without letting me catch her eye, and so I thought it best I stand back a way as Jeanne and her parents greeted each other and talked. For a time they talked about friends, about relatives, about the trip.

I was impatient and perturbed, but I said nothing and waited. Finally Jeanne introduced me. Her father shook my hand and said, "How do you do?"—a little indifferently, I thought. His eyes avoided mine, and he seemed to have nothing to say to me.

Her mother smiled at me, and asked me many questions: what were my plans, where did I come from, who were my relatives? She seemed genuinely curious to know who and what I was. Her mother at least was talking to me, and I was glad.

Throughout their stay in Anchorage, our relationship remained the same. Her father rarely saw me and rarely spoke to me. Her mother asked me many questions about myself and about my family, but all the while kept a strange, nervous aloofness that made me uneasy. Neither expressed approval or disapproval, except that her father once remarked, as I drove him to Jeanne's apartment in my dilapidated Ford truck, that I ought to have a more "respectable" car.

I saw little of Jeanne that week. It seemed she was hidden away in her apartment with her parents, and I worried that they were trying to talk her out of marrying me. But Jeanne told me later that she was the one daughter whom they would let make her own decisions; there had been some balking, but in the end they left it up to her. Happily, Jeanne was all for having me.

At the wedding my new in-laws were civil and polite, but seemed glum, distant and uneasy; they left the reception early and the next day boarded the afternoon plane. Her father shook my hand and bade me neither good luck nor bad, but simply said, "Goodbye, sir." Her mother waved, smiled nervously, and asked me to write.

Jeanne and I waved them off, and I was glad that they would be three thousand miles away and that the two of us would be left to our own ends. I had no reason to think they would interfere with our marriage. Nevertheless, it made me feel good that they were gone.

Jeanne and I walked back to the truck. For a moment she turned and looked at the sky, one hand shading her eyes. But the plane was nowhere in sight.

"Well," I said, "we're on our own."

She climbed into the truck without saying a word. Her silence worried me; I wondered if she were having second thoughts.

"Do you know," she said, "there isn't a thing to eat in the refrigerator."

"We could eat at the restaurant," I said.

"Let's not. Let's eat at home," she said.

"That's right—at *home*."

"Would you like some candles?"

"Yeah, candles at home."

I turned the key and pressed the starter. The motor turned over quickly.

We had three days for a honeymoon. We were much in love, our plans were indefinite, and we didn't care. And now we were going home.

The Anchorage airport soon diminished in the distance behind us.

3

ONE OF THE HAPPIEST TIMES of a new marriage is when the two of you buy your first house, and all the better if the house is a bit dilapidated.

That is, the house that newlyweds buy, like the marriage itself, should have many unfinished rooms, many windows and many places to build more windows, upgoing stairways and walls that are downgoing whenever it becomes time to expand and make changes. Walls must go up, walls must go down, dreams must be put to the music of hammer and saw. It must be a private place, exclusively and particularly your own, a place of vistas and super-vistas, and hence lots of interesting windows, skylights, and even cracks in the walls through which to peep, and wonder at the outside world, with cots for guests, with dogs, cats, creaks and crockery.

Twenty-two miles north of Anchorage there was such a house, perched, like the grandest of things that perch with folded wings, on a glacial moraine, an ancient mound of silt and gravel heaped high at this very place by a glacier long since turned to water and vapor and which at this moment is perhaps nothing more frozen and formidable than the cloud that waters the birch.

Jeanne and I first saw this house and its one-pipe plumbing system on a beautiful fall day, a day of golden birch and just-fallen and now-passed rain. The Alaskan countryside that surrounded the house was for the most part covered with birch so thick and so smitten by frost that the low, rolling hills were in yellow flames. In a few weeks the first winter snow would fall.

It was the Dutch front door, half log, half glass, that caught our eye as the real-estate salesman drove us up the hill and parked in front of the barn-shaped house with the tiny skylight over the upstairs bedroom, old-fashioned, full-length front porch, knotty-pine kitchen with built-in stove, oven and refrigerator, and with one water faucet, at the end of the only water pipe in the house.

When we arrived, the top of the Dutch door was open (purposely perhaps) and we gazed spellbound into the log living room with its brick fireplace built into the stairway to the upstairs bedrooms—one the master, one a nursery of knotty pine, with a built-in baby crib of skinned birch poles and a little mobile of paper birds hanging above it.

Jeanne, pregnant with Mark, thought it would be so convenient having the nursery next to the master bedroom, thinking of all the times she would have to get up in the night to feed him. An apartment-house-sized Diesel furnace—plus the fireplace—would provide more heat than is available in most hotels. It wasn't much more than half an hour's commute to my job. Jeanne could have the vegetable garden she wanted, I could have the spare bedroom to write in, and Mark, when he arrived—ah, my—would have his rustic and custom-built nursery.

But there were three hitches. The asking price, though not bad by high Alaskan standards, seemed more than we could afford. The one faucet spewed cold water and cold water only—and what to do about the Mark-diaper situation? The bathroom was vacant except for a disconnected bathtub, and about ten yards in back of the house was the toilet, an outhouse that actually had a Sears, Roebuck catalog—and a winter one at that.

The diaper situation, we soon learned, was easy: yes, even in Alaska there was a friendly diaper service. Just bring a bagful, on the way to work—and Out at Three. The outhouse! Well, I tried to convince Jeanne what a gloriously simple and rustic convenience it was. Just think: no plumbing to fool with, no leaky valves; it would make for Nordic stamina. But no! She insisted I install the one convenience she could not do without. That promised, albeit reluctantly, one more hurdle was cleared.

The hurdle most likely to topple us was the price.

In our seven months of marriage, by both of us working and living in a small apartment, we had saved a little over $1,000. The money was burning a hole in both our pockets: Jeanne wanted a house, and I had wanted to move north, to the Eskimo country, to live for a time with the last American nomads, the Aniktuvik hunters who roamed the Brooks Range and the Arctic slope, and to write a book about them.

Jeanne was at first excited by the idea of an Arctic adventure, but along came Mark-to-be, and for the time our adventures would have to be domestic ones.

So we chose as our first domestic adventure an ultimatum to the owner of the house: $1,000 down or else. (Or else we couldn't affort to buy it; but we didn't tell him that.) This was $2,500 under the down payment he was asking, and the realtor who acted as our intermediary thought we didn't have much of a chance. We waited a couple of days; no answer.

Three days. And then a phone call from the realtor.

"Are you *sure* a thousand dollars is all you can come up with?"

"We're sure."

"Okay. I'll try again"—accompanied by a telephonic shrug.

"So I guess we'd better start looking for another house," I told Jeanne.

"But there isn't another house," she said, "not like this one."

"So what do we do?" I said. "We can't come up with any more money."

"We wait," she said, "and we keep our hopes up." I was overwhelmed by her logic.

A day later, another phone call. It was the realtor's secretary, and she wanted to know if we would drop by the office and pick up our fifty-dollar deposit.

"Are you sure?" I said. "We hadn't heard that the deal had fallen through. I'm sure Mr. Allen would have told us."

"I talked to him the other day," she said, "and I'm sure he said your offer hadn't been accepted, and he hasn't deposited your check."

"Where's Mr. Allen?"

"He's out at the house now."

"Can I call him there?"

"You can try—but he was only going to stop for a moment. He's on his way to the Matanuska Valley."

I called Jeanne at the apartment and told her the news. "I hate to say it," I said, "but it looks like the deal's off. I'm trying to get hold of Allen now."

"Oh, golly," she said, "keep trying."

"I'll let you know," I said.

I felt a lot better when I called the house and Mr. Allen answered the phone.

"Well, fancy this," he said. "I was just about to call you."

"Yes?"

"Everything's okay. My client wants a little bit more a month than before, but he says the down payment's okay. Drop down to the office this afternoon and we'll sign the papers. Or maybe you'd rather wait till tomorrow. We can—"

"Fine—I'll be there in an hour."

And so we made a down payment of $1,000 on our one-faucet, twenty-three-acre pipe dream and would-be potato farm twenty-two miles north of Anchorage, and we decided that our pioneering spirits could stand the twenty-five dollars more a month house payment and whatever consequences might come, financial or spiritual.

That hurdle cleared, we splurged twenty dollars on a rocking chair, bought enough used plumbing to install an inside toilet, hoping the well would stand the strain, and soon quickly and happily moved into our first house, lighted a fire in the fireplace, and began collecting blankets, bottles and booties in preparation for the arrival of Mark, who would arrive in five months—give or take a few days—and who, so far as we knew at the time, might be a boy, might be a girl.

Not long ago a doctor of psychology said in an Iowa courtroom that a father is a biological accident, and this was his expert opinion. And of course he was right. Millions of children come into this world like the pop of an old-fashioned party surprise, even in this age of birth control.

When Jeanne announced the coming of Mark, it was indeed a surprise: we simply hadn't planned on it. It was also an announcement of great importance, this arrival-to-be of a combination of bits and pieces of the two of us, and something within us, our genes perhaps, began to well up in wonder and joy.

As is the custom in Alaska, where there is often a long distance between home and hospital, Jeanne spent the last few weeks of her pregnancy in town—three blocks from the hospital. She stayed at the house of a girl friend, who had been Jeanne's maid of honor; happily, she had a bedroom to spare.

Some nights I stayed with Jeanne; others I spent at the house, where I made sure that the furnace was working, that the pipes (the two we now had—one to the sink, one to the bathroom) were not frozen, and to feed Beezle (after the devil god Beelzebub—our dog that was half spaniel, half Malemute, and that was really half dog and half Beelzebub).

On the night of my birthday I had dinner with Jeanne at our friend's house in Anchorage. The baby was due any day now, but Jeanne was sure it wouldn't be tonight.

We had a steak dinner by candlelight, just the two of us. Tonight was the night I should fill Beezle's dog pan with a two-day supply (which he would eat in two minutes, and then lie flat on his side by the fireplace), and I left Jeanne about eight P.M.

"I'm going to bed," she said. "There's no reason to sit up and wait for the baby. I think he's a long way off."

"I'll come back in the morning for breakfast," I said. "See you then."

I drove out to the house. There was still patches of ice on the road, and it took me about forty minutes. I fed Beezle and disappointed him by not lighting the fire. He went upstairs and stretched out on my bed. I shooed him off and went to bed myself. I was half asleep when the phone rang.

It was Jeanne's girl friend: Jeanne had just been admitted to the maternity ward.

"I'll be in as fast as I can get there," I said.

Half asleep, I had trouble getting into my pants; Beezle, also half asleep, growled and pulled on one pants leg. It reminded me of the time when I was a volunteer Anchorage fireman and had made a leap for the fire truck in the middle of the night. The fire gong was still going, and the truck was pulling out of the firehouse. I was half asleep and my legs were tangled in rubber boots, pants and suspenders. I leaped for the truck and fell flat on my face. The truck went on without me. I hoped it wasn't going to be the same now: this was one fire I wanted to get to.

Thank God, the truck started. It didn't always. I think I turned the lights on, but it didn't matter; the moon was out and the road was bright. I drove over the speed limit. The truck skidded once, and I slowed down. There was a bang, and the front of the truck seemed to heel about a foot to the right. I had trouble holding the wheel.

I slowed down and finally pulled up to the side of the road. The right front tire was a mangled mess; about half of it lay in the middle of the road.

My fingers were numb from the cold, and the truck rolled and pushed the bumper jack over—after I had taken the wheel off. I found a rock and blocked one of the rear wheels. It took me twenty minutes to jack the front of the truck up, and it didn't look as though it would do much good: the spare tire was bald. But there was no choice. I drove the rest of the way at thirty-five miles an hour. It seemed I was driving backward.

It must have been eleven P.M. when I finally arrived at the hospital. The lone nurse on duty in the darkened lobby got up from her chair behind the reception desk. Her lap was full of knitting, and a ball of yarn rolled to the floor as she stood up. She bent down to pick it up as I walked to the desk.

Jeanne had given me an expensive bottle of sour-mash whiskey for my birthday, which I had found on the front seat of the truck as I drove in and now carried wrapped in a newspaper; the doors of the truck wouldn't lock and I was afraid the bottle might be stolen.

I asked the nurse to check my bottle at the desk while I went upstairs to see my wife; and would she tell me on what floor was the maternity ward?

My shirt, coat, face and hands were smeared with grease and road dirt. I held out the bottle of whiskey.

"Young man," she snapped, "it's long after visiting hours. You come back tomorrow."

"My wife's having a baby," I said.

"I don't care," she said. "You come back tomorrow just like anyone else."

"I'm sorry," I said, "I've come a long way, I've had a lot of trouble, and I'm going to kick the door down if I have to. Here." I handed her the bottle of whiskey.

Instinctively she reached out with one hand and took it. The newspaper was coming unwrapped, and she was having trouble keeping her knitting intact.

"I'm sorry," I said, "I've got to see my wife."

I didn't wait to see the outcome of her tribulations. I went through the door next to her desk and found the maternity ward myself. It was on the second floor. I found Jeanne in a bed in the hallway; as usual in long-wintered Alaska, the maternity ward was overcrowded.

Jeanne was more calm than I. "Hello," she said. "I think we're going to have a baby."

I felt deflated. Why so matter of fact? "How soon?" I said.

She had a book on her lap, a 700-page history of China. She picked it up and turned to page 10, as though I had interrupted something.

"Oh, maybe sometime tomorrow," she said. "The doctor said I could expect to wait awhile."

"For God's sake," I said.

So we visited for a time and talked about China and the Great Wall and how many years it took to build it. Finally Jeanne said it had been a long day and now she was sleepy, and I left. I was feeling rather sleepy myself.

I got up as usual at 5:30 the next morning. I had to be to work at 6:30. I checked by phone with the hospital: Jeanne was asleep—no baby.

At various times of the day I checked. And still no baby. Nor was the baby in sight when I visited at 4:30 that evening.

What I did after that I don't recall, but little remembrances come to mind: dog food, a box of candy, a steak, a patched tire, a drink at the Malemute Saloon, looking in a window at a mounted moose head, wandering around in a store looking at baby things, talking to a bearded man in front of the courthouse.

Perhaps I went to the moon and kicked stones, or maybe I went to Africa and whittled a totem, or counted stones in the Great Wall of China. Or maybe I paced off stars. Whatever I did, I arrived at the hospital at seven P.M., and Jeanne and baby Mark were waiting for me.

Spanked, swabbed and wrapped in a white blanket, Mark was presented for my inspection. He looked red and healthy, was fast asleep and didn't say a word. A strip of white tape on his right wrist said "Painter" and told all who saw it whose baby he was. It also reminded us that we hadn't decided what his name was to be.

Of "Painter" we were sure. We were sure also that he was not to be a junior, for we wanted Mark to be very much his own man. The name Mark we had tossed around a bit, mostly because we liked its sound. The name seemed to have distinction without affectation. So much better than Winston, Egbert or Terence. It was short and had a certain Anglo-Saxon masculinity and strength. But it was better than Bill, Joe or Sam.

Wendell was my middle name, and we decided that this would give our son a certain affinity for his father but not so much that his name might compel him to walk step for step in his father's tracks. And this name too was unusual and Anglo-Saxon but not too unusual.

So we decided that the name that might sound best on the white cards that children wear on their first day of school, on essays, term papers and return addresses, billboards, marquees and works of art, bridges, roadways and parks, trees and fences—that the name that would sound best would be Mark Wendell Painter, and this was the name we chose.

If there was at this point anything having to do with genes and omens, it had nothing to do with Mark's looks. He certainly didn't look like me, nor his mother—not yet—but bore a resemblance to W. C. Fields and Winston Churchill. But of course he looked like no one other than himself, Mark Wendell Painter, two hours old, with a wisp of dark hair and a funny pushed-in nose.

He had come easily, more or less on time, and he had not been especially hard on his mother. She had weathered six months of morning sickness, and when she first saw her son she said she would gladly have weathered six months more, so lovable was he.

The naming done, the birth certificate was complete. Mark was wheeled away in a plastic basket, into a room full of baskets filled with his peers, some sleeping, some wailing.

Jeanne, a bit woozy from sedatives and as calm as

ever, said she was very proud and happy and was wheeled at last into a room of her own, shared with a veteran of seven babies and, now, eight pregnancies, who grinned at my gift of a box of candy to Jeanne and told her own husband she would be back in a few days to do the wash.

Three days later, with Mark in Jeanne's arms and wrapped in two blankets, I drove the three of us home in the cab of my pickup truck. Beezle was waiting and anxious to be fed, the house was warm and cozy and I made it even cozier by lighting a fire in the fireplace. Mark's built-in crib of birch and pine was ready and waiting.

The sky was gray and cold, the blustery wind that had accompanied my own birth was not surprisingly absent, and the omens were warm and cozy ones: the flame of the fire, the heat from the furnace, the fire's glint on the log walls of the living room, Jeanne's happiness and my own.

4

IT TOOK fourteen sticks of dynamite to make our well bring forth water, and it never brought forth water but what it didn't pour, except that it didn't pour water. It poured forth nuts and bolts, wheels with broken cogs, bubbles and brine—but hardly ever water. And they came for miles around, from Chughiak, Chignik and Colby's Market, from Matanuska, Mister Merlin's and Moosehorn, to witness its birth—this birth of a well that came into the world with such a splendid bang that it knocked down all who came to witness, lifted the back of our house (not yet our house, but *our* house all the same) six inches off the ground, let it drop back four, and left it never the same again, ever.

There came Maud Moog, the smiling Eskimo lady, who had walked all the way from a fish wheel in the Copper River Valley almost 160 miles away—not to see this grand explosion but to marry a potato farmer half a mile down the road from our house; and it was the two of them, Mr. and Mrs. Moog, who rode half a mile side by side and almost popping open the doors of a surplus Army ambulance—once olive drab and now pea-green and peeling—so big were they, as most Eskimos are: short, very big and round, and immensely jovial and curious. They came to bear witness, along with perhaps a dozen others from up and down the road, to the wonderful works of the Dynamite Man, the local expert in home construction, road building, surveying and, lately, demolition, who had become famous for miles around when one day he "blew" the rock that had kept a road waiting. Pieces of it, some as big as a man's head, came from the sky and punched holes in the roof of Moosehorn Lodge, and all the windows that looked to the north were shattered and broken, so immense and meaningful was the explosion. But the road went through, though Maud Moog had cried, "Too much, too much, too much dynee-mite!" and clasped her sides in a fit of laughter.

And she said it again when she heard that fourteen sticks would be used to bring forth water from the well of our house long before it was our house.

Already 160 feet into the Alaskan earth, the well—so said the Dynamite Man—needed only a nudge to break it free of its own obstinacy, and it would be no problem, no problem at all, that the northwest corner of the house—the bathroom-to-be and half the kitchen—sat over the well.

"Too much, too much," said Maud Moog, who clasped her sides and stood a safe distance away, where flying boards and beams could not touch her.

"Who knows? We might even need more," said the Dynamite Man, and put his match to the fuse and dropped his bundle of wonders deep, deep, into the Alaskan earth and ran, as any good dynamite man should.

There were no flying boards, no flying planks or beams. Nothing flew at all, and the house hardly lifted off the ground. Unless you had a keen eye, the upward slope of the living-room floor was hardly noticeable; the wainscotting on the kitchen wall sloped only gradually—three inches in all in a distance of twenty feet; and though the northwest corner of the house rose six inches, it dropped back four. This too was hardly noticeable.

All who came to bear witness went home disappointed, for all the might of the Dynamite Man had only knocked them down. All who came picked themselves up and went home again, while, lo!, water gurgled forth, trickled, spewed and ran, deep in the hole in the Alaskan earth. The Dynamite Man smiled and said the well, though hardly a gusher, would give forth forever. And so said the realtor, and so said we when we bought this house, this well, this lore.

And it was the beginning of the end.

5

THE WELL went dry with neither bang, wheeze, nor whimper. It just seemed to happen one night when we were both asleep, as though the water, under cover of darkness, had decided to steal away.

When I got up the next morning to make a cup of coffee, the tap in the sink blew spray and rust and finally air. The toilet flushed once, and that was all.

I went to the basement and looked at the pump and pressure tank. I had had trouble with these before, but now they were working perfectly. But instead of pumping water, the pump pumped air. Had we been fish in a tank, we'd probably have been happy with all this air. As fish go, we were forced to flounder, as was Jeanne's spring crop of carrots, cabbage, broccoli, spinach and strawberries.

It was Jeanne who floundered most. We had never got around to hooking up the bathtub, which stood upright against the bathroom wall like a pop-art sarcophagus for a Mr. Clean, and Jeanne and I contentedly bathed in a twenty-five-gallon washtub. Mark was bathed in a yellow plastic tub all his own, with plenty of warm water heated in a five-gallon canning kettle placed over a Swedish primus stove. His diapers went daily to the Friendly Diaper Man. The toilet had functioned perfectly, and neither of us had been disturbed when at the height of a winter blizzard powdered snow came softly through the bathroom wall; it was the kind of adventure we liked. But now, with the bathroom only a namesake, the little white outhouse, next to the chicken coop and with boards so widely spaced you could poke your finger into daylight, became our all and only. Before now I had never known Jeanne to swear: "I hate that damned thing," she said. It was all she could do to keep from throwing rocks at it. And when one day the door fell off, she did.

The local well expert, in the now immortal words of Maud Moog, simply said, "Too much." It would cost too much to fix the well, even if it could be fixed.

And it would cost money we didn't have. Already we had spent almost every cent I had earned to replace the refrigerator motor, repair the furnace, repair the rear axle of the truck, pay off the balance of a winter fuel bill—which came to $360 for several hundred gallons of Diesel oil—and to pay the doctor and hospital bills for Mark's birth, which, though minor, now became major. The house payment was $150; electricity, phone and butane were hitting well above the thirty-dollar mark; and the cost of commuting forty-four miles each day to work, six days a week (with gas at forty cents a gallon), was becoming a burden. My $150-a-week salary just didn't seem to be covering it all. Jeanne wondered if we weren't coming to a crisis.

For the next few months I hauled water to the house,

fifty gallons at a time, in a surplus Army water barrel. We had lost the distinction of being the only house for miles around with its own well, but at least Jeanne's garden flourished, even if we had to water it with a tin bucket punched with nail holes. But worse than having lost our place of distinction, we learned from the realtor that the price of our house, should we ever have to sell it, had, like the water in the well, dropped considerably.

"I just hope we don't have to sell the place," I told Jeanne.

"But we're going to have to do something," she said. "What's going to happen when the winter comes?"

I knew she meant she would have to use that awful outhouse when the snow fell and the temperature seldom warmed above zero. And what would we do for water when the community watering place froze over?

That summer the clover in our backyard grew high and green in the long, warm days that refused to end until long after the children in the States, 2,000 miles south of the Arctic sun, had gone to bed in darkness. The skies were blue more often than not, which was a happy change from the usual summer overcast. Surprisingly, all summer the days were neither too hot nor too cool but warm enough to lie in the clover on a blanket with your shirt off on, say, a Sunday in July. July might have been hot and dusty, or overcast and cold, with the temperature seldom above sixty and the moist air making the mornings seem as cold as winter. But this was a different kind of July.

Marty Vorys, my trapper friend, had staked a wild mountain sheep, three months old, in our backyard, in the center of the sweet and succulent clover. Toward the end of August the ewe would be sent to a zoo in Washington, D.C., in a fifty-gallon gasoline drum with both ends cut out and replaced with wire. The zoo owner would pay Marty $1,250, a sale Marty would make reluctantly because he had grown fond of the sheep and would have kept her himself except that he needed the money. He had spent months in the mountains, in a tent high above timberline, trying to catch the sheep—now called Genie and staked in our backyard on a white piece of clothesline attached to a studded dog collar purchased at the five-and-dime.

Jeanne and I sat on a dark-gray Navy blanket, Mark between us in a sort of plastic bucket seat for babies that looked as though it had once been part of an airplane—a small one, perhaps, for babies. We fed Genie handfuls of clover, which she munched in her tiny sheep's mouth while at the other end she produced pellets, pellets in the clover, and looked at you just like a dumb but affable sheep chewing cud and producing pellets at the same time. She sniffed at Mark and pulled his knitted pink cap off with her teeth. It was the first time we had heard Mark laugh, for it was his first laugh, unless he laughed in the dark at night when we were asleep: an amazingly deep and throaty laugh, and we were pleased that at the age of four months he had a sense of humor.

Marty was a graduate of Yale and of Ohio high society and had given up an affluent and assured way of life in Ohio for a life of adventure in the Alaska bush, after brief layovers on the way to Alaska as a Montana cowboy and a Texas newspaper reporter. Even with his boots off he stood closer to the ceiling than to the floor; few beds and few doorways were made for his comfort. He detested phony, insincere people; loved books and the guitar; was so generous he once loaned a pleading deadbeat his last seven dollars and fifty cents; and had a sense of humor that lay somewhere between James Thurber's gentle surrealism and Mark Twain's hearty nose-thumbing.

He came to the house often and slept in the spare bedroom but seldom stayed more than a day or two because he was on his way to a hunt, coming back from one and anxious to get back to his cabin, writing a book, trapping a sheep, searching a stream for gold, or setting out on a lone expedition of picture-taking.

That August in Alaska was Mark's first Christmas, and my mother, who was visiting us, was his Santa Claus. Caps and bonnets, rattles and booties—gifts that flowed as if from a giant cornucopia, and most or all of them

Mark tossed out of his crib and onto the floor. It was a fascinating thing to watch, this thing called Mark flat on his back in a crib that from time to time exploded rattles, booties and plastic birds into the air. We picked them up and put them back. Again and again they flew into the air and onto the floor, until we tired of picking them up. I don't know whether my mother left because she tired of this stooping game or honestly had to report back to work on a day that was drawing dangerously near. Whatever, she insisted she had to leave. But there was no question, when we saw her off at the airport, that she was leaving reluctantly.

The girl with the faraway voice that seemed to come from another place, another town, or a neat, blue booth somewhere in the sky, announced that Flight 721 to Seattle would depart from Gate Three in four minutes. Or perhaps it was Gate Four in three minutes. The travelers who had crowded and pushed against the gate, like salmon pushing their noses at a dam in the stream when something within their damp psyches insisted they push onward, now flowed onto the runway apron and walked hurriedly toward the open door of the airplane, itself looking like a winged salmon, a bizarre aluminum flying fish that canned and packed people for instant opening at instant destinations.

My mother pushed onward, her large wicker handbag full of the traveler's booty. Glancing back as we walked toward the plane, she asked that we be sure to tell Marty that she enjoyed the ride to see the caged grizzly bear; thanks, too, for the ivory Bilikin luck charm handcarved by no less than an Eskimo, the souvenir spoon and the bottle of seal oil for cooking.

Don't forget, she said, to paint the outhouse pink and paper it inside with something elegant; and: "I hope you get the well fixed."

We nodded and waved goodbye, not wanting to tell her that we couldn't afford to fix the well. Nor did we want to tell her that the Alaska house was slipping away from us. We waved once more as the plane started down the runway and my mother looked back through one of the round windows over the wing and waved back.

6

WHEN, precisely, the end came, I don't recall. I suppose it began and ended on the day that men were told they would have to put down their bartered goods and go to work for money.

Had the man who could fix our well accepted barter we'd have had no problem—provided he had some use for the hundreds of pounds of corroded welding rod and the other junk that made up the huge pile of odds and ends that had been stacked by an unknown collector in the outskirts of our backyard. As it was, I took the boxes of welding rod, pieces of brass pipe fittings, thorny wreaths of barbed wire, and a couple of complicated-looking valves that weighed about fifty pounds each to the local junk man. My naïve eye had gauged the worth of this pickup-truckload at thirty dollars, relying largely on what I supposed would be the high price of used brass. Deducting ten dollars (the difference between its actual worth and the junk man's no doubt conservative offer), I decided we would make a profit of twenty dollars.

But the junk man was more knowing and wily than I. "A dollar for the whole lot." This was his offer.

"Nuts," I said.

He countered with an offer of two dollars—and that was final.

"Three dollars or I'll take it all home," I said.

He grumbled something and motioned to a shirtless Negro in striped gray coveralls, who immediately began to unload the truck. The junk man pulled three one dollar bills from a folded wad as thick as most men's billfolds, and I went home disappointed and mad as hell.

The twenty dollars I had anticipated would neither have bought us a new well nor part of one, but money was becoming so scarce it would have given us at least a warm feeling—at least as much warmth as if we had put a match to two ten-dollar bills and cupped our hands over the flame.

My salary was considerably less than a bonfire, and the furnace to which we fed it required more and more of this legal tinder. I managed to make ends meet and to pay off the incidental expenses that kept plaguing us by writing and selling articles from time to time.

Up to the time of our buying the Alaska house, I had written only fiction. Discouraged by having failed to sell it, I began to wonder if I could ever sell anything, so I tried writing articles. To my surprise, I sold the first article I wrote to the *Christian Science Monitor,* and I felt considerably encouraged when the editor asked for more.

For a while I felt as though I had been given wings. The writing I was doing for the Anchorage newspaper that employed me bored me stiff. I covered city-council and local public-utility district meetings, and I just wasn't interested when the city council "approved the city engineer's request for the installation of 600 feet of sewer pipe on L street . . ."

My exposure to city government was a disillusionment, and I couldn't begin to write what I felt in the local newspaper; the newspaper was too much a part of it, and it supported the politicians I thought were insane.

The *Monitor* editor asked me to write about the Alaska scene: about the move for statehood, the land itself, the people, their politicians. It was the only newspaper writing that ever gave me satisfaction. The editor asked for more than the cursory treatment given so-called breaking news events by the other newspapers I have worked for; the *Monitor,* I was told, had no call for a hasty, pasted-together and superficial sketching of events, and I found myself in the happy position of having to write critically of the things that were going on around me.

When Jeanne and I lived in the Alaska house I wrote for the *Monitor* and wrote fiction too. My newspaper job was a daily chore that kept me away from my work. But it was my newspaper job and the *Monitor* that provided the money we so badly needed.

For years I had been trying to sell my fiction to the national magazines, but all I got in return were printed rejection slips—and rightfully, for most of my stories were terrible. As if to prove I could sell, I wrote an article—a true story. It was my first magazine sale; I sold it to a boys' adventure magazine. Pleased with this, I hopefully returned to magazine fiction. It didn't sell.

For a time I did all three: working six days a week on the newspaper, writing deadbeat fiction and paying articles after work and on weekends. We needed the money, I needed to write what I felt, and it was getting me down.

Things were happening and things were about to happen that were getting Jeanne down too. Fixing the well was beyond our budget and out of the question, and thus too was any possibility that the outhouse would be "out" and the bathroom "in" by winter. Water would be a serious problem when the pond froze over and I would have to haul water from work. This meant adding another hour to what was already two hours of winter commuting; and the long hours in the winter darkness, without neighbors and despite the consistently jolly company of Mark, Jeanne looked ahead to with despair.

Jeanne's inability to make friends quickly or to be casual among new acquaintances baffled and perplexed some of those who sought her friendship, and it made her isolation in the house painful.

She was neither class-conscious nor standoffish, but she sometimes gave that impression in the presence of those who had little in common with her, inasmuch as she never knew quite what to say, and her emotions were too honest to allow her to pretend. Unfortunately, some of our acquaintances felt rebuffed by the calm reserve with which she met social encounters that were vastly new to her. I think perhaps I was the only one who knew how much it pained her not to be able to make the small talk on which most acquaintanceships are founded.

She surprised me once by telling me that her first meeting with a "working man" had been in Juneau, shortly before she had come to Anchorage. By this she meant a man who worked with his hands for a weekly salary. In Iowa she had known only her parents' friends and visitors, of which there were few, and these were landed farmers, publishers, bankers and businessmen. As a child she had learned to think of the "working man" as an itinerant who lived in a shack by the river, had neither land nor education and was more than likely a no-account.

Her meeting, in Juneau, with a construction worker made such an impression that she made special mention of it in her diary, analyzing his motives and ambitions as though she were Herodotus observing his first Hottentot.

Our nearest neighbor was a seasonal construction worker, one of a breed that had built in Alaska just about everything that bore the unwritten label "made by men." Like many of them, he worked in the few short months of summer, made enough to keep him through the winter, lived out of town in the "low rent district," in a cozy tarpaper shack, hunted, fished, played cribbage long after the Late Late Show on the local television, went dancing and drinking with his wife at a nearby bar on Saturday night, and got up in time for a late lunch Sunday afternoon.

Short, wide, gruff and good-humored, he wore a thick red and black checked shirt of prickly, hairy wool wherever he went, and wherever he went his wife went too, and wherever she went she wore a thick red and white checked shirt of prickly, hairy wool, and her whiskey voice was almost as husky as his.

They visited us on several evenings over a couple of weeks, and they came to talk, to become acquainted, to drink beer, and to sit by the fire. He talked to me about hunting bear and moose, building roads and bridges, the best fishing places, and how to keep down the fuel bill in winter by tacking sheets of transparent plastic over the windows. She talked to Jeanne about the local beauty operator's habit of telling dirty stories and drinking on the job but being one hell of a hair stylist all the same, about the divorced woman down the road who had knocked on their door in the middle of the night to complain that the Indian hitchhiker she had brought home with her went half mad when she rebuffed his advances and had tried to set fire to her dress. She talked a little about cooking and a little about sewing, and then told anecdotes about the Saturday-night dances and the time the bartender got drunk and threw a bowl of potato salad at the cook, who was drunk too, and threw onions like baseballs at the bartender.

It was the kind of talk, a kind of life, which Jeanne knew nothing about. Few things our neighbors had to talk about struck a common chord; Jeanne responded by maintaining a polite silence, by being obviously perplexed and occasionally amused at the rough, stock humor that passed for party talk.

As the visits went on, our neighbors became less and less at ease and more and more inclined to grope for the words that would bring a common response from Jeanne, grew perplexed at not being able to find them, began to sit silent for long periods, and eventually didn't visit at all. The woman stopped visiting Jeanne during the day, and Jeanne became anxious and had guilt feelings because she had found nothing in common and wanted desperately to have friends.

Jeanne recognized our neighbors as kind, generous people with a charming if salty sense of humor; but they couldn't fill her need for a woman confidante and the kind of conversation that stimulated her interests, which, unfortunately, did not include tipsy hairdressers and bartenders whose idea of a tossed salad was an airborne one.

The only other woman who came to visit Jeanne during the day was a Russian, a huge, strong woman with three unusually energetic children and whose estranged husband dropped by from time to time for something to eat, a shave, and a good night's sleep in a clean and sober bed, and then he wouldn't trouble her again for weeks. One night's stay—that's all the husky Russian woman allowed him; more likely than not, she would tell him she had more important things to do than worry about him and would put on her pack sack, hike two or three miles into the birch forest, shoot a moose, clean and quarter it, and carry its parts back to the three hungry mouths that waited in the half-tarpaper, half-log nest she had built herself.

Nothing disturbed her, nothing got her down, not even the fire that roasted most of her kitchen to an indelicate charcoal brown. "In two minutes flat," she told Jeanne one day in her slightly Russian accent, "I tore down the whole goddam kitchen and builded it once again." It was more like two weeks flat, but in her half-frenzied, self-sufficient and determined spasm, it was but all of two minutes.

Her rare visits boosted Jeanne's morale and revived her zest for the now rough and pioneer life in the Alaska house, but they never lasted long enough to make Jeanne overcome her aversion to the outhouse and the menace it made of the coming winter. Her spirits were always high on those days when she had been visited by this always happy, resilient and forceful Russian woman whose voice vibrated the half-log walls in our living room and shattered the thousand and one malicious icons of coping of which pioneering is made.

Jeanne's days in the house, alone and with no one to talk to, eroded her morale; housekeeping was anathema, and knowing little about it and having been inculcated with her mother's dark observations on this sometimes dank and dusty art, she spent her time reading and tending to Mark, whom she looked after assiduously and with tender concern. The art of decorating just did not exist in her mind. A bare bulb dangling in the living room would drive me nearly insane, but Jeanne gave it no notice; she simply turned it on when light was needed, and used it, with utter common sense I sincerely envied.

Our biggest problem concerned with lights was that if our expenses kept on the way they were going, we might not be able to pay the bill and have any lights at all. In light of this—a constipated well that no elixir would make right again, an outhouse whose wintery overtones chilled Jeanne to despair, my own despair in trying to write fiction, paying articles, and keep a six-day-a-week job, commute, haul water, and still enjoy a reasonable home life—we decided there was only one way out.

The house itself had been everything we had wanted, in spirit and in essence. We loved its windows and Dutch doors, it stairways and varnished wood, brick and logs, porch and peeled-log porticoes. If only we'd had water and money and a few neighbors who shared Jeanne's interests and would come to visit during the lonely days. Mark, however, seemed quite content with it all and complained no more than most babies, and then only about erring diaper pins, thirst, hunger, and the lack of constant cooing and tickling.

Practicality, unfortunately, overcame the romantic attachments that remained. I made a small sign, painted by hand with black paint on a piece of plywood, and nailed it to the base of a tree at the foot of our driveway and along the sometimes busy highway to Anchorage: "For Sale, 3-Bedroom House. Inquire Within." So that prospective buyers would be sure to find us, I painted an arrow at the bottom of the sign, pointing upward, toward the house.

For us, the arrow pointed downward, away from the house and toward Anchorage and destinations farther south and farther *down,* toward a pit with a trampoline bottom that would send us bouncing in all but the right directions.

7

A YEAR PASSED and Jeanne, Mark and I had left Alaska and were living in an all but busted boom town in the center of Washington State. Janet Lizette Painter was just learning to walk, with the help of Jeanne, Mark and myself. Mark's help was mostly confined to pushing—a shove from behind that would send Janet on her way.

This last year had gone poorly for us. Jeanne was upset at my dissatisfaction with my small-town newspaper job. She was growing weary of my pacing the living-room floor and wishing out loud that we were all of us immediately somewhere else. My black moods were making her uneasy and she was beginning to feel insecure and doubtful. Our duplex apartment was too small, the rent a strain, and a contorted bedspring was giving both of us a back-ache.

We had had to repossess the Alaska house, after being unable to sell and having to settle for a lease. The strange man from Nome, who had leased the house, vanished one night, two weeks after the November payment had come due. A tiny sign on the front door of the house succinctly explained what was holding up the payment: "Gone Fishing."

Desperate, we immediately moved out of our apartment in Anchorage; we couldn't afford to rent it and pay for the house too. The steep road to the Alaska house was three feet deep in snow, and I couldn't afford to have it plowed out. So I packed our furniture up the hill on my back, and when I finally got it all in, I discovered why the strange man from Nome had gone fishing: the furnace had expired. We couldn't afford to fix that either, so I packed our furniture down the hill again and into the truck. No heat. No water. No money. Jeanne, Mark and I slept at a friend's house until I could find an apartment we could afford, a too-small duplex, and each month in the months thereafter the owner raised the rent—five dollars each time, with no limit in sight.

By late April, when the rent for our one-bedroom, wall-to-wall claustrophobia apartment began to approach the moon, Jeanne and I began to wonder if there were some other place in the world where life would be different.

Jeanne was pregnant then with Janet, and we couldn't find a decent two-bedroom house for less than $200 a month; this meant more like $250 after you paid the heating and utility bills.

The spring breakup was beginning to break our spirits. The front yard was a colossal mud pie; the condensation on the thin plasterboard walls made puddles on the floor; the washing machine—in the living room for lack of space—one night leaked a puddle of oil on the floor.

What to do about my writing career? This became a crucial problem. I had had enough newspaper experience and had made enough magazine sales that it was likely I could strike out in journalism and probably land a job as a magazine or newspaper feature writer. I had moved up to the job of city editor of the Anchorage *Times,* but it was a job I had no love for; nor was there the prospect of more pay or a better job.

My *Christian Science Monitor* editor had asked me to fly to Little Diomede Island, walk across the frozen Bering Sea to the invisible international line separating Russia and the United States, and write an eyewitness account of what it is like standing at the only place in the United States where Russia can be seen with the naked eye.

It struck me as a good enough idea and a great adventure, but I couldn't get time off from the newspaper and the *Monitor* couldn't afford to pay me more than a few dollars and nothing for plane fare.

Janet's coming squelched my plans to spend three months with the Brooks Range nomads in the Arctic, interview the chief, and write a magazine article and a book. I put the idea away for another time, and Jeanne and I worked out our plans on how best to prepare for Janet's arrival.

The coming of Janet, as had been Mark's coming, was one of those miraculous surprises, and it couldn't have happened at a more unsettled time. We were taken aback when the doctor told Jeanne the news, and for a time we hoped for a rewinding of the sanguine red tape that was about to ensnare us. But there was little hope that nature would undo the ineffaceable results of its own capricious undertaking, and so there was little Jeanne and I could do but wait out the inevitable, and love and cherish, as inevitably as nature, man and woman, and our own two selves would have it.

As for a career in journalism, I decided at this perhaps crucial point to give it up. I would stick to short stories, humor and satire. Someday, somehow, I was sure it would sell. Jeanne was too, and I decided I would apply for a job as a copy editor on some small paper in Washington—hopefully, an undemanding job; I would write after work and on weekends. I would find a job where food and rent were cheaper and the weather was less likely to keep Mark indoors six months of the year.

I wrote a master job application, and Jeanne and I typed and mailed a flurry of copies. In a few weeks I was given a firm offer of a job as copy editor on a small daily newspaper in Bremerton. I had been to Bremerton when I was about fifteen years old and remembered the place as a wooded village by the waters of Puget Sound and a short drive from a magnificent Pacific Ocean.

The pay seemed about right, and a copy of the newspaper listed two-bedroom homes renting at $75 a month and less. The job would open in thirty days, and Jeanne's father had generously offered to have Jeanne and Mark stay at the farm in Ames for the coming of Janet while I moved our furniture, pots, pans, and books to Bremerton; Mark, Jeanne and Janet would join me as soon as possible after Janet's birth. I accepted the job. Unfortunately, I lived to regret it.

Three weeks before I was to report to work in Washington 2,200 miles south and a seven-day drive, Jeanne packed two suitcases for herself and Mark, and I mailed a carton of their things ahead of them. I drove the two of them to the airport to see them off. We had purchased tickets in advance, and the plane would leave in a few minutes. In a matter of a few hours they would be in Minneapolis; from there it would be a short hop by air to Des Moines, where they would be met by Jeanne's parents. But they were not to get there—not today, not for another two weeks. I couldn't bring myself to see them off.

Jeanne agreed to stay another two weeks and I was as happy as if Jeanne and Mark had just arrived at the airport after a long absence. We celebrated by going to town for dinner. Two weeks later we waved goodbye as resolutely as we had planned. Mark and Jeanne sped through the sky on hired wings, and I found myself very much alone and wishing they hadn't gone.

A week later I was gone myself, speeding away from Alaska as fast as four wheels would take me, though as I got farther and farther south I more and more wanted to turn back and return to Alaska. The closer I got to Washington, the more I began to miss the spirited Alaskan wilderness. The wilderness was now becoming parks and campsites. Twisty, turning wilderness roads walked by Indians, moose and bear now became highways and then freeways traveled indifferently by speeding cars and trucks; people began to look sickly, stooped and desperate, as though they too had come hurtling out of the Alaskan wilderness into a maze of hopelessly blind streets and hallways, offices and factories, where frustration, smog and smashed cars were as omnipresent as the sun's light each morning when the alarm clock sounded.

By the time I got to Bremerton, I felt sick. Three years in Alaska had made me impatient with the small-town gentility and repression I found here: the people on the street, the clerks, the people I met at my new job—all seemed smitten with pettiness, as though their motions had been squelched by an oppressive need to knuckle under.

The people here—so many of them retired government employees—were so different from Alaskans. Alaskans, it seemed to me, were generally *big*. Their emotions ran big and deep. They ate more, drank more, were impatient with petty rules and regulations. Alaskans seemed young, and they had young thoughts. It had surprised me to learn, when I first went to Alaska, that there were more college graduates per capita there than anywhere in the United States. This was evident in the people I had met, most of whom, especially the young couples, had come to Alaska to be individualists and to live unbridled by any standards other than their own.

Many Alaskans wrote poetry and painted, and often the poems were mediocre and the paintings bad, but they conveyed feeling, feeling for the *bigness* of Alaska and the Alaskan way of life. So many Alaskans were genuinely interested in what was happening in Europe, the States, Southeast Asia—wherever books, magazines, radio and television and their own travels by air and by ship took them, and it was surprising how many Alaskans had traveled the world, to discover in Alaska a truly cosmopolitan yet wilderness mecca of sorts.

So many Alaskans, even those without so-called educations, seemed sophisticated—sophisticated, perhaps, in the sense of being *of the world,* of being alive, human, and emotional—not mannered, not pretentious, and not suffering from an acute awareness of having membership in a tiny, artificial world of constipated emotions and calculated interests.

Alaska had been far from perfect. Everything had cost too much: food, rent, housing. The difference between a life of hardship and a life of reasonable creature comforts was likely to be a couple of thousand dollars you didn't have for a down payment on the right house—especially if you were on a small, fixed salary and had to live near or in town, where the pleasure of having just hot water, heat and ample space could run well over two weeks' salary. All the social and individual ills were here too; the wilderness and its frontier towns and cities were neither assurance against nor a cure for a man's battered psyche. It was just as easy to find a neurotic and frustrated man in the midst of the Alaskan wilderness as in the midst of New York or Los Angeles.

But Alaska *had* wilderness and big spaces, and its attractions were expansive and broad, so that those who came often came to break away from any kind of *establishment* that would inhibit their search for an individual meaning in life. Perhaps it was an illusion—this condition of personal freedom and expansiveness in Alaska; but if this did not exist in fact, the illusion then was a forceful, overwhelming one. And if a choice must be made between living a life of expansive illusions and living a life of statistical and factual certainty where there is no room for illusions at all, then perhaps a life of illusion is to be desired. My life in Bremerton offered few illusions.

Bremerton had trees and open spaces and even a few contented and yet exciting people; but its spaces seemed fenced and posted with signs that warned against trespassing, airing the dog, and picking flowers. Only the nearby waterways had even an illusion of openness and vitality—if you could find the way through the water skiers and the people in buzzing plastic boats.

My job on the Bremerton newspaper was hell, but it was a tepid hell. My job on the Anchorage newspaper had not been my calling, but it had had exciting moments. The reporters and editors I had worked with were fiercely independent and drove the thoughtful, quiet but internally excitable managing editor insane with their eccentricities and surprises. The Anchorage paper had had bedlams, breakdowns, and bizarre happenings.

The Bremerton newspaper was a monumental comedown, a saga in reverse. All but a few of my fellow employees seemed pallid and frightened, either of their jobs or themselves. The news seemed petty and trivial, and the managing editor seemed to me to be a petty tyrant who stood over your shoulder, badgering words out of your typewriter, and whose bad breath was constantly in your face, which made his petty injunctions prodigious.

Here, in this packed office with the faded, sweet-pea green walls, adventure was the recounting of a ride in a station wagon to buy two potted plants for the patio, which sold for seven cents less at the Payless, but the Payless was another half hour's drive, and somebody was coming over for pinochle.

I was bored to desperation.

I was glad when, early in July, Jeanne, Mark and one-month-old Janet arrived. I had been alone for almost three months, and one adventure I find intolerable is loneliness and the absence of my family. I was anxious to have them back.

But our meeting at the airport was marred. I found

Jeanne standing at the bottom of the airplane's gangway with Mark in a leather harness and a single leather rein. I took it off and angrily threw it in a trash can. I told her I supposed that the harness had been her father's idea. I told her that harnessing children might be acceptable in Iowa but not to me. Later, I was sorry and frustrated: I knew she had had all she could do to manage Mark and Janet alone on the airplane, and Mark was not one for sitting still. Yet, I couldn't help being angry.

And I further made Jeanne unhappy by having rented a small cottage, along Puget Sound, surrounded by tall pines. She cried when she saw it, because it was surrounded by trees, and trees, she said, gave her claustrophobia—and the house was almost hidden by them. Perhaps hers was a reaction to our imperfect meeting at the airport, and I deserved the let-down it gave me. Before she had arrived I had written to tell her I had found an apartment for rent in downtown Bremerton. I described it in my letter and described also the beach cottage. She wrote back that she preferred the apartment in town, but I talked her out of it and accepted the condition that I promise to install a washing machine before she arrived.

It was after she cried that we came together, properly and happily, after having been separated by the spaces of half a continent for almost three months.

If Jeanne had sought retribution for my ill-timed outburst at the airport, she had it, and rightfully, for I was dejected by her crying when she saw for the first time my place of trees by the water's edge. And now we smoothed it out and talked it away. Jeanne dried her tears on a corner of Janet's yellow baby blanket. She held Janet in her lap, and we turned our attentions to our newly born, whom Jeanne was proud to present and I was proud to hold, and we admired Mark, who had grown a bit, and then the three of them went to bed and to sleep, dead tired, after a long trip home.

In the weeks and months that followed, we became acquainted with our lively and generous neighbors, Jeanne seemed to forget the claustrophobic trees, and we went clamming on the beach, walking in the woods, and on sunny days I often pulled Mark down the rutted road, in his red wagon, along a wire fence where blackberries grew. We plucked them on the spot and ate them, Mark examining each one with care for bugs. We picked bucketsful and brought them home to Jeanne, who made pies.

Janet seemed quickly to grow from baby to babe, and when her young stomach was ready for it, Mark and I stood by her crib and fed her berries, which she alternately ate with a little bird mouth and threw on the floor.

My writing was going badly and I knew it. My job was going worse. I hated every minute of it, and by October I was fired. I was told I just didn't seem to fit in and was indifferent to my job. The editor was right on both counts.

Jeanne seemed to take it matter-of-factly. "Golly," she said, "what do we do now?"

This was characteristic. Her words scarcely revealed the worry within.

"What we do now," I said, "is I look for another job."

And now we were in this busted boom town of Moses Lake. Larson Air Force Base, booming in the war years, had been the town's mecca. The base now reclined in postwar inactivity and with it the once booming town. High hopes had turned toward the nearby airplane and missile factory, which each day mass-produced rumors of a wholesale shutdown that eventually did materialize. But there was always the sugar-beet refinery—a massive blockhouse of cement silos, hard white smoke and dust.

The federal reclamation project had brought in vast quantities of water, in cement waterways that snaked through a desert that now bloomed only in bits and patches. Desert homesteads produced the sugar beets that lay in dry and dusty mounds here and there along long roads to virtually nowhere. But neither corn nor beets nor sorghum would make this unpromising town bloom. Small businesses seemed to come and go in the night, leaving behind unpaid bills and disgruntled creditors in snap-brim hats, who sat in the neon-lighted coffee shops, where day-old slices of pie were indifferently displayed in glass cases upon which frustrated flies had vented their displeasure, and talked of ways of promoting the annual

Crazy Daze Sale and developing the lake—dank with algae and a curious gray growth that had been traced to sewer-plant effluence—for tourists with plastic motorboats and water skis.

A little bit of joy came rolling out of the flat and worn horizon when a large construction company began to advertise for workers. A few businesses sprang up overnight; the whorled white film on the windows of a few of the vacant stores was erased with wetted sponges and replaced with signs that told of rug remnants, photographs for the whole family, lawn furniture, and men's work shoes. The bars and beer taverns became a little more lively and musical on Saturday nights; the Baptist and the Church of Christ pews became almost full on Sundays.

On the hill, the one eccentricity in an otherwise flat and colorless town, the housing tract began to blossom forth with the yellows, greens and oranges of moving vans and U-Rent trailers. Bicycles, bedsprings, and beige and gold-flecked bedroom sets for a time lay on the little dried lawns with dusty cement walks that inevitably paralleled the shadowless wall of a tiny pinkish garage. Spirits ran high in the mornings in the coffee shops. The men in tight black snap-brim hats of tightly woven and slightly shiny straw began now to talk about the coming high-school football season and how, if the new coach shaped up the kids (and at a Kiwanis luncheon at the Chinese restaurant he had solemnly made this promise), the home boys would be on top. The seasonal playoff would be held at Moses Lake at the same time as the big retail sales promotion, and there was some talk about calling the promotion Dollar Days Galore.

Meantime, the big construction company hired its fill and work was begun south of town, on the underground missile-launching silos. Night and day, under sun and white tungsten floodlights, the men worked feverishly to meet the government deadline, as if hurriedly to protect this already burned-out, would-be mecca from a fiery bomb that would be sent, no doubt by mistake, by impassive Russians in funny, frumpy hats.

I had come here looking for a job, and I was hardly Jason setting out in search of the Golden Fleece: just myself, father of two, husband to my wife, failed writer, fired worker. And I had traveled sixty miles to the east, sixty miles farther away from the Alaskan wilderness and sixty miles away from the green if tainted woods and the shimmery and white-capped waterways of Puget Sound, to this besmirched oasis of 15,000 outstretched palms. I had been told that the local newspaper, though perhaps destined for bankruptcy, needed immediately a reporter of the local news events: the pancake feeds, the Crazy Daze, the Lions and Kiwanis, the politicians, the missile silos, the men in the snap-brim hats, the backyard barbecues of the dusty four hundred.

Desperate, I applied for the job. My credentials passed, and the job was mine. And now I was more desperate than ever. But at least I had a job. The pay wasn't much, but if we couldn't *live,* we could at least eat.

I took the job without knowing I would be covering high-school sports, in and out of town, in addition to being the city-hall reporter. From 6:30 to 10 A.M. I wrote sports. From 10 A.M. to noon I covered, by foot and by phone, the city hall, the chamber of commerce, Kiwanis, police and the ubiquitous men in the snap-brim hats.

I knew nothing about sports. For weeks I wrote fabricated but detailed accounts of high-school basketball games. And for weeks I had bad dreams: I saw thousands of giant, spidery boys entangled in a phantasmagoria of flying basketballs, legs, and smelly tennis shoes. For nights on end my dreams reverberated with the ping-ping-ping of a giant basketball being dribbled down an echoed hall of eternity. I finally gave up going to the games; they were driving me insane. Fortunately, a morning paper carried the games in detail. I rewrote these, adding events of my own imagination.

I hated this town, this life. Jeanne did too. At night I came home feeling dried out, depressed, angry and frustrated. Our plasterboard duplex apartment was too small, but it was the best we could afford. The men in the snap-brim hats called me at home, at night. They came to the door with news releases day and night: Crazy Daze, Dollar Daze, Dollar Nights, Dollar Basketball Games, Dollar Pancake Feeds, Dollar, Dollar, Dollar. City-council candidates called me up at 9 P.M. to tell me they supported the local Dollar Daze 100 per cent; they would use the tax receipts to promote the Lake; they would cut taxes, hold down expenses, and bring in more Dollars. All day, all night, all weekend, it seemed, the phone rang. But it didn't ring like other phones. It rang like a register ringing up two, then four, then six, then eight Dollar Daze sales in a row. Every time I picked up the phone I was in a rage. When I hung up, I was in more of a rage. I threatened to tear the phone off the wall and throw it in Moses Lake.

My depressions and rages were getting Jeanne down. At home I was either horribly silent and melancholy or raging and cursing.

We had made no friends; it seemed that only the men in the snap-brim hats came to visit. The windows needed washing, the house seemed cluttered with toys, diapers, baby bottles. Everywhere I walked, everything I touched seemed smeared with Karo syrup. I was angry with Jeanne's bad housekeeping, and Jeanne was afraid that my frustration was really my dissatisfaction with our marriage, with marriage in general, that I thought she and Mark and Janet were dragging me down, that I wanted to be free and away.

I took long walks, alone, through the streets at night, when it was cool. I went down the back alleys, where the men in the snap-brim hats couldn't buttonhole me. I peered into garbage cans and incinerators, into stacks of boxes in back of stores, as though trying to divine from the scatological effluvia the meaning of this place, my life, my future.

I walked and wondered how I could explain to Jeanne that there was nothing wrong with her, nothing wrong with our marriage. It was just me, that's what was wrong: I couldn't stand this town, this life.

One night I walked by the train tracks and a string of boxcars went hurtling by. A bum with a rolled-up blanket on his back clung to the steel ladder on the back of one of the cars like a grinning spider clamped to the back of a shooting star. How I envied him. I imagined myself on the car behind him, hurtling down the tracks, toward the mountains of Idaho, the sea, Alaska, a great lake in the wilderness.

But I thought of Jeanne and Mark and Janet, sitting in that godawful plasterboard house and wondering where Papa had gone. Why didn't he come home? And what would they do?

No, if I climbed onto a boxcar, I would take them with me. I would pile us all on, Mark, Jeanne, Janet and myself, and we'd go whizzing out of town: three puzzled spiders and a grinning one, clamped to Papa's shooting star.

Poor Jeanne, puzzled by my frustration, trying desperately to weather my raging unhappiness—outwardly calm, hugging the children close, herself wanting to be more than just a housewife and patiently writing, for small pay, social events for the morning paper eighty miles away and using the money to buy a new bedspring for the two of us. Arid phone calls, arid callers plagued her too. The neighboring man and wife got drunk and had fights that rattled our walls; their beer bottles and milk cartons littered our lawn.

I went home. The kitchen and living room were cluttered with toys, diapers, and baby bottles. I went to the kitchen for a glass of water. The bottom of the glass was stuck to the shelf with syrup. Desperate, I picked up a plate and smashed it in the sink.

Jeanne jumped up from the couch. She was frightened. "What's happening?" she said. "What did you do?"

"This place, this small-town newspaper—it's driving me crazy," I said. "We've got to do something. We've got to get out of there."

"Tonight?" she said. She looked numbed.

I would have given anything to have gone that night, but I told her I had to start writing job applications—immediately.

I would have taken a job on the moon, but Jeanne was more level-headed.

"Why don't you get out of the newspaper business," she said, "and get a job writing for a university? They have lots of good jobs. We could live in a university town, and you'd have time to write too."

Her calm, cool logic was soothing. I felt better now. We would work this out together. We talked for a long time, quietly and eagerly, about the pros and cons of college jobs, where to apply, could I put up with the academic flim-flam that had driven me from college, could I get a job right away. We talked about Alaska. We agreed that we missed it, both of us, but we knew it would be the same old story if I returned to the Anchorage paper: poor pay, more of the newspaper work I now despised, inadequate housing for Mark and Janet in the long winter. Australia—that was a possibility too. Jeanne still wanted to go; so did I. But how would we get there? And so, yes, a university job might be an acceptable compromise.

I sat on the couch with my arm around her, her head on my shoulder. For the first time in months we felt at peace. Eight months in Moses Lake had been too much for the both of us.

8

MY APPLICATION for a job as a writer at Washington State University had been accepted, and I had made it through the interview. In a few days I would report for work. I had quit my job and we hurried off, as fast as we could, to the university town of Pullman, fifty miles east, near the mountains and lakes of Idaho, a city of seven hills green with spring, fan-leafed maples, pines and flowers. Quaint old houses with weathered shingles grew like shady trees in its hills.

If Bremerton had been hell's brink, Moses Lake had been its wasted pit, the smoking bottom of an absurd wishing well where to make a wish was to snatch in vain at a plummeting dollar. But now we had arrived at the green and watered university town of Pullman, a veritable Walden Pond, with our camel's load of books, blankets, and clothes, our past troubles, like a frenzied circle of footprints in the desert, left behind us. Here was a new beginning, neither perfect nor promised, but promising all the same.

If life at Pullman was ostensibly dull, grass-grown, mowed and planted with flowers and maples, it was intrinsically a time of pause, recapitulation and forward-going, and thus exciting. Its dullness, at least, was neither deadly nor deadening. We had discovered, here and there in these half-haloed shrubs, trees, flowers and green hills, interesting and exciting people who found in Pullman a few moment's pleasant pause in their lives, an escape from freeways, cities, city streets, impersonal deadlines, jobs that demanded a pint of blood each day and a fragment of your brain and gave in return a bowl of crumpled paper sprinkled with IBM perforations to eat or rub in your hair—whatever was necessary, according to the instructions, to restore lost blood and bits of brain.

Now it was our turn to lie on the grass and think, to look ahead with patience and no need to snatch handfuls of grass in driving, nagging frustration. It was our time to take pleasant walks in the nearby forests and parks, to play with Mark and Janet in the city park below our house, and to go swimming in the public swimming pool, where the water was blue and cool and the sun fell hot and white on the wet cement along the pool's edge.

It would end, and it would end too soon, in a time of winter, but it would end not forever, only for the moment, even if that moment seemed forever.

March 10, 1962, city of hills and trees and pleasant days. And today was Bean Day, a sort of family get-together, except that only the four of us came and no one else had been invited: an unplanned *happening* at home, one day when the weather was nice.

First there was Jannie-Bean, now closer to three than to two; in three months we would burn the birthday candle to the little blue three and put it away for another year. I don't remember why I chose this nickname. Perhaps it had something to do with Jeanne's once bending over Janet—who lay in the bottom of her bunk bed rubbing her eyes and blinking doubtfully in the light of new morning—and saying, "Hello, old bean—time to get up." So, from time to time, Janet was called Jannie-Bean.

And then came Mark-a-Bean, more nearly three than four, for his birthday had come and passed six days before. From Jannie-Bean to Mark-a-Bean was an easy and logical step, and these nicknames somehow seemed right.

More and more Mark began to call Janet Jannie-Bean. To his mother he would say, "Jannie-Bean ate a flower," ate this, did that. Jannie-Bean this and Jannie-Bean that. He frequently addressed me as Hal, and sometimes he called his mother Jeanne. In the backyard one day he told me that Jeanne was in the house baking stuffed green peppers to feed to his turtle eggs, of which he had none, but they existed all the same and therefore needed nourishment, and stuffed green peppers were as good as any. And then he went inside and said, "Mama, the turtle eggs are hungry."

Jeanne said, "Go tell Papa, and maybe he'll find you something to feed them."

Mark came back to the yard and said, "Hal, the turtle eggs are hungry, Hal. Mama said you would feed them, Papa."

"Ask Jannie-Bean," I said. "Maybe she has something for them."

"Janet doesn't know anything about turtles," he said.

"Then let's go to the kitchen and see if Mama will give us a stuffed pepper," I said.

"Yeah, Hal," he said.

In the kitchen I said to Jeanne, "Mr. Mark-a-Bean wants a stuffed pepper for his turtle eggs."

"Oh, he does, does he?" said Jeanne. "Well, Mr. Mark-a-Bean, let's see what we have."

Mark suddenly pointed a finger at me and lurched: "You're Papa-Bean," he said.

"And that's Mama-Bean," I said, pointing and lurching at Jeanne, who pointed at Mark and lurched and said, "You're Mark-a-Bean." Then Janet came in, dragging a small board.

"Well, who's this?" said Jeanne.

Janet stood and thought for a moment. Mark giggled. We waited for Janet's answer.

"Janet doesn't know anything about turtles," said Mark.

"I do too, Mark," said Janet.

"I'm Mark-a-Bean," said Mark. "That's Papa-Bean. That's Mama-Bean."

"I know a story," said Janet.

"Be quiet, everybody," I said. "Janet's going to tell a story," I said.

"Janet doesn't know anything about turtles," said Mark.

"Quiet," I said. "Let's hear the story."

"I flew out of my window," said Janet, "without any wings. Then the birds saw me and came and sold me some eggs and some feathers and some wings and bird mouths—four bird mouths. And then I was a sea gull and I flew away forever. The birds gave me a Yogi Bear mask and I put it on but it didn't fit over the bird mouths, so I gave it back and I was a sea gull again, and I flew and flew away forever and ever.

"Then Mama and Papa cried. They cried and cried because they didn't have any Jannie-Bean. Then I was a sea gull and I flew in the window and Mama and Papa cried, so I took off my bird mouths and said, 'I'm your Jannie-Bean!' "

"You're Jannie-Bean," said Mark.

"You're Mark-a-Bean," said Janet. She abruptly turned and, dragging her board behind her, went downstairs to the backyard, and that was the last we saw of her until dinnertime.

Jeanne now began to make notes of the things that

Janet and Mark did that amused her, and she made notes of some of the more interesting people we had met and the adventures we had had in Alaska. She hoped someday to write about our adventures in the Alaska house.

She made notes about the morning Janet, unfed and in pajamas, had walked to the refrigerator, opened the door and pulled out a big, brown, partly scorched potato.

Janet took a large bite that puffed her cheeks, and then walked matter-of-factly to the garbage can. She bent over and spit out the mouthful and threw the scorched potato in after it. She turned to her mother and said, "It's much too weak and wan," and shuffled indifferently, on the padded bottoms of her pajama suit, back to the bedroom.

Jeanne wrote about the day when Mark had asked her about our deceased cat, Lobo, who had died of distemper because, as Jeanne explained to Mark, "he wouldn't let Papa catch him to take him to the doctor."

"Lobo was stupid," Mark answered, and added that he himself got shots to keep *him* from getting sick.

Then he asked his mother, "If I make myself dead, will I be a spirit and see Lobo?"

His mother said yes, that if he made himself dead his spirit would leave his body and he would probably see Lobo; but she really preferred, she said, that he stay home, just the way he was, and not go away to see Lobo the cat.

He wanted to know more about what happens when people die, and did Gramma Horner—my mother's mother, who had died a few months before—have a spirit too, like Lobo the cat? Jeanne explained to Mark, as best she knew, the nature of death.

One day Mark asked his mother what love meant, and Jeanne told him that love was "what Mama and Papa felt about Mark and Janet" and, hopefully, what Mark and Janet felt about Mama and Papa. Mark, she wrote, went away satisfied that he knew the answer. I like to think that she had rung a bell with a tiny golden hammer and that Mark was knowingly informed—though the word *love* is a mystery. Only in the wordless lexicon of our days and nights together did the word have a meaning.

Jeanne sewed clothes for the children and none for herself. Cooking, which once made her impatient, now captured more and more of her time and imagination, as though she had discovered that to set a hot and faintly steamy rib roast on the family table was not only to satisfy three, four appetites but to stimulate them as well and create an undefinable glow within and without the stomach.

This was a far cry from the day I had gone to her bachelor-girl apartment in Anchorage and found her heating a white porcelain pot of stewed tomatoes and dropped-in pieces of bread, which she heated and ate indifferently, as though food was merely a logical method of keeping alive—an attitude she attributed to her Iowa childhood.

She enjoyed having guests for dinner, especially John and Carol—our former upstairs tenants—who had bought a house of their own on the other side of town but visited often; and often we visited them and their new baby, Sean, born brightly of Carol and John.

Carol, however, disliked cooking, and we joked about it often, even John, who came to our house in the afternoon—after lunch—munching a pepperone stick and drinking a can of Metrecal from the Chinese grocery just down the street. John and Carol were both indifferent to the art of cookery, Carol more than John perhaps. She preferred slow-cooking stews that simmered and bubbled self-sufficiently while she read her books of ancient music or played the violin in the bedroom.

But they enjoyed good food all the same and were always pleased and hungry when they came to our house for dinner and Jeanne served stacks of juicy tortillas piled indulgently with melted cheese, lettuce, and hot sauce—Mark, Janet and baby Sean sitting at a small table of their own and making a splendid mess of everything.

Carol came to see Jeanne during the day, and Jeanne went to see Carol, and they discussed history and civil rights, the neighbors next door, me, John, Mark, Janet and baby Sean; took walks with baby strollers, waxed irate and amused at the local weekly newspaper's spastic, far-right editorials that pointed to "Pinkos" everywhere and spoke in dark-red undertones of suspicious glimmerings in the university's newly formed chapter of the American Civil Liberties Union.

Several hours of the day Jeanne gathered news for the morning daily in Spokane. There was no society news required of her—only the news from the city council, the courts, and the planning commission, in which Jeanne took a genuine if often amused interest. The affairs of politicians, big and small, had always drawn Jeanne's interest. She enjoyed writing about them and looked forward to interviewing the principals and having intimate access to high places and otherwise enjoying the powers of the press, which gave her a feeling of being in command and of being commanded by the strong sense of civic involvement inculcated by her publisher father.

This too was a far cry from her self-enforced civic involvement in Anchorage shortly after our marriage and after she had quit the newspaper, when she sold cigars and candy at the hospital for the benefit of the hospital's Gray Ladies. It was a job she abhorred but kept, out of a coercive sense of duty—but quit when it got her down and she decided that the job hardly conformed to her own sense of realism and hardly satisfied her desire to do more than serve just for the sake of serving.

Jeanne was pleased with herself when the article she wrote in Pullman, on the impoverished life of the children of the state's migrant workers, was published by an influential Seattle newspaper and came to the attention of a state senator who promised an investigation.

On Sundays she took Mark and Janet to Sunday school, and I stayed home, contentedly agnostic and indifferent to the church. The question of whether there might be a God rarely came to mind, though from time to time I wished there was one so that I might shake my fist at him and throw rocks. My sense of being independent of any so-called predestination and preplanned fortuities gave me cause not to attribute my personal experiences, good or bad, to something called God. War and gross inhumanity made me wish there was a God, but when I imagined God I always saw a nineteenth-century drunk in bowler hat and three days' beard, leering over a five-cent schooner of beer while the world desperately tugged on his coattails like a small boy trying to get his father off the bar stool and home to his mother with what was left of the pay check.

My notion of gods worried and puzzled Jeanne, who wondered what *good* would be left in the world if God was dead, drunk, or indifferent. I answered by saying I thought *good* came before God, that *good* was what men did that the *word* good best defined, and that those who had to be told what *good* was would never learn anyway, so why bother? Bad you can teach; you can teach a child to murder, steal and fight a war. That's easy. But how do you teach compassion and love, if this is what *good* is made of?

Janet and Mark were getting love and compassion at home, and I figured that's where *good* begins, if it has to have a beginning. Sunday school exposed their minds to rules and regulations, some good, some bad, about which they would make up their minds anyway when the questions moved them. Meantime, Sunday school was fun for them. They came home stimulated with stories about baby Jesus and Moses, whom they looked upon as exciting characters in a good book of children's stories.

Theology and dogma they neither understood nor gave a hoot about, and, to Janet, baby Jesus was a baby three blocks away whose birth had been Christmas in July, with fireworks and all. Mark came home with stories of not being able to find his snow boots in the piled jumble on the floor, and how Stevie had hoarded the toys in the corner and caught hell from the Sunday-school teacher. Whatever, they enjoyed it, and that was enough.

In Anchorage, Bremerton, and Moses Lake, Jeanne's God had been a demanding, stern and trying God, who confused the way and yet demanded dutiful perseverance in achieving the one goal, which was itself a mystery. In Pullman her God had undergone a transformation and had become more an observer than a doer—an important but not awesome light and essence that sat at a large desk in a small corner of the mind, more like an understanding minister, who smokes a pipe and suggests you solve your own problems and "let me know if I can be of help." And her new God made her happier, and his local Congregational minister was far more interested in the social-action calendar of the day than the theoretical nature of God, good and evil, and the consequences of committing sin. God's new minister made her happier too. And this made me happy; her will was her way.

Jeanne was surprised but not shocked when I came home on a hot day in June and told her I had been asked to resign my job at the university. She was angry and impatient with the reasons given me for my called-for resignation but not at all uneasy about what might happen to the four of us. This too was a far cry from Bremerton and Moses Lake. Here in Pullman we seemed to belong; we had friends, friends who were close and dear to us. We also had $3,000 in stocks, but we were determined not to use them and had put them in a safety-deposit box. Our duplex, with the upstairs rented, made our mortgage payment a little more than fifteen dollars a month. There was no cause to panic, nothing much to worry about.

My fiction had been going well, even if I hadn't sold any. I was satisfied with what I was doing. Instead of rejections, now I was getting notes and letters from the editors. The outlook was hopeful.

My being asked to resign puzzled me, but here it was: I was being asked to resign because my punctuation in the biweekly faculty news bulletin did not conform to the academic mode. Regretfully, I was told, the faculty demanded a pedantry to which I appeared indifferent. Cited for my consideration was my having abbreviated January in one story and then spelling it out in another, in the same issue.

Shortly before this I had written an account in the faculty news bulletin that supported the newly formed campus chapter of the American Civil Liberties Union, then under fire by the local newspaper editor, who was finding Pinkos everywhere. My article had caused a stir in the newspaper, which in turn caused a stir in the university's public-relations office, where great sensitivity was maintained in matters of public image—partly out of fear of the conservative farmers, who, it was said, had a great say about legislative funds granted the university and partly out of past brushes with hunters-down of Pinkos and liberals.

My editorials in the university news bulletin had attracted a following among the young liberals, by far in the minority but outspoken and sympathetic. I ignored my editor's warning that I had gone too far in expressing my feelings against atomic weaponry and academic chicanery. The university, he warned, was a citadel of transplanted Midwestern conservatism, and I was being called a beatnik—my beardless chin being no assurance against it. Since I was editor of the faculty news bulletin, I intended to write my views to the full; that I was being called a beatnik seemed ridiculous and hardly worth worrying about.

Whatever the reasons, I was asked to resign and had little choice. I was given three months in which to make it official, a time of grace I took in full while Jeanne and I charted the future.

We talked about selling the house and going back to Alaska, and Jeanne suggested we consider Australia. That island continent still held a fascination for her, as did China, to which she was drawn by Edgar Snow's fascinating accounts of intrigue and Oriental inscrutability and which was, in her mind, a vast, unopened box of journalistic adventure where she could write of need and poverty and capture the attention and inspire the help of the more bountiful countries of the world.

But we decided that we had too many good friends here, that we were probably in a better financial position than ever before, should I want to free-lance full time. My fiction was getting better and better responses from the editors, I had recently developed a passionate (if sometimes disillusioned) interest in photography—in which I found a visual language akin to my writing—

and I was doing surprisingly well with the sale of picture stories.

We finally decided that it would work out best if I combined writing and photography and welded the two into articles—except that I had very recently sold my camera in disgust because I had decided my pictures were mostly bad and meaningless and that, therefore, photography was too. So I went back to writing. Now, when Jeanne and I decided I would free-lance full time, I figured I would have to sell a few articles to buy a camera and begin anew my picture-taking and reconcile myself and photography.

If our plans of free-lancing worked, we figured we would someday go to Australia and Asia on our own, to write and take pictures, and back to Alaska, to write and do picture and story books. It was a grand dream we both shared, and Mark and Janet would of course come along with us. Both of us felt strongly about having well-traveled, well-exposed children. Janet, now three, had a remarkable facility for words. Mark, approaching five, seemed mature and intelligent, and both had an immense curiosity that we tried hard to satisfy.

Both children were easy to talk to and to reason with. Always we talked things over with them and never talked down. Their world of innocence, naïveté and constant wonder and curiosity fascinated us, and we tried to fascinate them with ours, the adult world, and with what it had to offer—at the same time trying to nurture and let bloom all the natural, exotic, and incremental charms of their green-growing childhood. They seemed to be happy children.

When my resignation became effective in September, we had charted our course, and we looked forward to splendid years. Jeanne had taken a job as a reporter on the Moscow, Idaho, daily newspaper, eight miles east of Pullman, in an adjoining college town. Each day she drove to work and took Janet and Mark to one of Moscow's day nursery schools for working mothers, a Catholic school open to all for a very reasonable fee, where sisters watched with a constant eye for hell-raisers. I stayed home alone and wrote in the basement.

Jeanne's earning our living troubled neither my conscience nor hers. We fancied we were being modern, emancipated and practical. We had planned it this way, and it was neither a stigma nor a sticky question among our friends. If she were satisfied with the arrangement, I was too—though secretly I hoped the arrangement would soon be reversed when my stories sold. There was no question that it would have been better had I made the living and Jeanne stayed home and looked after the children. But if we were to achieve our goal, this was the way, and we stuck to it.

I usually made breakfast for all of us and did light housekeeping and fixed dinner for Mark's, Jeanne's and Janet's return in the evening, though I was always happy when Jeanne fixed dinner—it was better than mine.

Mark enjoyed the day school, though often Janet brought back reports that "Mark didn't get his sucker today," the sucker being the reward at day's end for non-hell raisers. Mark, we were told, liked to wrestle, run and jump when he was supposed to be doing other things. And sometimes he got a sucker and sometimes he didn't. Janet always got hers, but day school was not easy for her. While Mark was self-sufficient and remarkably outgoing and gregarious, Janet was shy and held herself close to her mother. She often dawdled at her breakfast because she did not want to go to day school.

Jeanne was happy with her job. For the first time she was a full-time news reporter and not a society editor, and her editor was more than pleased with the way she was handling Moscow's most sensational court trial in years.

No one had ever remarked that our life in Pullman was Bohemian, nor did we bother to give a name to our way of life. We were doing much the same as the college teachers, artists, writers and photographers who were our friends. Most of our friends had children too, and they lived in a way that simply appealed to them and to us.

We all enjoyed conversations on just about everything. Some of us played recorders, some the guitar and piano, some of us nothing at all. Some of us went to church, some of us didn't. We were liberal in our politics, and we were liberal, I suppose, in our views about most things.

Jeanne, more than ever before, was happy and pleased with our circle of friends. We seemed to have in common a desire to determine our own lives, unconcerned that we were either conforming or not conforming to any particular mode. We went in the direction our emotions and special and individual needs and propensities took us.

This time in our lives, in the lives of the four of us, was meaningful and promising. We had love, we had good friends, we had good things to eat and good things to talk about and to think about, and we had hopes for the future. And the future seemed not too distant and would probably be not too different, except that we would want to travel more and see the things and places we had so long wanted to see, and Mark and Janet would come along with us.

9

JEANNE telephoned one of our close friends, Bev McConnel, who lived a few blocks away. She asked if Bev and her husband, Pat, would come to the house after dinner that evening. Pat, who taught business law at the university, was also a lawyer. Over the phone Bev said she was sure Pat could help out with the advice Jeanne was asking.

Bev was tall, Pat short. If you were to judge them by their physiques, they were as incompatible as an upper-case "T" and a lower-case "g" side by side in a spelling game. But any physical comparison was grossly misleading, and when you got to know them it became quite apparent that both were *big* and as compatible as the "i" and its dot. They gave of their time, compassion, and home life when good causes—civil rights, migrant workers' needy children, and simply friends in need of help—beckoned.

They were busy and young and lived in an old white house fifty years late in its quest for modish distinction and elegance among the town's former farm folk. They shared their house with three lively and galloping children—two boys and one an elfin girl with her mother's warm, deep eyes. The three were playmates of Mark's and Janet's, and often Bev and Pat, Jeanne and I exchanged baby-sitting favors, along with the others who belonged to the sitting pool.

I looked forward to having Pat and Bev over that night but it was a little disconcerting: Jeanne had asked Pat to draft her will.

Perhaps a week before, Jeanne and I had been reading a book on palmistry, and, out of curiosity and a certain willingness to challenge the fanciful powers of the occult, we read the instructions on how to read a palm. At the time I was very much interested in photography and how a photograph of a person told so much about that person's character. Wondering if the palmist's art might offer an insight into the photographer's, I borrowed the book from the library. Jeanne, reading her own palm according to the instructions, said, "Look. I have a short life line." She rubbed her palm with the other hand, as though erasing the line away, and then looked at the other palm. "This hand, too," she said.

Neither of us had faith in the palmist's professed powers of telling the future. If we hadn't been momentarily intrigued with the book on palmistry, we might just as well have been passing the time with one of the children's games.

But Jeanne seemed disturbed. She was all but silent the rest of the evening. We never again mentioned our ostensibly cursory brush with palmistry—not that we were overwhelmed and awed; I, for one, simply forgot about it, and I supposed Jeanne had too. It wasn't much more than a week later when Jeanne made arrangements to have her will drawn.

Pat and Bev came to the house in the evening, and it had been decided before hand that this was as good a time as any to draft both our wills, though Jeanne's main concern had been her own. The four of us sat at the kitchen table, each of us with a small glass of red wine. The kitchen walls were yellow and glossy and usually gave a feeling of bright warmth; but tonight they seemed cold and institutional. The wine in my glass looked purple and sickly and tinted with the yellow of the wall.

I felt the draft of the macabre and I had a momentary nervous shiver as we discussed the details of our wills. It was as though we were talking about two dead people who, by some quirk in time, happened to be ourselves, and I was glad when later we discussed other, more lively and pleasant things.

One detail was Jeanne's $3,000 in stocks, recently given to her by her father—this in addition to his earlier gift of stocks Jeanne had cashed to buy the duplex we now had owned for about six months. She directed that the stocks, along with other minor stocks, go to me—if ever it became necessary to execute the will.

Janet's and Mark's future guardians she was especially concerned about. She made the provision that I would be both executor of the estate and guardian to the children, the usual arrangement in these matters. But she was concerned about what might happen should neither of us survive Mark and Janet and about who might step forth to fill the vacuum.

She asked Pat to make a provision that Mark's and Janet's guardians—should neither Jeanne nor I survive the children—be her favorite cousin, Ginny, and her bearded psychologist husband, Thornton. Jeanne was confident that Ginny and Thornton occupied the same ground in matters of child rearing and most things in general as we did.

I agreed. Thornton and Ginny were only a few years older than we; their ideas and outlooks were young, thoughtful, compassionate, and well tempered with good humor. Pat, however, advised Jeanne that it was doubtful that a provision appointing Ginny and Thornton guardians would stand up in court. Such a provision would be risky, he said, unless firm legal arrangements were made with Ginny and Thornton beforehand, and to make them would be long and involved.

Anxious to get on and be done with this unpleasant business, Jeanne made the provision that her parents be named guardians if neither Jeanne nor I survived the children. I did the same. The assurance of guardianship by immediate family provided against the danger of a court-appointed guardian, and we figured we could thus make any other arrangements privately, among the family.

Jeanne loved her father and mother; there was no question about that. But she hoped that Ginny and Thornton, or perhaps our friends, John and Carol, would be Mark's and Janet's guardians and tutors for the simple reason that her cousin and her husband and our friends were young and of a similar mind. Her own childhood had been a happy one, but that time had long passed and her parents were getting on in age; her wish was merely a practical one.

A few days later Pat brought our typed and completed wills to the house, and Jeanne and I signed them. We put them away in the tiny gray safety-deposit box at the bank, and I looked forward to forgetting the matter. Her will, as well as mine, I supposed, were only pieces of paper whose intent was no more than Jeanne's practicality. They would grow old and yellow in the little gray box in the vault at the bank.

The day was Wednesday, December 5, 1962, and the next day Jeanne would drive Janet to day school and leave Mark home with me, since Janet had recovered from a mild bout with the flu and Mark had not. Scarcely three months ago Jeanne had made out her will; but this was hardly on our minds.

Janet usually pulled out of colds, the sniffles, and the flu more quickly than Mark. She was as bouncy, busy, and bubbly as usual but not very eager to go to day school. She was never eager to go on any day, but tomorrow she would have to go without Mark, and that would make it worse.

Mark, however, was anxious to go to school, for he had been given a choice part in the school's annual Christmas pageant—but his stomach wasn't up to it. He was to be Jack Horner, and he was something of a celebrity among his playmates. He had only a few lines to say. But his script had been issued well in advance by the veteran director, a wise, elderly sister who apprehensively was guarding against bad reviews by first-night parents.

Tonight, Jeanne sewed Mark's costume to completion: a shirt with a foot-wide Jack Horner collar, blue stripes and big buttons. For bottoms he would wear a pair of olive-drab tights, already well worn and with a wide rip in the seat, which Jeanne had mended. Then we had a dress rehearsal.

Mark sat in his diminutive wooden rocking chair, in tights and foot-wide collar, in a selected corner of the living room.

"Now, Mark," said Jeanne, "do you remember what to say?"

"Yeah," said Mark, "I'm Jack Horner."

"Mark's Jack Horner," said Janet, who perhaps felt a bit upstaged and climbed into Jeanne's lap. Jeanne sat in the big rocking chair and Mark in the little one.

"You're supposed to say more than that," said Jeanne.

"What?" said Mark.

"Don't you remember?" said Jeanne.

"Mark forgot what he's supposed to say," said Janet.

"I did not," said Mark. "Janet forgot what *she's* supposed to say."

"I'm not in the play," said Janet. "I'm going to watch Mark be Jack Horner."

"You've got two more lines to say, Mark," said Jeanne.

"You sewed my pants too tight," said Mark. "There's a lump where the hole was."

"Stand up and let me see," she said.

Mark stood up and bent over for Jeanne's inspection.

"My," she said, "there is a lump. Maybe you'll have to stand up to be Jack Horner."

"Jack Horner *sat* in the corner," said Mark.

He sat down.

"The lump feels better now," he said.

"Do you remember your lines now?" said Jeanne.

"Yeah," said Mark. " 'I'm little Jack Horner, as I sit in my corner, I'd like a new Christmas pie.' "

"Good for Mark," said Jeanne. "We'll just have to give Mr. Mark a Christmas pie."

"I want a pie too," said Janet.

"Then we'll all have pie," she said.

We didn't have any pie in the house, so we had ice cream instead. And because the ice cream wasn't pie, we called it pie. Mark had Jack Horner pie. Janet had pumpkin.

Mark said the ice cream made his stomach feel better, but he still didn't feel well enough to go to school. Most of the day he'd been drinking juices; he had even balked at his favorite breakfast cereal, pop-and-crackle stuff that was mostly silent even when you bombed it with milk and slices of banana.

Janet ate a full breakfast as usual that day; her cheeks were pink, while Mark's were telltale pallid. We decided that Mark would stay home with me and Jeanne would take Janet to day school. With Mark home without Janet, I would be able to write in the living room while he played, lounged, or whatever. With Mark and Janet home sick together and kept in the house all day, they were as hard to manage as two bears, sick or well: squawks and squeaks were the mode of the day, in addition to broken toys, records, and great traffic jams of toy dump trucks, wooden trains and Janet's rocking horse, which always had to stay inside the house on the days she had to. Sometimes we all raised hell together. I filled their room with cardboard boxes, and we crawled in and out, popped up, sprang out, painted on windows and doors, trap doors and secret passageways. A big, yellow cardboard packing box still sat in their bedroom, a fragment of the house of several nights before. Several times squashed and flattened, it looked like a drunken parallelogram about to say "O."

A few weeks ago I had had new heavy-tread tires put on our tiny Volkswagen, since I was worried about Jeanne's driving on the highway to Moscow on winter days when it snowed. Usually the snow melted almost as quickly as it fell, but when the snow stayed on and made difficult going on the highway, I drove Jeanne, Mark and Janet to Moscow and picked them up later. Recently it had snowed, but it was warm and the snow didn't stay. The streets were wet, as they were most of the winter. I was not concerned about Jeanne's driving herself and Janet to Moscow the next morning.

In the morning I saw the two of them off. The few words of goodbye we said at the driveway that morning were the last words we would speak to each other; Jeanne's and Janet's voices I would never hear again.

10

JEANNE WAS DEAD.

Janet was dying.

I called Jeanne's father from the hospital. "I have bad news," I said. "Jeanne is dead." I didn't know how else to put it.

For a long while he was silent. Then he said, "Oh, golly." It was the same expression Jeanne had used whenever something catastrophic happened, like the day before our wedding when a fire had broken out in our apartment-to-be and burned some of Jeanne's favorite history books. It had hurt her deeply, but that was all she had said: "Oh, golly."

I broke the silence and tried to tell him what had happened. Jeanne was taking Janet to nursery school. No,

Mark wasn't in the car; he was home with me; he wasn't feeling well. The car skidded on ice and struck a school bus head on.

He didn't ask about Janet, but I told him it looked bad; the doctor didn't think she would live.

He didn't say very much. He seemed to grope for words. "We'll come as soon as we can," he said finally. "We'll catch the first plane we can; we should be there tomorrow morning."

I hung up the phone and stood in the office of the university hospital administrator looking out the window, through the Venetian blind, at the black asphalt street wet from a recent snow that had since melted. The sky was silver gray and intensely light. A green 1954 sedan was parked across the street in a white-lined space marked Reserved for Doctor; it was shiny and hard and looked brand new. It didn't look real. Nothing did.

I don't think I cried in the office. I couldn't. I couldn't believe yet that Jeanne was dead. An hour ago I had said goodbye. I had helped Janet into the back seat. She wore a red parka with white imitation fur around the hood. She had wanted to wear her favorite dress that morning, the red and white checkered one her mother had made. The day was cold, and under her dress she wore black tights.

I waved as they left the driveway. Janet was standing up in the back seat, and she waved back through the little oval window in the back of the Volkswagen. When the car had turned the corner, I went back downstairs and tried to coax Mark to finish his breakfast. He was still in the yellow pajamas his mother had made from one of his old baby blankets.

This morning I let him dawdle more than usual; his stomach was still uneasy. The breakfast dishes were still on the table: Jeanne's, Janet's and mine; Janet's glass of milk was only half finished.

I read a book while Mark poked and dawdled at his Cheerios. I must have been reading for about fifteen minutes when I heard a siren. At first it sounded like a police car in pursuit of a speeder; but the siren kept going.

It was still going until the sound of it was lost in the distance.

I went to the kitchen window and looked out, not in the direction of the siren but in the direction of the city park below. The trees were black, tall and gaunt; a few had patches of snow around them. It was one of those bleak days when the sky was like old and dirty snow, and the whir and swish of the heavy early-morning traffic seemed to make the morning even bleaker. All December, every December was like this; only the colored lights of Christmas would save it.

I looked for my pipe and finally found it on top of a stack of books on the floor. The warm yellow flame of the wooden match, as I lighted my pipe, made me feel better. I sat down at the table, across from Mark, and stared out the kitchen window, fascinated by the dirty-snow sky and the black trees and still holding the burned-out match in my hand.

A few minutes later the phone rang and I didn't want to answer it. But I perked up a bit when I thought maybe it was John calling. On the way to the university, lately, he had been stopping by for coffee, and we often spent about half an hour talking. He usually called before he came.

Mark didn't seem to hear the phone; he never did—maybe because nobody ever called him. Someday I'll call him up and surprise him, I thought.

I picked up the phone and was tempted to say, "Good morning, John," but then I thought it might be somebody else, though only the people who knew us ever called this early. But the man's voice was new to me.

"Mr. Harold Painter?"

"Yes," I said. It was one of those voices you hear on the phone when you're behind in your bills. I wasn't behind in any bills, but it sounded like that anyway. Maybe it was a job offer; I'd had several lately.

"Mr. Painter," he said, "could you come to the university hospital right away?"

His urgency baffled me. Whom did I know at the hospital? Why did he want me? I didn't know what made me think of Jeanne and Janet, and I was afraid to ask the question. What else could it be—but it couldn't. Why was he calling me?

"Is anything wrong?" I said.

"Mr. Painter," he said, "your wife and daughter were brought in here a few minutes ago from a traffic accident. I'm afraid it's serious. You'd better come right away."

Come right away? What does that mean?

"How serious is it?" I said.

"We don't think your wife will live, Mr. Painter. We're doing everything we can. We're not sure about your daughter. I suggest you hurry."

I didn't know what to make of it. His voice, his words didn't sound real. Nothing like this ever happened to you; it didn't happen to anybody. Perhaps in the confusion the doctors had made a mistake: Jeanne and Janet were all right after all. But I had to hurry to the hospital—not because there might not be time; I had to hurry to ask Jeanne what had happened. She would be in a clean white bed and she would smile and tell me not to worry. Janet would be crying, but I could calm her. I had to hurry.

I didn't know what to say to Mark. I put him in his blue snowsuit and told him I had to hurry to the hospital, that the doctor told me Jeanne and Janet had run into something in the car and the doctor wanted to tell me what had happened.

"Did Janet hurt her arm?" he said.

Suddenly he looked very lonely, small and helpless. I picked him up and carried him out the door.

"I hope she hasn't," I said. "I'm going to take you to Bev McConnel's, and you can play with the boys. I'm going to go see Mama and Janet. I'll tell you all about them when I come back."

What was in his mind I couldn't tell. He was quiet and looked puzzled. When I took him to Bev's, one of her little boys asked him what he was doing in his pajamas. Mark didn't answer. He ran into the back room, where the other children were playing with blocks.

Bev looked worried. I told her Jeanne and Janet had

been hurt in a car accident. I didn't tell her more; I didn't want to. I didn't want to believe that it was any worse. They were just *hurt,* that was all.

Bev offered to call Jeanne's young minister friend and ask him to drive me. But it seemed too long to wait. I walked to the hospital, about half a mile up the hill, as fast as I could.

The administrator was waiting for me at the door.

"Are you Mr. Painter?" he asked.

I don't think I answered. I must have just looked at him, waiting.

He took me by the arm, to the registration counter. A woman in a white hospital dress was sitting at a desk just below me, typing. If she heard him, I didn't know, didn't care. She went on typing and I envied her.

He said it simply. "We did all we could, Mr. Painter. Your wife died a few minutes ago."

He said Janet was in serious condition and it was doubtful she would live, but they were sending her to a brain specialist in Spokane, eighty miles away.

I don't know what I said to him. I asked to go into his office. I wanted to be alone.

I looked out the window, through the Venetian blind, looked at the gray sky, the wet pavement, the glistening car across the street, the long green building. The gray sky—I kept staring at the gray sky.

Paul, Jeanne's young minister friend, came into the room. He didn't say a word. He just looked at me, holding his hat in his hand.

"I hope Jeanne was a happy woman," I said. "I hope she knew she was loved. That's the most important thing in the world. I hope she knew she was loved."

He didn't answer. He was in his late twenties, a few years younger than I, and I think he was lost for words and I was glad. I was glad he didn't say anything about God, life and death and the Church. That would have made me angry.

The administrator came into the room and told me I could see Janet now. She was on a guerney, in the hallway. They would take her to a brain specialist in Spokane. I had to hurry; the ambulance was waiting.

When I saw Janet, a nurse was pushing her guerney down the long corridor, toward an open door and an ambulance. She was covered up to her chin with a white sheet and her head was wrapped in bandages. Her eyes were black and blue and swollen shut. A hospital attendant carried her clothes in a transparent plastic bag.

Why didn't she open her eyes and ask for Papa and Mama? Why didn't she come running into my arms, excited and with her wonderful little imagination at full tilt, and tell me that she and Mama had had a funny thing happen to them, that a lot of men came and let them out of the car and a policeman gave them a ride home and Mama would be coming soon? Why couldn't I take her in my arms and tell her that everything would be all right?

Someone asked me if I wanted to ride in the ambulance.

I said, "No." I couldn't.

Janet was unconscious. I didn't think she was alive.

Jeanne's minister, Ted Edquist, was at my side. He said he would drive me to Spokane; we would follow the ambulance.

This was much better. I wanted to believe that some miracle would happen on the way to Spokane—something that couldn't happen if I sat in the ambulance holding Janet's cold hand and looking at her swollen face, her unfeeling body.

I don't know how long it took to get to the hospital. I remember only looking at the cold winter landscape and thinking that something had come between me and the world, an invisible wall that turned everything—the earth, the sky, my friends, my family—into cold glass.

The brain specialist met me at the entrance to the hospital. "There is a chance, a slim one," he said. He said Janet had the worst kind of concussion: the front of her head was shattered and had pushed bone into her brain. He couldn't promise anything.

He was too objective, too medical. I understood, but I wanted to rail against it, to say nonsense, he could save her. He wanted to, but he couldn't.

She lay in a coma for four days, in an oversized baby crib, naked, on a refrigerated sheet that kept down the high temperature that itself threatened to take her life. Her right leg was broken and in a cast. The white cast seemed so ludicrous, so hopeless. It just didn't seem to matter; it was so incidental, so meaningless.

Once I held her hand. Despite her high temperature, it was cool and moist. I hoped that the touch of my hand would awaken her. I hoped she would feel my love, my nearness, that something would flow from my hand to hers. But her hand did not feel mine. It twitched, opened and shut itself, over and over again. Janet had always been active and fidgety; she bored easily and was forever busy with one thing and then another. Now her hand seemed restless and nervous.

I looked at her swollen and bandaged head, her closed and bruised eyes, and I feared that if ever her eyes were to open they would look upon a crazed, upside-down world. But it didn't matter; I would hold her and love her all the same. I would be tender and patient even if I were angry that this beautiful child had been robbed of sight, sense and sound. It wouldn't matter. I would love her all the same.

But whatever it was that flowed from my hand to hers was not enough. Nothing in this world, neither love nor hope, was strong enough to give her life, to open her eyes and make them seeing again. She and I were never to have this joy nor this pain nor this awakening.

On December 10, 1962, four days after her mother's death, Janet died without having regained consciousness. It came, painless and unbeknownst.

Jeanne and Janet were gone.

PART TWO

Voyage to a Sunken Island

1

FROM THE MOMENT of Jeanne's and Janet's death, nothing seemed real, nothing seemed right. I found myself on a dark voyage, oddly alone and restless, unable to sleep at night—as though I lay in the bunk of a sailing ship and had vague sensations of passing strange islands in the darkness of the night.

I didn't know where the ship was going, and at times it did not matter. Even during the day I had dreams of passing islands, islands that rose and fell in the sea, from which voices beckoned and hands reached out.

Who commanded the ship I did not know; and at times the ship sailed beneath the sea, and I kept wondering where Jeanne and Janet were, as though I ought to know but couldn't remember, and the ship sailed on, driven by dark currents, and strange, luminous fish swam ahead, behind and over, and I wondered when the voyage would end and where it would take me.

I stood over Jeanne's open casket, in the mortuary, my hands clasping the wide, dark edge, feeling with my fingertips the silken lining that Jeanne lay upon and did not feel at all. Her father and I were the only members of the family to see her in death; there would be no open casket, no casket at all, at the funeral service.

Dwight Bannister stood next to me, holding his hat behind his back with both hands, bent slightly at the waist, leaning forward a bit. Neither of us spoke to the other; neither of us looked into the other's eyes. A few minutes before we had sat in the undertaker's office, a few steps down the hall from the darkened room in which Jeanne lay, a room of heavy drapes and opaque windows, slightly perfumed and with candles burning and a wreath of flowers on a wire stand with a card attached. A light hidden in the ceiling, like the lights used in the imaginative display windows of department stores selling expensive but imitation period furniture, evenly illuminated Jeanne's body and made her hands and face seem unnaturally pink and shiny, as though she had used too much liquid rouge. In the office the undertaker, tall, balding, matter-of-fact and businesslike rather than obsequious and overly sympathetic, had expressed his hope that Dwight and I would be satisfied with his handiwork, and had observed that it had been especially hard, "considering the nature of her injuries," drawing his hand demonstratively across his chest so that we might understand, without his having to use the words *crushed* or *cavity*. Before we went in to see her I made the final arrangements and asked that the casket be shipped to the Bannister family plot in Ottumwa, Iowa, as Dwight had requested—Dwight and I had discussed it on the way to the mortuary. This finished, he pointed the way to the room in which Jeanne lay and left us. And now Dwight and I stood side by side looking down at Jeanne.

There was no mistaking her. This was Jeanne, Jeanne Painter, my wife and Mark's and Janet's mother—and Dwight's daughter, the young woman who had gone to Alaska and met a young man and had borne his children and who would all too soon lie beneath a small matter-of-fact headstone in the town of her Iowa childhood, a headstone that would read "Jeanne Bannister Painter" and beside it a similar stone for Janet Painter.

Jeanne wore her favorite dress, a gray one with faint white stripes and a large round, white collar. But it was not worn well—there was a hollowness about the chest. No, this was not Jeanne. Only her dress. The dress was there, but Jeanne was not. She was not wearing her glasses, though she wore them every day in life. Of course not—there was no reason to wear them now, no reason to wear one's glasses in death. Her hands were folded across her stomach, and on her left hand was her wedding ring, silver, with a small diamond mounted high on a tiny filigreed pedestal. She lay in perfect repose, perfectly still and unmoving. This was unlike her, for she had been a restless sleeper, turning in the night, from side to side, often needing more room than our double bed was able to give her. No, this was not Jeanne. This was not my wife. I had seen Jeanne on the morning of the accident, waved goodbye as she drove around the corner, Janet looking through the back window of the Volkswagen. And this was the last I had seen of her.

And Janet! It would be the same with Janet, and that I had seen her after the accident—seen her alive but in a coma—made little difference. She was *alive* in the hospital, but there was no life in her. And four days after her mother's death, on the evening of the day of her mother's funeral, it was final. The last time I had seen Janet was when she looked back from the window of the car; this was the last time. There was no other Janet.

How could I explain to Mark what I could not explain

to myself? It should have been simple to explain that Jeanne was dead, to say she would never speak to us, never see us; that we would never see, never speak to her. For the fact was simple: she was dead, and we were not.

I tried. I tried to explain what could not be explained, not by me.

How could I possibly give Mark in words what had been lost in life! And I wanted badly to replace the ineffable absence, now and in the eternal future, of his mother's presence and his mother's love. I wanted to replace it with some acceptable understanding that not all was lost, that this world, though sheared in half, might be whole again.

My feelings about his future were dark. I saw a small boy alone in a dark, quiet house. His father was gone, at work. During the day an old woman, or perhaps a young, indifferent girl, kept the boy's time occupied with toys and games, gave him scraps of paper to draw on, magazines to thumb through on the floor and to cut pictures from, kept him *busy,* always *busy* and *occupied*—a woman who went away at night, to whom the man wrote out a check for her services, who went away at night and came back in the morning, a few minutes before the boy's father went out the door to work. Before he left he gave the woman instructions for the boy's lunch.

I had to tell Mark what had happened, even if I could not explain away the terror and the unreasonableness. I knew it would be wrong—and cruel—to tell him some fiction, that his mother had gone away awhile and would be back. When she didn't come back, what then? But how do you take a small boy in your arms and tell him that his mother is dead and that tomorrow will be just as nice a day as yesterday?

I sat on the edge of Janet's bunk, the bunk under Mark's. Whenever I had something to explain to Mark, something he would have to think hard about to understand, I sat him on my lap or squatted down beside him, so that our heads were on about the same level; to have stood above him, looking and talking down, would have missed the purpose.

Mark stood in front of me, pressing himself into my knees. I held him lightly by the waist. His arms hung loose at his sides. One of his fingers poked lightly at my knee.

"What, Hal," he said, "what do you want to tell me?"

I wondered if he would cry and ask to have her back. He seemed thoughtful, a bit preoccupied. I assumed he knew only what I had previously told him: that Jeanne and Janet were in the hospital and that we might not have them back. He hadn't asked me about them, but since the day of the accident he had been unusually quiet.

"Something very sad has happened, Mark. Mama is dead. I'm afraid we won't see her again."

"Did Janet have a broken arm?" he said.

He had asked this before, and I wondered what images, what thoughts were going through his mind.

"No," I said, "she broke her leg and hurt her head very badly. The doctor is afraid we might not see Janet again either."

A frown crossed his face, scarcely causing wrinkles in his young skin but contorting his eyes, cheeks, and mouth, as though he were trying very hard to think of something. He kept his eyes on my knees; one finger drew circles and lines on my kneecap.

"Did Mama go away in spirit?"

"Yes. Mama went away in spirit like Gramma Horner—do you remember?"

He nodded, his finger still drawing lines and circles.

"Will Mama turn into weeds?"

"In a way. When people die, the earth absorbs their bodies. This gives life to weeds—and to flowers. In a way, Mark, this is a beautiful thing. Mama will not be sad. Maybe she will turn into a beautiful flower. The flower will die too, but it will bloom again and become another beautiful flower, over and over again."

"Do flowers have spirits?"

"Yes, flowers have spirits. But it is a different kind of spirit. The spirit doesn't talk, it doesn't see, and it doesn't think. The spirit just gives the flowers life and makes them beautiful.

"There is something I want you to know that's very important."

"What, Hal?" For a moment he looked into my eyes. His finger had stopped drawing invisible circles on my knee, and now lightly brushed my forearm, slowly, back and forth.

"Mama wanted you to know that she loved you very much."

"Did she say that, Hal?"

"Yes, she said it many times, and she told me you made her very happy because you loved her. Mama was very sad because she knew she wouldn't see you any more. When she was here, she told me you were a very good boy and that she was proud of you. She always said you were a very big boy. She loved you very much, and you made her very happy. Do you understand what I'm saying?"

"Yeah, Hal," he said.

I didn't know what else to say. I pulled him close to me, so that his head was in my shoulder.

"You're a very big boy," I said, "a very big boy." I didn't want him to know I was crying.

2

JEANNE AND I had on at least one occasion discussed funerals; our attitudes were hardly reverential. Of course we talked about funerals as though we were discussing something that happens to someone else—not to you. I don't recall what brought the subject up, unless it was something that *had* happened to somebody else. Whatever, we talked about *our* funerals with an especial chilled detachment.

My own feeling about funerals was tempered in part by

my having gone to my grandfather's funeral at the age of perhaps thirteen and having overheard the funeral director say to one of his aides, "Can't we get these people out of the chapel? We've got another one at ten." This made my grandfather look rather silly, lying there with his proud goatee jutting almost above the rim of the open casket. I thought it an excellent idea when, afterward, my mother, my aunts and uncles, and I went swimming. The water was cool and cleansing, and I had a fond, snug memory of the grandfather in life, and this was enough. I'm sure he would have gone swimming with us, had he been able, though he might have been concerned about getting his goatee wet.

Where Jeanne had acquired her own notions about funerals I don't know. She thought them "silly" and commercial, and, with practical concern, she wanted her body given to medicine. But as I say, we talked about funerals as though we were talking about something that happens to somebody else, and I never thought I would be making arrangements for Jeanne's funeral. When that time came I had no intentions of carrying out her wish to be given to medicine. And only reluctantly I consented to having a funeral.

I too felt strongly that funerals were commercial enterprises that did nothing for the dead and put the living eternally in debt. My experience with Jeanne's funeral more or less confirmed this. Jeanne's minister—something of a realist—confided to me that the funeral director was upset because I had ordered a closed-casket service and that the casket not be present at the funeral, which of course meant a paucity of expensive flowers and the loss of transportation and handling fees. The minister was annoyed at this obvious commercialism, and so was I.

My grief was personal and individual—as I would suppose is everyone's grief; and I expressed it in my own way, in a ceremony of my own making, in the basement of my house.

As ceremonies go, it was grossly informal. I gave hardly any thought to its being a ceremony—if that's what it was. I simply sat down at the desk in the little room next to the coal furnace and wrote two letters: one to Jeanne, one to Janet.

I don't remember all that I wrote. I remember only that I wrote in my letter to Jeanne that I loved her, and I wanted above all else that she had died knowing she was loved by me, by Mark, by Janet. In my letter to Janet I wrote much the same. I put each letter in an envelope and told the undertaker to enclose them in Jeanne's and Janet's caskets. In Janet's envelope I put her Yogi Bear spoon, which we had got by sending away a cereal boxtop. The spoon had been a big thing in Janet's life; she would never eat her breakfast without it. I wanted it by her side, in her casket.

I thanked Jeanne—how inadequate was my thanks—for what she had done for all of us, for how happy she had made us, and for her wonderful ways with the children. I tried desperately to have my letters make sense. For God knows what reason, I tried to make my terrible handwriting legible.

I requested a funeral for the sake of Jeanne's parents. I knew it was important to them that there be a funeral for their daughter. Though it was not my way, it was *their* way. I assumed they needed this as much as I had needed to go to the basement and express my feelings with letters that would never be read.

Dwight and Margaret grieved deeply; I was quite aware of this, though neither was emotionally demonstrative. Only when I suddenly went into the kitchen and found Margaret alone and clutching her face with her hands, in a strange, tearless and frantic gesture, did I realize the depths of the emotional turmoil within. Outwardly, Dwight was no different than when I had seen him on the few times we had visited; he appeared calm, reserved and quiet. I never saw a tear in his eye, never saw his face contort, never heard his voice quaver.

But Margaret revealed what lay beneath. In the plane, on the way to Pullman, Dwight had confided to her, she said, that he regretted not having put his arm around Jeanne more often. It was only a hint, but, if I had correctly gauged Dwight's apparent impassivity, beneath it lay strong emotions that were put to long-term resolve. His regretting not having put his arm around Jeanne more often was ostensibly sentimental, and it was not like him to be sentimental when Jeanne was alive and near him. Then he had been much more than *sentimental.* His love for her had expressed itself in a deep and practical concern for her well-being, her achievements, her goals. His emotions never failed him in this; they were constant and persevering.

He never wore his emotions, never let them rise to the surface and burn out. He dedicated them, kept them burning in his actions. Now, with Jeanne gone, there must have been so much left to burn; tears would hardly extinguish the flame within.

Dwight and Margaret gave no indication of what they thought of my coming to Jeanne's funeral in a buttoned sport shirt and a corduroy jacket, without a necktie. Their thoughts on this they would express much later. I didn't try to explain, to anyone, why I dressed as I had. Neckties and dark suits are neither expressions of love nor of sorrow, and Jeanne had well understood my strong feelings against having the clothes I wore picked for me, as it were, by a team of social directors, when I knew perfectly well what I wore on a particular day, at a particular time, had nothing to do with what I thought, what I felt, or what I was. I'm sure Jeanne would have thought me weak and foolish had I come to her funeral in dark suit and tie. I supposed at the time that this was a matter strictly between Jeanne and me. An Iowa court would prove me wrong.

3

THERE WAS NOTHING now in Pullman—only the endless winter sky: gray, dark, always threatening to rain or to snow. The snow, if it fell at all, would be wet and sodden, falling in large, watery flakes that silently struck the window and clung to the cold but warmer-than-air glass until they dissolved into thick blobs of half-frozen water, like the remains of large, turgid insects crushed underfoot. But the rain and the snow never fell. The sky was a gray hard mass that a falling rock might have punched a neat hole through. I wanted to leave this place, to get out from under this sky, as quickly as I could settle my affairs.

I had sent Jeanne and Janet away, to be buried in Ottumwa, Iowa, where Jeanne had been born and had spent most of her childhood. I had seen no reason to keep them in Pullman, and Dwight had asked that Jeanne be buried in the Bannister family plot, in the cemetery not far from the old Bannister house and the now rotting and boarded-up Bonnefield house.

The Bannister house and the Bonnefield house, one a block away from the other, where Margaret Bonnefield and Dwight Bannister had spent their childhoods. The Bonnefield house—big, impressive, stately, one splendid and rich, Margaret's white-haired mother living in a set of tiny rooms in the back, in the salvaged clutter of an opulent past and being quiet in the night so as not to disturb the boarders downstairs. The Bannister house—square, brick and substantial, down a pleasant, tree-lined alley, with none of the Bonnefield grandeur, none of the tall wooden columns that made the Bonnefield house unlike any other house in this staid, modestly wealthy but unassuming Iowa town.

Dwight's father had been a beloved small-town doctor who easily made himself the friend of children, who mumbled a lot but spoke wisely of history and the ways of men, if you listened closely. Dwight's mother had been an able lawyer, wise in finance and business.

These two old houses that Dwight and Margaret had left long ago, one a banker's nightmare of ruin, the other brick and indestructible and rich with the past. The Bannisters and the Bonnefields, two proud old families, both with long, impressive histories of an American dream begun in the Revolutionary past and finding realization in the American Midwest, where a new dream celebrated the past—and the past alone—and allied itself with the future in the hope the past would not be lost. Not far from these two old houses Jeanne was buried, where the shaded lawn rose to a knoll. This had been Dwight's request.

I could think of no better place—certainly not Pullman; Pullman was only our stopping place, and the land here was not our land. I might have chosen Alaska; so much of Jeanne's and my past, our dreams and ambitions, were rooted there. But Alaska was very far away. None of Jeanne's relatives was there, and I did not plan to return. For whatever it meant, I agreed with Dwight: Jeanne would be buried in the town of her childhood.

Dwight was deeply concerned about Jeanne's eternal resting place, and he was also deeply concerned about Mark's future; he asked to take Mark back to stay with him on the farm in Ames until I "settled my affairs," as he put it, and made a new home for the both of us. He offered also that I come along, and suggested that otherwise I consider "following the example" of the pioneers who when their wives died would send the children to live with the grandparents: the father would break new lands and return for the children when the time came. I turned him down; I did not want to go to Iowa myself, and I wanted to have Mark close to me. I preferred that Mark stay with John and Carol, or Ginny and Thornton, if it came to my having to travel to look for a job—and hopefully this would be for only a short time; and Mark, with either family, would be close, since I was certain I would resettle in California. Dwight left his offer open.

Ironically, it was upon Jeanne's death that Dwight, Margaret and I seemed to develop anything resembling familial rapport. I somehow felt close to them, as though our mutual emotions over Jeanne's death linked us when it seemed there had been little to link us before. Jeanne's and my marriage had not accomplished this. It seemed now that her death had. For the first time I found reason to open myself to them, to speak freely of what I thought and to discuss my plans for the future.

Margaret asked a good many questions, and once surprised me by suggesting that I find a nice young girl and remarry, or cash in the stocks I had inherited from Jeanne and travel to Europe, where my Alaskan friend Marty now was—and leave Mark with her and Dwight in the interim. Margaret and I talked in earnest about photography and writing and how I planned to make my living from one or the other and was constantly torn between giving up writing to photograph and giving up photography to write, how I felt compelled to have to choose one over the other. This question troubled me deeply; Mark's and my future was wrapped up in it, and I felt strongly that I had to concentrate on one or the other, give everything I had, if I were to succeed. As always, I was torn between having to make a living and doing what I wanted to do. I wanted to explore the world about me, to sing praise and to find fault, to fix my thoughts in some indelible stopping of time. Sometimes I chose the camera, sometimes the typewriter. At times photography seemed hollow and trite, and sometimes writing seemed to miss the all-important nuances that could not be expressed in words. Margaret and I talked about this, and we talked about the past and the future, freely and with mutual understanding, I thought. I was glad that this had come about, and I was sorry it had come so late and had been brought about as it had.

Dwight, as usual, said little, asked few questions. Often, when Margaret and I talked, Dwight sat in a rocking chair in the corner of the room, his legs stretched full length, his eyes cast down at the floor or the tips of his shoes, rocking almost imperceptibly. When I spoke, I spoke to both, but it was Margaret who most often responded.

Into Margaret's and my conversations about photography and writing Dwight occasionally interjected thoughts on making it work as a business. When I talked about photography I knew he was thinking about a shop, a business—a commercial enterprise weighed in a value system of dollars and cents—something I had not the slightest intention of becoming involved in. But this didn't matter.

What mattered was that I thought Dwight's reticence in my presence was simply a condition of his deep introspection. I would have liked him to have been more talkative and open, more revealing of himself. But in this newly acquired feeling of closeness, this didn't matter either. I accepted it as I would accept any of the idiosyncrasies of any other relative, and his being Jeanne's father made me even more willing to accept him, whatever his manner. I did not find in his silence any reason to think that he might be quietly refuting my points of view.

Dwight did not seem overly concerned about my having inherited Jeanne's stocks, about $3,400 in cash value and representing a portion of the estate accrued by a succession of Bannisters. I asked Dwight if I might give him back the stocks and hoped he would turn me down. I was greatly relieved when he said the stocks were mine to use as I saw fit. He suggested I hang onto them, perhaps reinvest, or use them for Mark's education. I didn't tell him I had planned to cash in at least part of the stocks, if it became necessary, for my immediate use—for fear he would change his mind.

I was sorry to see Dwight and Margaret off at the train station in Spokane. With them would go part of Jeanne. There was little ceremony, little to-do at the depot. None of us—Dwight, Margaret and I—was demonstratively sentimental about arrivals and departures; our thoughts on this we kept to ourselves.

The depot was old and empty. It had seen grander,

more expansive times. Waiting for the train, the three of us walked through the long, brown corridors and stood for a time in the ancient lobby. Dwight and I talked about the former glories of the railroads, Dwight rendering a knowledgeable account of the financial debits and credits, the changing economy, that had brought the downfall. I pretended to listen as my eyes roamed the lobby. I kept thinking of coming back and doing a photographic essay on the echoic anachronism of a once-grand railroad depot. Later, I mentioned something about this to Dwight. He held his hands behind his back, his head slightly bent forward, his eyes downcast. He changed the subject.

The train pulled in, and Margaret and I exchanged promises to write. I promised to keep the two of them informed of Mark's and my venture into the future. I shook her hand, and then I shook Dwight's.

I tried to think of something to say to Dwight that would convey my feelings. I was sorry to see them go, and I wanted somehow to express how badly I felt over our mutual loss of Jeanne. But I couldn't find words.

Dwight smiled and looked a bit embarrassed as he shook my hand. He always looked embarrassed when he smiled; I didn't know why, but it didn't matter. It didn't bother me now, as it had when I had first met him in Alaska, that he called me "sir" and not "Hal" as he shook my hand and said goodbye. It was an acceptable idiosyncrasy now.

I had terribly mixed feelings about the house. I wanted to sell it. I wanted to keep it. I wanted to enshrine it. I wanted to burn it. The four of us had been happy there, and had I been in another frame of mind I might have continued to live there and cherish every stick of wood of it. But the house gave me a terrifying sense of claustrophobia, longing and frustration.

To sleep there was to lie awake most of the night, in a waking dream that had neither images nor sounds. There was only a vague foreboding, sensations that seemed to come from the darkened walls and the ceiling. It was impossible for me to sleep in our bed. I slept on a cot in the living room. Sometimes I slept in the bunk under Mark. I wanted to be alone, and I wanted everyone I knew to be in that house. The night was always an emotional turmoil.

I made arrangements to sell the house as quickly as possible, never mind the financial loss. Had it not sold quickly, I might have given it away.

There seemed to be no point in keeping the house for the sake of keeping Mark there. Mark's home had always been where Jeanne and I had lived, and we had lived in several places, always bringing Mark's security with us—and his security was our love. I was convinced that the security of a house is second best, something to be grasped for when love is missing. Mark had never been a thumb-sucker, nor did he ever cling in infantile desperation to a blanket; and I didn't think he would have to cling to the house of his deceased mother and sister. If there were to be any clinging, it would be one of us to the other, Mark and I. I packed all of Mark's toys, his bunk bed, pieces of his furniture and the clothes rack he had made from the forked branch of a dead tree, and I packed all my household possessions and some of Jeanne's and Janet's things in boxes and crates.

All of it I sent to California ahead of us, to my foster parents' home in Santa Rosa, to be stored and kept.

Death, I discovered, was inglorious. Only in retrospect does death's tedium—the tedium of the bill collector and the insurance adjuster—drop away, like the leaves of a dark, giant oak, and unveil a foreboding, almost romantic figure.

Jeanne's and Janet's death was followed by an endless succession of bills, forms, questions, and financial arrangements. The state, mindful of taxes, impounded my safe-deposit box. I remember sitting in an anteroom at the bank while a fat, frumpy and indifferent woman, sent by the tax office, kept an overtly watchful eye on me lest I sneak out a taxable bond or a fistful of currency, of which there was none. I resented her implied possession of Jeanne's and my belongings. She was rude to me, and I was rude to her; I didn't try to hide my resentment.

The insurance adjuster was friendly and helpful. I had expected a sonorous, pontifical condolence that concealed resentment over having to pay off on the car insurance policy—up to $3,000 medical payments for anyone injured in our car, including funeral costs. He told me he had children of his own. He had read about the accident in the paper. It was terrible, he said. He meant it. He had no part in the confused accounting that followed, and patiently helped me to untangle it. Doctor and hospital bills came in months after the accident. Duns came when something went wrong in the insurance firm's accounting office. I wrote explanatory letters to the doctors and the hospitals, but I was answered with more duns and, once, the threat of a collection agent's visit. The insurance benefits fell short. More confusion, more bills. They seemed never to stop coming.

I couldn't make sense of my bank account. Once a month I had sat down at the desk in the living room and made out the checks that paid our creditors. To break the tedium and boredom, I rarely entered the names of firms in the tiny ledger in the front of the checkbook. I drew pictures and symbols instead. The electrical power company was sometimes a zigzag flash of lighting, sometimes a lightbulb, sometimes a smiling sun. A dripping water faucet or "H_2O" did for the water campany. Our other creditors—the grocery store, the garbage collector, the furniture mart, the gasoline and insurance companies (fortunately, there weren't many)—all had pseudonyms as well as pictographs. Many of the envelopes our bills came in contained advertising; I took the ads from one firm and put them in the envelope with my check to another: tire ads went to the telephone company; furniture bargains went to the garbage man. This helped to while away my impatience and frustration with trying to sort pieces of paper with numbers on them and add columns of figures that never twice totaled the same.

If I had paid a bill for $1.78, I entered it in the bankbook as $2, and so on. This way, I figured we'd come out ahead; we never did. We were never behind in our bills, but Jeanne was always over my shoulder correcting my arithmetic. I tried hard to figure out my debts and credits, future expenditures, anticipated income, and all the monetary trifles entered in the bankbook shortly before and after Jeanne's death. But the only thing I was sure of was that the bills would keep coming, I would have to keep paying, and there was little cash at hand.

Financial disaster, no; confusion, frustration and uncertainty, yes. Friends of Jeanne and mine had raised about $200. Another $200 had come from an extraordinarily generous couple whom I had never met but who, by way of the church, had known and admired Jeanne. This kept the furnace going, and it put food on the table.

Somehow my lawyer was able to keep the state from tying up my bank account. It was too small, I suppose, for the state to covet it. The stocks were tied up and would be for months, in probate, as were Mark's and Janet's savings accounts—when I wanted desperately to cash in everything and clear out of Pullman forever, to get all this macabre business over with.

When six months later I got a $300 hospital bill for Janet, I would have paid twice, three times that much to get it off my back and out of my mind. Through some accounting error, it had not been paid by the insurance company. More letters, more duns. This nagging exchange went on and on: transportation fees for caskets, fees for the anesthetist, special nurses. No one seemed to know who was supposed to pay.

Perhaps a month after Janet had died one of the sisters from the nursery school called and kindly reminded me that Janet, while traveling to and from the school, had been covered by the school's insurance policy. She wondered why I hadn't applied. Much earlier she had sent me a form to fill out, but I had thrown it away. The thought of obtaining cash for Janet's death had made me sick.

Now, after sitting around the house and waiting for the estate to be probated, I had a practical change of mind. I applied, and two weeks later a check for $1,500 came like a wind from a fresh new planet. I packed up our belongings, bought Mark a good, warm traveling coat and a stocking cap, piled our things into the car, said goodbye to our friends, made a brief visit with my mother, and headed for California.

"Come on, Bucko," I said to Mark, "we're going to see Grandma and Grandpa McNelly, and we'll find a nice warm beach and maybe take a swim. How does that sound?"

"Fine, Hal," he said.

The car broke down the day we were to start. No matter. I had it fixed. It cost me $60, and I had the money to pay for it. And it made me sick, this money. Why is life and death so encumbered by money? Is this the thin dividing line?

As soon as the car was fixed we rolled down the freeway. At the end of the freeway were sun and blue sky. I wondered how much they would cost. No matter. As long as I had dimes and quarters, the sky would continue to play its song of sun and cloudless days. I felt like throwing up. And Janet, what was Janet thinking? A penny—no, my life—to hear her speak her thoughts.

4

THE OREGON COASTLINE was blue, golden, and coldly serene. Long white waves, born of blue waters, slid up to the shore and then back to the sea, without benefit of wind. The air was chill, even at three o'clock in the afternoon when the light of the sun—the sun still keeping its winter's distance—lay hard and golden on the deserted beach.

In the motel manager's eye it was still very much the winter season. He answered the door in leather slippers, carrying in one hand a folded newspaper and in the other a pair of horn-rimmed glasses. The manager's wife, in some sort of loose-fitting smock, leaned around the door to see who or what I might be, and then retreated behind it when she saw me looking at her as she looked at me. I had interrupted their winter-season solitude.

The beach at this time of year held little attraction for the summer people, those who regaled in the easy, barefoot freedom of hot sun and hot sand. Only those came now who found pleasure in solitude, or who had no choice but to take winter vacations, and people like me, who sought for the moment both sun and solitude at this place at the land's end.

Mark had never tasted fresh, cracked crab before. He had his first taste of it in the cabin—a large red crab I had picked up in the fishing village where we had stopped that morning. We had walked up and down the piers, looking at the fishing boats, and I had asked a fisherman whether there were any sailboats in the harbor, and was told there were not. This disappointed me, for this was a beautiful place for a sailboat—despite the dangerous bar at the mouth of the harbor. In the back of my mind were vague thoughts about the possibility of buying a sailboat, and Mark and I sailing the coast, or perhaps sailing to Hawaii. I bought a cooked crab instead.

Mark said he thought he would eat some of the crab if I would too. But the expression on his face, as he ran one finger lightly over the crab's scaly red back and one of its sawtooth claws, raised doubts. I bought some bananas, milk, cheese, and cold meats too.

I brought the crab, wrapped none too neatly in a newspaper that was already beginning to smell, to the cabin, where I put it in the refrigerator. A quart of milk in a square red carton, a white butcher-paper parcel of cold meats and cheese and the crab wrapped in a newspaper—that's all there was in this refrigerator that might have held huge bowls of spaghetti and soup, remnants of roast beef and lamb, vegetables and fruits, and home-made pie. The little white light in the back of the refrigerator seemed to be made of luminous ice; I supposed it went out when I closed the door.

Mark and I took towels and went swimming in the heated pool. The water was warm, pleasantly warm, the glass enclosure steamy and full of the sounds of splashing water made by Mark and me. We had the pool to ourselves, and the sea seemed very near, as though it were above and around us, as though we might have been swimming in a ship's pool, far out at sea.

This was a far cry from our stop of several days in Portland, where I had applied for a job and then turned it down because the town was even more gray and overcast than Pullman had been—a pleasant town in the sunshine, but otherwise dreary, and it stayed that way most of the year.

There was none of the bright colors, none of the sunshine and stimulation here that I was looking for. And there had been that morning I had gone to apply for the job and had left Mark at the day school. I was terrified as I watched Mark being taken by the hand by the large and pleasant-enough woman in the flowered smock, and led to a half-empty room of scuffed and broken toys and somber children who scarcely seemed to notice Mark's arrival.

God knows, I had never before had to fill out a form explaining that Mark's mother was dead, that he had had all the proper shots, that he used to have a sister, that, yes, I could afford to pay for graham crackers and milk and lunch. In a panic I snatched him out of there at the day's end and fled Portland and sped like hell for the beach and the sea.

I put Mark on his back, in an inner tube, pulled him around the pool behind me, and from time to time sent him spinning and sometimes left him bobbing in the center of the pool as I swam under and around him, pretending to be a seal and a dolphin and once a shark that bit his toe and made him yowl and thrash and say do it again.

I had never seen Mark frightened of the water. Those times when we had gone swimming in the airy, sunny pool in the park in Pullman, Mark had let me carry him on my back as I swam across the deep end; his arms had clung tightly around my neck. Now he bobbed about the pool, hanging half in and half out of the inner tube, unmindful that he couldn't swim and that the water beneath him was well over his head.

He was reluctant to leave, but I suggested we take a warm shower and comb the beach.

"Maybe we'll see a whale or the bones of an old sailing ship," I said.

"Yeah, Hal," he said. "Maybe we'll see a big, big whale and he'll eat us up, but a crab will pinch him and he'll spit us out."

We went to the beach, Mark in his gray, hooded sweatshirt and carrying his tiny traveler's bag, a canvas airline bag my mother had given him at the start of our trip and which now was filled with bits of driftwood and seashells gathered during the morning's sojourn on a sunny beach now far behind us. Wherever we had stopped after leaving Pullman, Mark had gathered mementos—loose-lying fragments of a time and a place. In a box in the car were rocks, flowers and weeds that had passed from his hand to his bag to the box, the bag being emptied and refilled at each new place where we had stopped to browse and wander about like tourists. He kept the bag sometimes on the seat beside him, sometimes on his lap as I drove. At night he kept it by his bed and fingered and talked about the contents before he went to sleep.

We started down the beach, and two children, a couple of years older than Mark, popped from a sand dune and ran ahead of us, beckoning Mark with wayward glances and significant pauses as they worked their way toward a large camel-like creature of driftwood with its head high and visible for perhaps a mile up and down the beach.

Mark ran ahead and soon caught up with them and presented his traveler's bag for inspection, all of them squatting on the sand and examining the contents. Suddenly there was a cry—the boy snatched something from Mark's bag and made a bee-line for the camellike creature.

An indefinable sense of panic engulfed me as I saw Mark stand upright and bone-stiff. He had dropped his bag by his side, and it lay upset in the sand. He cried in despair. I ran to him.

The little boy and the girl ran with all their might as I ran for Mark. A sand dollar flew from the boy's hand into the sand. They disappeared into a cluster of bright-green bushes and white cottages.

I knelt and pulled Mark into my arms.

"Why did they *do* that, Hal?" he said.

He picked up his bag by one of the half-round canvas straps; the other strap flopped like a dog's ear as he held the bag at his side, the weight of the contents pulling the bag open so that I could easily see inside, see several bits of driftwood and the assortment of seashells.

"It's all right, Mark," I said, "they didn't mean anything by it. Come on, we'll go find your sand dollar."

I couldn't explain to Mark why they had snatched his sand dollar; it was as if I had suddenly been asked to explain why his mother and sister had been snatched away.

I tried to find the stolen sand dollar, but it was lost, sunken in the sand perhaps. We went looking for more sand dollars, and other shells too. We found hundreds of them. We filled his traveler's bag and a pound coffee can besides. Mark seemed satisfied with his newfound plentitude of sand dollars and assorted seashells; he seemed to forget the lost sand dollar.

Mark slept that night with his tin can and traveler's bag of seashells on the stand next to his bed. He slept soundly. I almost envied him—but I knew better.

Beside me slept Mark, and beside the two of us I felt only the darkness, and I lay awake most of the night, listening to the steady thump and swish of waves pulling away at the land.

5

THOUGHTS OF THE FUTURE perplexed me as we sped down the highways toward California. My plans were vague and uncertain, and the only thing I was certain of was that I wanted to put the past behind me as quickly as possible.

I knew I would have to find a steady source of income in the not-too-distant future; but I didn't want to worry about this now. I worried about it anyway; I couldn't help it. I didn't want to spend the money I had in the bank for the simple reason it might run out when I wanted it most. And I didn't want to cash in the stocks I had inherited, but I figured on cashing them in anyway if the bank account dwindled. If only Mark and I could have got along without money! I would have burned my bank-book, every stock certificate and government bond, in a flaming pile beside the road. I would have pushed the car over a cliff, and Mark and I would have strode off into the woods. We would have climbed mountains and swum lake and stream. Just the two of us, Mark and I.

Cars, automobiles, motor vehicles, whatever they are called—I detest these snorting tin monsters, these ambulant, 100-mile-an-hour millstones, these quacking tin ducks, these two-bit missiles to nowhere that go bouncing down the highway like bent silver dollars.

I would rather walk, crawl, thumb a ride on a three-legged elephant, a droll, loping beast in pursuit of its own snout, than climb into a four-speed coffin, body by Fisher, funeral by whoever can afford to pay for it, and go in smoggy pursuit of the highway's end. But how necessary they are—these pursuers of instant destinations. They get you *there,* quickly and surely—with exceptions, of course.

And how else can one leave the past behind and make the future an immediate possibility? Whatever lies around the corner—this is the future; and the little tin missile will get you *there*. Watch, and the past recedes in the rear-view mirror, at a rate curiously in relation to the local speed limit. A cop will let you know if you're proceeding too quickly; you'll get a ticket, an invitation to a temporal day of judgment, from a roadside metaphysician doing business on a two-wheeled crystal ball with a screaming red siren. Heaven is just beyond the toll gate and every galloping mile thereafter. Hell is a flat tire on the Fourth of July when the rest of the world goes whizzing by on hot little tires.

Mark and I went whizzing through Oregon, past trees and mountains. I didn't know where I was going, even if I consciously steered for California, scooting out from under the gray skies that overtook us the day after we had left the beach.

Cars, money—I would have burned them all. The forests and mountains might have been enticing. In another frame of mind I might have put a pack on my back and a tiny one on Mark; the two of us would have taken to the hills for God knows how long. I would have found a cabin, by a perennial stream (in Alaska perhaps), and Mark and I would have cut wood, fished the stream, hunted our dinner, gone snooping in meadow and dale. I would have kept him constantly by my side as we climbed mountains and glaciers, as we sat by the fire at the day's end, as we hunted, fished, and otherwise pursued our tandem existence. But what an impossible dream in this age we live in! No, there would have to be schools and money and time spent away from home, cars, roads, and an indefinite plunge into a *positive* future that would be right for our times. And besides, I couldn't stand being alone, just the two of us, in the wooded mountains. It had been easy years ago, when I had taken to the woods by myself and stayed there alone and comfortable, feeling neither lonely nor morbid, but free-wheeling and content.

Now it was different. I wanted to see old friends and

relatives whom I was fond of and remembered well from the years past. I sped for California. We stopped only long enough to get a good night's sleep after a long day's travel and for Mark to have a bath. He delighted in splashing in warm water before he went to bed, and I liked an interminable hot shower. We stopped at motels where the tub was big and hot water plentiful. I let Mark splash till the walls ran wet, and then I dried him off with a big towel as he giggled, squirmed and danced, showed him the way to his pajamas on the bed, read him a story, talked awhile, and then tucked him in and doused the lights. I had trouble sleeping, and I would stay up long after Mark had fallen asleep, reading or practicing angles of view with my camera and mentally taking pictures of the things, places and faces I had seen that day that had retrospectively fastened themselves, like pictures on a wall, to my imagination.

How thankful I was for my past romance with photography. Words were useless to me now; I couldn't write. Even to write a letter was difficult. The words would not form, and I seemed to be unable to define my own thoughts and to take a concise viewpoint, of anything, that could aptly and neatly be expressed in words. Shortly before I had left Pullman I had bought a 35-mm camera (my third—I had got rid of the two before it) and all the necessary enlarging and darkroom equipment. Even before I had sold the house I had plunged into photography, plunged into the darkroom in the basement.

Things, faces, gestures, places, shapes and planes, configurations of light and shade, light and darkness, always have fascinated me to the point of obsession. It was never enough for me to take a single picture of a thing or a face and let it go at that. I would take dozens of pictures, from different points of view, not trying to capture what was in front of the lens but what was behind it, in the picture, the essence I saw in my imagination. Snapshots, literal representations—these won't do; they miss the point.

The camera—any camera—is an ingenious piece of junk. The camera must be loved and cursed and shaped into a delicate carving tool of the imagination. It must not be used as a saw, to hack out a piece of landscape for instant hanging.

Demoniacally perhaps I pushed my camera to the limit shortly before leaving Pullman, when the house had been deserted by relatives and only Mark and I were there to occupy it.

As I looked back, there were pictures I had taken that had seemed prophetic, pictures taken months before the accident. There had been the picture of Janet, alone in a field, standing not far from a rusting, unearthly threshing machine; in back of her, not quite over her head, a hawk hovered, and behind the hawk, from over a rolling hill with a few dark trees in silhouette, a cloud seemed to rise like smoke from a distant fire that was rapidly spreading over the landscape. And then there was the picture of Mark which I took a few months before his mother's death: Mark alone, in a chair, a deserted chair—his mother's—next to him; Mark wore an expression of melancholy longing. These pictures haunted me from the moment I saw them. Only in retrospect, I suppose, were these pictures prophetic. Nevertheless, they haunted me—as all photographs have haunted me.

After the accident I was haunted by the unreality of the faces, the things, the landscapes I saw. My camera became a means of penetrating the unreal to re-establish the real. I spent hours in the darkroom, late at night and in the early hours of the morning, fixing the ephemeral images of the world about me in the indelible, timeless configurations of a new reality: a photograph—more real, more tangible than its fleeting counterpart.

The interpretive eye of photo-journalism had fascinated me too, and I half planned to renew my past, moderate success in this. I re-established contact with my photo agent in New York, troubled, as I had always been, with the nagging feeling that I was morally entitled to enjoy a pursuit of the spirit only if I could obtain from it a contribution to my livelihood—another sorry instance, I suppose, of my being influenced by the perverse American notion that an artist is self-justifying only if he is paid, and that to pursue one's art out of personal conviction and the pleasure it gives is to traffic in the deadbeat merchandise of the devil.

I would now, as I had in the past, sporadically pursue photo-journalism, spending more time and money than I might receive in return for the pictures, taking on my own an assignment that might or might not be of interest to a paying editor, obsessed with doing a picture story as thoroughly as my interest in the subject demanded—and hoping I might be saved from financial disgrace and ruin by a major sale. Always my relatives—ironically, the Banisters were silent—were after me to "settle down, get a decent job." And in this I always failed them; no "steady, decent" job has ever left me satisfied and not itching to get the hell out and pursue my own works, unfettered by the dollars-and-cents trivia, the compromises of the spirit and the emotions, the petty but all-encompassing machinations that make "steady, decent" jobs a pinch-penny hell of colossal frustrations.

What jobs I might hold, what ends I would pursue, I didn't know as Mark and I sped down the highway toward California and the sun. The sun, tranquility, quietude—these I pursued. The future, earning a living, finances, Mark's having to begin his first year of school in September, a time when we would have to be settled, turning my photography into a means of livelihood, satisfying my obsession with picture-taking—these questions pursued me, and I had no answers. A prolonged vacation in the sun—this, perhaps, would provide the answer, and for this I sped to California, as fast as the four demonic wheels of my car would take me.

6

MY FOSTER PARENTS were glad to have us in their home near Santa Rosa, and Mark and I were glad to have them.

San Francisco, my friends and relatives there were not far off. I didn't know how long we might stay, though my foster parents generously offered to keep us for as long as we liked. I had thoughts of going farther south, to San Diego perhaps, where I knew the beaches and the sea would be warm and the skies blue and sunny.

But there were sun and blue skies now in Santa Rosa, and for the next few weeks Mark and I used my foster parents' home as home base for frequent excursions into the hills and valleys and the vineyards of Sonoma County. We buzzed up and down steep mountain roads, went twisting through narrow roads transformed into green, shady and sun-dappled tunnels by giant oaks and, here and there, blossoming fruit trees. Sometimes we parked and took to the hills and the vineyards by foot. The February, and soon the March, sun rose bright and golden almost every day; the skies were blue and whistling with white clouds in high, spring winds: beautiful days of blossoming green.

One of these memorable excursions took us whizzing down a narrow road, across a bridge, and I swung the steering wheel rapidly and sharply left, lest we go crashing through the ancient adobe walls of the Glen Ellen Hotel. I found myself suddenly alighting upon the time-arrested center of a flowered wheel that idyllically turned on a creaking wooden axle set in yesteryear. Perhaps my having suddenly come upon this village on a bright spring day made me more than willing to suspend my calculated disbelief that what existed here now had existed here now, here now in 1875, 1780, 1963, in 1850—whatever the theatrically fused date of my belated arrival. The scene itself was simply set: a long, narrow street (extending interminably the leg of the "L" that began its incongruously short foot at the bridge), happily protected from the highway builder's notions of progress by the doggedly adobe hotel; a log-cabin saloon where Jack London had been one of the hell-raising regulars and which now wore a cocked-hat sign that heralded its establishment in 1875; a flower and trinket shop that kept alive, in postcards and ceramic bric-a-brac, the tourist's love of historic immediacy and thus abetted, with commercial candor, the local business establishment's determination to keep this village as it *was,* regardless of when and whatever it was. Thus this narrow street into the past remained narrow and questionable—but plausible, and if I doubted the vendor's sincerity, I neither doubted nor questioned my being captured by this place: it had come at the right time, at the right place, one spring day when the weather was right. Snug little cabins and houses (chock-full of writers and artists, I was told) were hidden in the tree-dense hills, an atmosphere that would make me feel intangibly at home the three months I was to rent a cabin here, after looking long and hard for a vacancy.

The cabin I rented was a two-bedroom place about half a mile out of town, on perhaps half an acre of tall grass and tall shady oaks with dark elephantine limbs that hung over the eaves. One of the bedrooms I converted to a darkroom; Mark and I slept in the other. I moved in a few odds and ends of the furniture I had sent ahead of us from Pullman, a few pots and pans and plates, a few of Mark's toys, and that was it.

I thought perhaps this cabin in a sunny clearing on the fringe of the past, surrounded by vineyards, hills, valleys, countless trees, would do well as an interim resort, a place to idle away the spring and perhaps part of the summer. But I was wrong: there would be time on my hands, yes, but no idling, no tranquil moments of quiet speculation in the sun.

During the day I paced the house and paced the yard.

I couldn't sit still, and I couldn't keep pacing. Mark and I made countless trips into the hills and vineyards, and I took many pictures of clouds, mountains and landscapes. Often I stayed up a good part of the night, developing film and enlarging the pictures I had taken during the day, making many of them over and over again until I was satisfied. I couldn't sleep anyway, and I was glad I had something to keep me busy.

Several times I went to San Francisco to do a picture story on speculation for the magazine trade, and I left Mark with my foster parents. Driving sixty miles, I figured, to the city and back again would be too much for the both of us. I thought also it was just as well to put my idle time to earning money, since my bank account was getting smaller rather than bigger.

I had hoped to find a family in town in which there were several children and at least one Mark's age, with whom he might stay during the hours I would be gone on picture stories, and I had inquired before I had rented the cabin and was told by the kindly old woman who ran the flower shop that she knew of just the family, or, rather, just the woman (a divorcée, I assumed), who had two lovely children Mark's age. I paid her a visit—only to have my apprehensive feelings about Mark's having a baby-sitter become an obsession.

When I went to meet the prospective baby-sitter it was just as the kindly woman in the store had told me: indeed, there were two lovely children Mark's age—but I found the two of them locked in a bedroom while their young mother sipped a bottle of beer with a boy friend who greeted me at the door with a look that suggested I was being taken for a rival from out of his paramour's sketchy past. I made some excuse and left, feeling terribly sorry for the two kids locked up in the bedroom and terribly worried about Mark.

I was obsessed with wanting Mark to have a mother—something I could not possibly give him—and I was fanatically alert to any influences that threathened to rob Mark of even a modicum of his mother's upbringing.

I rationalized that there were probably devoted baby-sitters in this world, but I couldn't conceive of one who would give Mark the constant, loving tutelage he had had from his mother. I was convinced that Mark needed a mother as a fish needs water, a woman and mother whom he could count on always to be at hand, always helping and unconditionally loving. No baby-sitter would do, and his mother was dead.

Years ago I had learned to keep away from sailboats lest I get carried, if not sailed, away. I should have remembered this now, and I did, but it didn't stop me.

Early one morning, after breakfast, I piled Mark into the car and announced that we would go looking at sailboats in the harbor at Sausalito. Within the hour we were standing on the dock in back of the harbor yacht sales office. Below me, floating in a state of auroreal radiance, was a Mermaid, a twenty-two-foot sailboat with varnished mast, an open cockpit, and a varnished, open hatch that revealed the small space below decks, where two long benches on either side would serve nicely as twin bunks.

I envisioned Mark and me on a three months' cruise of the Bay and the Bay delta—1,200 square miles of navigable water in all, and it has been said a man can sail these waters a lifetime and never twice set foot on the same shore. At summer's end I would sell the boat, and Mark and I would have had the perfect summer I had been looking for.

After two days of thinking about it and trying without success to be fiscally sensible, I cashed in half of the stocks I had inherited and headed for the yacht harbor. But just as I got there the Mermaid was pulling away from the dock, steered by a rather contented-looking man with two children and a woman at his side. Some fortunate family had got there before me, and I watched, heartbroken, as the Mermaid was sailed away.

No matter. Two weeks later I made a down payment on another sailboat, a twenty-six-footer with three bunks, a galley, head, and auxiliary engine—a little more expensive than the Mermaid, but within my means and easily financed.

I loaded the boat with two sleeping bags, fuel for the Primus stove, food, a few books, many bottles of orange juice for Mark, warm clothes, wool seaman's caps—one for each of us—a radio, and Mark's traveler's bag, now stuffed with fishing line, a toy saw, a rubber mallet, and a couple of brass rigging shackles.

We sailed in gales, and we motored in hot, windless sunshine. We got wet when the spray and sea came rampaging over the bow. We got cold and hungry, and when we did we went below, ate hot food and wrapped in blankets. Mark took to the water like a young seal, and in a very short while he memorized an amazing assortment of the names of the many parts and pieces of the boat, and visitors to the boat often were amazed when Mark took them on a lecture tour and expertly explained the ingenious working parts of this marvelous contraption that flies with sails into the face of the wind.

His seaman's cap pulled tight over cold ears, his bright-orange life preserver fastened with a man-line to a cleat in the cockpit, the boat hard-heeled on a starboard tack—Mark looked like a young Joshua Slocum, an ancient, peach-fuzzed mariner of tiny ships and fearsome seas, dragging a finger in the water off the submerged lee rail, as if to test the current, and the next moment asking for a tin cup of orange juice.

We sailed when the storm warnings flew, and big yachts flew for port with sails furled, leaving behind only the will-o'-the-wisp vapor of their heated engines. High winds and high seas didn't bother Mark, and they didn't bother me. Pushing our way up a thirty-foot sea with foaming breakers, the Golden Gate Bridge trembling in the wind above and small foreign cars swaying on the bridge's deck, we topped the peak and flew troughward, the bow plunging three feet under and throwing spray halfway up the mainsail, cold green sea water coming down the deck at us in fire-hose torrents. I wanted to yell out my joy and bless the world for such a bucking, rollicking sea and the cleansing, powerful wind. Cold sea water and wind—what elixir! Every sea we topped was the top of the world, and every gust of wind blew from my mind the images, the morbid thoughts of Jeanne's and Janet's death in a smashed car. And there was more—there was a feeling of pure joy, a feeling of having smashed down the malevolent forces of nature, feelings of having made a truce with an invisible adversary, a feeling of lifting myself above the earth in a marvelous machine of flying sails and wood, the bowsprit rising skyward in a hallelujah triumph of ithyphallic primacy.

But at night it was different. When the wind had died and the Bay was calm; when the docks had been deserted by the Sunday sailors, the tourists, the bright Sunday sun; when the dock lights flashed on and turned even the most brightly painted boats into half-luminous, half-real, mauve-green creatures that lay at dockside like spectral, sleeping whales—at night, when we had come in from sailing, tied up at the dock, stowed the sails in bags and settled down to eating in the yellow light of the cabin's single brass kerosene lamp; when afterward I stepped on deck and smoked my pipe, Mark lying below in his sleeping bag in the forward bunk, the light out, the fog drifting down from the Sausalito hills, the docks deserted and creaking—when this time came the images, the morbid thoughts returned. Everything I saw looked unreal, cold, pointless. The waters beneath the boat became an abyss, cold, endlessly deep and lonely, inhabited by strange fish that gaped and haunted.

Even that gentle afternoon when Mark and I sailed to the wooded cove off Angel Island and anchored for the night, the spectral images were much the same. The sun was setting, and behind us the sky was red and golden. The green waters of the cove were still, and I put the Primus stove on deck and boiled corn on the cob in sea water for our dinner.

The corn would be sweet and succulent, hot and running with butter. The evening was quiet and cool. A gentle tidal current swung the boat in a gentle arc at the end of the anchor line, the anchor securely caught in the sandy bottom; the people on the beach, children still in their bathing suits, parents starting barbecue fires and fanning at mosquitoes, the big white house at the head of the cove, the trees, seemed to be swinging gently past us, in a slow procession, and somehow it seemed appropriate that the people on the beach should wave to us as they went moving quietly by, as though they should remember us from something we had done together—a play, perhaps.

But the tranquility, the calm—even the beauty of the evening—made me nervous and uneasy. Even with Mark beside me, dangling a hookless fishing line over the side, I felt alone; the shore, a few yards off, seemed to be separated from me by a sheet of hard glass.

That night, when I put Mark in his bunk and pulled the ends of his sleeping bag around his shoulders, I held his hand as he went to sleep. Perhaps I was projecting, I wasn't sure; nothing was clear to me. I saw him lying there, alone in the bunk, and I was overcome with a sense of desperation.

Then and there I dropped my plans for a three-month voyage to the sunny island in arrested time. The island had sunk even before it had appeared on the horizon—and where was the horizon?

What followed was sporadic weekend outings, an abortive voyage of fragments, on days when the docks were alive with people and when the day flashed with brightly colored sail bags and crisp white sails run up the mast for a luffing Sunday airing.

Wherever I went, wherever I had gone, wherever I was, night and the evening, dusk and darkness, the empty hours between that time when the sun sets and the sun rises, overtook the daylight and all thoughts that I might naturally and rightfully belong to the world about me. I seemed not even to belong to myself, as though part of me had gone on an implausible expedition into unknown, unnamed catacombs, with a candle and a dried piece of bread wrapped in a piece of crinkled waxed paper. The other part of me had stayed behind, to muse vacuously in the sun, until the dusk, when the images of the dark expedition came from all directions, so that a sleek, bright-red sailboat bobbing in the twilight became a Stygian barge that had risen from under the sea and waited to

Jeanne and Mark. Alaska, 1958.

Left, below and opposite: *Jeanne and the children in Pullman, Washington, 1961. Mark was three, Janet two.*

Mark, four, shortly before his mother's death.

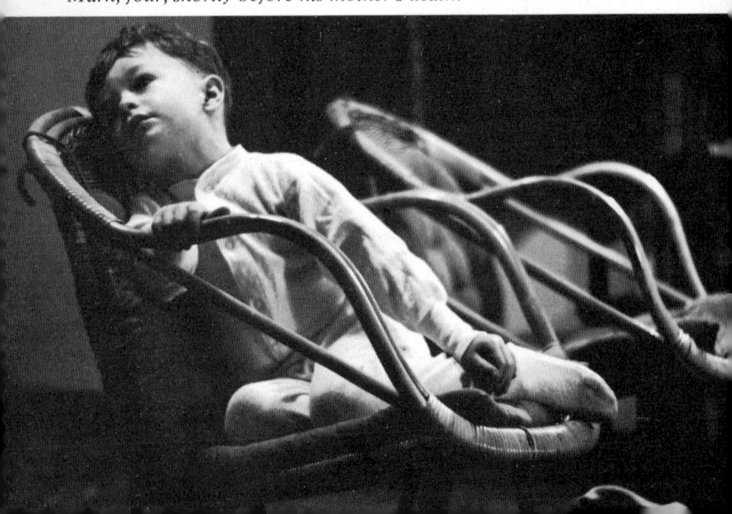

Margaret and Dwight Bannister at their daughter's wedding in Anchorage in 1957.

Mark taking riding lessons in Santa Rosa, California, 1963.

Mark on the Oregon coast.

Mark and I, a year and a half before the custody trial.

William Allen, our Washington, D.C. attorney who represented us before the U.S. Supreme Court. Marylyn stands in the doorway of our house, which figured in the Iowa Supreme Court's decision.

take me to the scene of the dark expedition. It had been like this since December. Only playing the radio, which I kept by the side of my bed as I tried desperately to sleep, kept me from stepping aboard the boat that lay waiting throughout the night and which submerged and returned to the bottom of the sea at dawn, when I would turn off the radio and fall asleep, knowing that the daylight had returned as the colored objects in the bedroom or in the cabin of the boat regained their natural hue.

The voyage had become a nightmare, a sunken boat wallowing in a sea of broken glass, and I was trying not to cut my feet as I ran for shore with Mark under my arm.

Where I was running to I had no idea. Once on shore, I leaped into the car and went in search of a job. This was a mistake too. Everything was a mistake. Nothing was right, nothing whole, complete. Everything was in fragments. I expected the steering wheel to come off in my hands and to see the four wheels of the car go rolling on ahead of me while some mysterious force carried the car backward, as though winding me up by the invisible wake of my travels.

Late one dark night I crashed into a fence. The experience was real, but it seemed to be imaginary. I left the disabled car along the road, with its smashed front end securely embedded in a steel post, mutely testifying to my having swerved suddenly to avoid a wrong-way approach onto a darkened freeway.

The accident left me without a car. I bought another, a $150 gem of the highways that broke down completely after three weeks of sparkling appearances on the state's highways and byways. "Shoot it," advised the mechanic who gave it a thorough going-over. I gave it to the mechanic and said, "Here, you shoot it." I promptly made a down payment on a third car, this time a $400 one—which broke down too but at least was worth the fixing. I detested cars then, and I detest them now.

My venture into photo-journalism wasn't working either. My sales were few and far between. And my pictures! I looked at them and decided they were meaningless—junk, pieces of paper. Once again I concluded that photography was trivia: photographs didn't say anything. They were mute, dumb, stupid. They didn't *sing,* they didn't orchestrate. They were just silent pieces of paper that conveyed not a whit of *feeling.* I put my cameras, my enlarger, into a box and sold them for half, even two-thirds off.

I went looking for a job on a newspaper, determined to find one as quickly as I could. Something to keep me busy. And in two months Mark would have to begin his first year of school. Get to it, I thought. Find a job, an apartment, or a house. Settle down, I thought—now, before something else goes wrong. Save what money is left. Save the boat.

Every time I thought of the boat I saw it sinking at the dock. When I went to look at it, it was as watertight as ever and floating sensibly and perhaps a bit indifferently at dockside. When I turned my back and walked away, the boat took on water and only the lines that held it to the dock kept it from sinking. It sank in my sleep, and it sank in my waking dreams.

I reported for work in mid-July, on the Contra Costa *Times,* a sensible newspaper that four times a week published the affairs—some carnal, most of them civic—of a sprawled, interlocking mish-mash of suburban cities born of freeways and the vaporous, mutating sperm of migrating Fords. My editor was intelligent, progressive, and had a marvelous sense of humor, and I found good friends in my fellow reporters. But suburbia! The city-council meetings, the planning commissions, the chambers of commerce, the high-pressure, high-hope machinations of the suburban shamans who preached life-giving marvels and built a dreary doom of tract homes and apartment houses that had all the charm of crematoriums that slowly burned their tenants to crisp figures of desperation—these made me want to smash my car into the side of one of the countless pizza parlors I passed each day when I made my rounds of the outposts of progress along the scorched freeways.

My job, this was a mistake too. It wasn't right, not for me. But nothing was right and as it should be. I knew this before I took the job. The job kept me busy, and this was enough; but it wasn't enough—not during the day, not at night.

I had left the Glen Ellen cabin. Mark had gone fishing and camping with my foster parents. I hate house-hunting. I grabbed an apartment near the newspaper. Glen Ellen was gone. The boat was sinking. My car had turned over onto its back in the night; smoke and steam poured from its black, greasy entrails as it lay upside down and blocking the apartment-house driveway. Several men in business suits and snap-brim hats and a naked, pregnant woman pushed the car into the swimming pool.

I detested the apartment. I detested it before I moved into it. As soon as I moved in I found a bill that had been shoved under the door. It was from the four men in the business suits, who charged me for having pushed my car into the swimming pool. There was a note from the naked, pregnant woman; she wanted me to come to her apartment. The baby was mine, she said—I had willed it in my sleep.

My apartment was cold, clammy, empty. All night, all day, cars and trucks roared by my window; they smashed through the thin walls and went rumbling through the apartment. They went under my bed and out again, through the wall. I dreamed of the naked, pregnant woman—about to give birth to the universe, perhaps. I had her note. Somebody was honking. My car was in the driveway again, upside down and smoking. I heard curses, and then the splash. I would have to pull it out again in the morning, and now I couldn't sleep.

Something was happening to Mark. He wasn't Mark any more, not Jeanne's Mark, not my Mark. He was changing, becoming somebody else. He was saying "ain't" now, and his sentences were becoming short, his words monosyllabic. He was parroting hollow conventionalities—closed and shut thoughts, as though an extraordinarily striking flower, a flower so tropic and sensitive, so attuned to the flow and ebb of the universe, had been closed, by hand, in the midst of having its expansive day in the sun. I blamed my foster parents—and this was wrong too.

He had spent a wonderful month with them, on a fishing trip that had made them all happy and tan. And now they offered to look after Mark, to start him in school, to give him a home that had both a man and a woman, both loving, both present, twenty-four hours a day. Mark was tan, healthy, amazingly happy in light of the tragic visitation of a little more than half a year ago. But I couldn't see this. I saw only Jeanne's death all over again. I saw Jeanne slipping away.

I made a desperate grab, and I was unfair to Mark, unfair to my foster parents.

My foster mother and I had petty but explosive arguments over differences of opinion about what should and what shouldn't be done in the way of rearing Mark. We clashed on bedtimes, on clothes, on the question of who was boss.

I got angry one day when she wouldn't let Mark put on his shoes and socks with his own two hands: this had not been my way, it had not been Jeanne's. Such a petty thing, but it made me angry. There was more of this, and I saw the break coming—more fragments, more pieces.

I was determined that not so much as a figure of speech should be erased from what had been the workings of Jeanne and me. I wanted to arrest time and preserve in Mark all that was left of my wife, and, yes, my daughter, and that time when the four of us were together, and what was ours was ours alone.

I had made up my mind there would be no hired baby-sitters for Mark. I decided that Mark would not stay with my foster parents—and he would not stay with me, not until I picked up the fragments and put my pieces back together again.

I wanted desperately for Mark to have at least the trappings of security, a home with a man and a woman who if they could not be his father and mother would at least be his loving mentors, who would be there—both of them—when he awoke in the morning and when he went to sleep at night. I wanted them to be there when he went to school and when he came home.

My foster parents would have generously provided this; their desire to look after him transcended generosity and the helping hand. They *wanted* him with them, to love as a grandson. Mark would have been close to me, hardly more than an hour's drive away.

But I chose a place half a continent away, and I might as well have picked the moon: a farm, in Ames, Iowa, where there were horses and sheep, a great expanse of green-growing things, and two people who had been his mother's parents.

The vibrations would be there, his mother's vibrations. Jeanne's parents and I, we understood each other now. There was a bond that had not existed before and which transcended even the bond between my foster parents and me. Jeanne's blood was in their veins. They had Jeanne's eyes, some of Jeanne's gestures and mannerisms.

At the last desperate moment I called the Bannisters—and, yes, they would set their vacation ahead and come to California a few weeks earlier than planned, and of course they would be more than happy to have Mark, to get him started in school, until . . . They came, and they came quickly.

Mark did not want to go. He didn't fuss, but he didn't want to go. "I want to stay in California, with Hal," he said.

I tried to explain what was happening, that he would be gone only for a while. I wanted him to have faith that as best I could, as quickly as I could, I would put all my pieces and fragments back together, and things would be right again for both of us. "Okay, Hal," he said—as though he were going to the store, on his own for the first time, and had memorized twenty items to go into a sack of groceries. It was not this easy for him. But he accepted my word.

I had rented a motel room for Dwight and Margaret not far from my apartment. But Margaret said she and Dwight would rather stay at my apartment. This meant I had to sleep on the floor, but it didn't matter. They slept in my bedroom. Margaret, as usual, was curious: she had found a book in my bedroom, an Alan Watts book on Zen Buddhism. "Is Zen Buddhism a sex cult?" she asked. She had seen the cover of the book, showing a nude man and woman. I laughed.

My foster mother was crying. She was angry and hurt. Why was I taking Mark from her?

The Bannisters were quiet, smiling, nodding, happy to be of help. Dwight wore that enigmatic, slightly embarrassed grin, eyes downcast, hands behind his back, holding his hat, rocking on his heels, slightly bent at the waist, nodding.

My foster mother was warning me. "Don't do it—you'll never get him back. They don't like you. They didn't even want you to marry Jeanne."

"Mom, that's not true," I said. "You don't understand the Bannisters."

"You wait and see," she said.

I didn't want any more mistakes, any more fragments and pieces. Mark would be taken, in loving hands, to a safe and secure place, as close to his mother as possible. I had faith in Dwight and Margaret Bannister. I was sure they would take good care of Mark. They would do all they could to make him feel that the world was a solid place, that all would be well in time, when his father would come to get him. I was certain they would preserve that part of Jeanne, and of Jeanne's and my days together, that remained in Mark and that certainly I would remain fixed in Mark's eyes and in his hopes for the solid future.

It was hardly a pleasant and happy arrangement—Mark in Iowa, I half a continent away. But it would work to good ends, this I was sure. Time would do this, and I was grateful that Dwight and Margaret would help. Mark and I would be together again, hopefully soon—as soon as I could put down the demons, the nightmares, to retrieve, or to push ahead and find, whatever was necessary to restore the whole.

7

On and off, for almost a year, I lived on my boat, which I recklessly named *Ahab* and which I sailed on weekends. One of my friends, who knew me well, once said, "Why don't you get the hell out of that floating coffin?" and I suppose he was right. But it was so much better than a coffin on land, and I couldn't afford to rent an apartment or a house and to keep the boat too, and I had to keep it, not only to recover my investment but to recover something more. I did not want an apartment or a house anyway; houses and apartments made me uneasy, especially at night, when the walls closed in and the emptiness got to be too much. On the boat, at least, I often got a good night's sleep, and I felt much more at home on the water, where ebb and flow, rise and fall seemed so much more natural and *right* than did solid ground.

For a short while I rented an attic room, and I hated every moment there; but it sufficed in that the room prevented my clothes—those clothes I wore to work: coats, pressed shirts, and neckties—from molding, as they would have on the boat, and kept them unwrinkled and presentable. And I welcomed the bathtub, something I did not have on the boat.

On weekends and those nights when I did not have to work late and attend some civic meeting, I went to the boat and occasionally I sailed in the evening. It gave me a good feeling to be alone and on the water, away from land, and the good feeling remained as long as there was light in the sky.

Once when the Bay became dark, I sailed for the ocean, by midnight or later sailing under the Golden Gate Bridge, where the sea swells began and the boat began to climb and rise. Beyond the bridge was an expansive darkness, and I could hear but not see the waves breaking against the rocks as I made way in the outgoing current close to the north shore. The only lights now were the red and green ones, port and starboard, on the sides of the cabin, and the kerosene lantern on the floor of the cockpit, lighting the compass.

The green light, now close to the water, went rippling ahead of me like the light of a luminous fish barely below the surface, as the boat heeled on a slow and easy tack. The red light glared blindly at the sky, its light lost in the darkness.

In the darkness ahead of me, about twenty-two miles away, were the Farallon Islands, themselves dark and unseen, their presence revealed only by a flashing light that rose and fell with the oncoming swells.

I had to go to work in the morning, and even if I turned back now it would be two hours before I could tie up at the dock and climb into the bunk and sleep for the few remaining hours of the night. I knew I should turn back, but I couldn't. And then it began not to matter that I might not report for work at all. The darkness, the night, the ocean were compelling.

Margaret wrote often and told me how well Mark was getting along in school and how well he was getting along in general. He was happy on the farm, she said, and was constantly talking about his father—and bragging about him too. "Only Hal," he had told her—she wrote one day—could put together the toy plastic car someone had sent him as a present. She sent it to me, at his insistence, and I spent part of an evening with a tube of glue, putting the tiny convertible together and being careful to follow the diagram and to have Mark's final approval. I was glad it had been sent to me, and that evening was one of the most pleasant I had had in months.

I didn't write to Mark regularly, but occasionally I called him on the phone. My letters were read to him by Margaret, and she read him two poems I had written and tailored, I had hoped, to his flair for whimsy.

I was pleased when Margaret wrote that Mark had enjoyed them both—though she had enjoyed "Yogre the Orge's Band" more than he—and that "Clever Sam on the Lam" had inspired Mark to do as Sam did and take up residence in a culvert beside the road. Mark's residency, she assured me, however, had been terminated before it even began. He was pleased and interested, she said, and this was enough to make me happy.

When I spoke to Mark on the phone he was most often taciturn and formal, intimidated perhaps by the shiny black magic of the telephone, and often the extent of his conversation was "I'm fine, Hal. How are you?" Or there might be his brief mention of riding one of the horses on the farm or a nature project at school, in which a chicken egg or a duck was the prime object of his scientific speculations.

Shortly after Mark had begun school, Margaret wrote to say that "son Mark" was doing amazingly well and that "I'm happy to report that his health, disposition and exuberance are all at high peak." In all, she painted a pleasant picture of a happy and busy boy who found life on the farm in Iowa much to his liking; and for this I was thankful. All was well with Mark, and this is what I had wanted when I had sent him to stay with Dwight and Margaret on the farm.

Thinking back, I try to recall the exact moment when I decided to turn back, to swing the tiller about and head back to the dock, the shore, where the lights were. But I recall no exact moment, and remember only going and then returning and having a vague awareness, the feeling but not the words, that it was not in me to live alone in black-burning veneration, even though there were moments when I demanded and wanted to do something like this, when the nearest I could come was to think of sailing my boat across the ocean, alone and with black daring. But I had stopped. I turned back.

All sorts of sensations and impulses had taken hold of me since Jeanne's death. There was an afternoon when I had gone into a large department store to buy Mark a coat and myself a pipe, shortly before we were to leave Pullman. I was on my way out of the store when I saw a young salesgirl—nineteen or twenty, perhaps—bending over a glass counter full of purses. Her hair was long and honey-blond and fell nearly to her soft, round shoulders. She was neither pretty nor plain but struck me as being uniquely handsome; her breasts looked firm and soft beneath a knitted dress that revealed also firm hips and thighs. She looked very healthy and simple, like a girl who from the age of ten, with neither confusion nor single-minded hysteria, knew she wanted only to be a wife and mother, who had not reasoned it out but felt it in her thighs and breasts, in the feeling it gave her to be close to a man—and I wanted to make her pregnant on the spot. Mine wasn't love, and it wasn't infatuation. Never in my life had I felt like this. I wanted her pregnant, about to give birth to a child.

And it didn't stop with her; I suddenly wanted to make every woman in the store pregnant. I ogled every bare knee and calf, hips and breasts. I fantasized luring the young salesgirl into a dressing room and pulling her clothes off and making her pregnant. I didn't want an affair, I didn't want to marry her. I wanted her pregnant, this instant.

The experience was overwhelming then, as though I had witnessed an allegorical play in which I myself had played a part and had watched from a distance at the same time—and it was drawing me now, as I turned back the boat, the remembrance of the brief time in the department store sustaining itself in a dim but meaningful light, the light of a white and open door seen from the end of a dark hallway and reflecting the light of the moon, the moon in turn reflecting the light of the sun, the door reflecting the commingled light of both.

I desperately wanted a mother for Mark, but I was not inclined to go looking as though I were shopping at the supermarket, as I was not so purposefully minded that I could pick, weigh and choose the woman best apt to succeed as a mother, regardless of her possibilities as a wife.

I hoped I might find a woman with whom I would fall in love, who would love me and love Mark.

Not quite a year after Mark had gone to the farm in Iowa, I met Marylyn, in the dressing room of a community little theater not far from where I worked and had my attic room. Our meeting that night was brief, but pleasant bells were rung. I had had other dates before this and had come close to marriage, but had found myself in a confusing relationship that had been mutually dissolved for lack of a common meeting ground. My meeting Marylyn was indeed, as my eccentric and brilliant Polish friend had suggested one day when we discussed it, the workings of Kismet and a raft of obscure forces of good fortune.

For perhaps half an hour, an hour after our meeting, Marylyn and I talked across a crowded table of little-theater players, over glasses of beer; signals and signs came through as we talked about film-making, sometimes having to shout over the voices of the others. I wanted to hear more.

I took a chair next to hers, and she told me she was writing a script for an animated cartoon called *The Judging Machine*. As she related it, I caught a glimpse of a woman who was intensely and charmingly curious about what goes on in the head and who combined her ratiocinations with the artist's impulse to create out of thin air. It didn't take much to find out from the friend who had introduced us that Marylyn was twenty-nine and unmarried, warm and outgoing, that she had a master's degree in film-making, and was, as my friend put it, "very independent, artistic, and charming."

From the start we uncovered a good deal held in common, from an interest in films, books and graphic design to boats, music and civil rights. Marylyn warmed to my interest in her, and I in turn warmed to her interest in me, which is I suppose the way most romantic attachments are begun. And like most romantic attachments, ours progressed from dinner date to dinner date, to movies, to sailing, to my being invited to meet her parents.

Within a few weeks I knew I had found a woman who would be a good wife and a good mother—and more than that, for she wanted no tract homes in her life, no frumpy conventionality. She told me she would happily live in a tree house as long as she had love and affection, no matter how hard the wind blew and the tree shook. She played the guitar, cooked well, was clever at decorating, read a lot, enjoyed long conversations, and seemed to combine books and the arts with good food and a sensibly moderate concern for housekeeping, in a generally romantic outlook.

What might have been a stumbling block was not at all: we disagreed on God and the Church, but we mutually welcomed the dissent. Despite her fidelity to her Roman Catholic faith, Marylyn was hardly a parchment-bound Catholic who crossed herself and clapped her hands over her ears when I argued against the faith and God in general.

It was less than a year since Mark had gone to stay with his grandparents on the farm in Iowa, and now Marylyn and I were planning to be married—and I wanted Mark to join us as quickly as possible. When I knew I was in love with Marylyn, I wanted us to be married soon. I did not feel the need for a long courtship, nor did Marylyn, and I was thankful that Marylyn was as eager as I to have Mark. On our first dinner date, at Marylyn's cottage, I had shown her photographs of Mark—and Janet too—and she had said she thought he looked very bright and handsome. She asked many questions about him, then and thereafter, wanted to know his favorite foods, his bedtimes—did I think he would like her?

"Oh, I hope he likes me," she said one evening when we talked about him—and about marriage. She threw her arms around me. "I'm scared," she said. "Oh, Hal. I want him to like me." I had no doubts, no doubts whatever. All the pieces, the fragments—things were coming back together now.

I called Margaret Bannister and told her of my having met Marylyn, that I was convinced that Marylyn was going to make my life and Mark's pretty close to whole again.

Margaret was matter-of-fact, and I noticed a certain hesitance as she asked questions: What did Marylyn do for a living? Was she an artist?

I knew it was difficult for Margaret when I discussed the possibility of my remarrying, and I knew it was difficult when I talked about Marylyn and tried to convey my enthusiasm, my bright feelings about the future. But I was concerned that Margaret's response was generally hesitant and negative.

There was no question in my mind that things were going to work out well. Mark would have a home and a mother. He had been well provided for in the interim, and now it was time for him to come home. There would have to be a new beginning, yes, and he would have to make adjustments. So would Marylyn, so would I. But all the essentials were here and waiting, and now it was time. The dark voyage was over.

I thought often of the wedding and wanted Mark there, to celebrate the homecoming, to witness the wedding and the bright celebration of the coming together of the three of us. I wanted him to know, to feel that he was of this wedding, this union, so that it would be quite clear in his mind that he was home, that now there was a triple alliance against the forebodings of the past.

I envisioned the reception after the wedding—the plank table under the big walnut tree in the backyard of Marylyn's parents' home; Einer, tall, laughing and with the trace of a Danish accent, popping champagne corks while his granddaughter Jill scooted about with a slice of salami in hand, her mother, Ellen, Marylyn's younger sister, chasing after her . . . The afternoon sun streaking through the leaves of the walnut tree and giving cool brilliance to the white tablecloth set with silver candleholders from Denmark, plates of cheeses, potato salad, pickles, olives, salami, thick slices of sour French bread, Italian candied almonds—and thick slices of pizza, made by Rose from an old-country recipe so that the pizza would be unquestionably Italian, as was Rose, Marylyn's mother, who would be smiling pleasantly and often and seeing to it that her guests had full plates and as many refillings as their appetites required . . . Mom and Pops, my foster parents, sitting in lawn chairs, Pops telling Einer about a likely fishing spot on the San Joaquin River, Mom listening and smiling . . . Jim, Marylyn's brother-in-law, who had swapped days off with one of the men at the firehouse, taking a picture of my mother, Charlotte, who would ask him to send a copy to her home in Washington . . . Marylyn's friend Sylvia, and her quiet, physicist husband from New Zealand, admonishing their exuberant and mischievous son, Michael, as he uncombed his slicked-down hair with his hand and the funny, characteristic tuft of blond hair flew up in a peacock's tail on the back of his head.

And Mark—Mark would chide Michael, tell him he looked like a bird and would giggle, and then run off as Rose called him over to the table to fill his plate, took him by the hand and explained he could have anything he wanted, short of champagne, and I would say that he could even have a tiny glass of that if he wished. Marylyn and I would take him by the hand and lead him around the table, filling his plate as he went with whatever he wanted. Rose would go into the house for a small liqueur glass, which she would give to Einer, who would insist it be full, reminding all of us that when he was a boy in Denmark he regularly drank goblets of beer at the age of four. Mark would put his glass to his lips—but not before Marylyn would insist he give a toast and would poke a finger into his ribs. We would all wait to see what Mark would say in toast, but he would probably giggle and say, "But I only *eat* toast," and we would laugh and end up making a toast to Mark instead.

Mark would be coming home.

PART THREE

The Alien Corn

1

SHORTLY after I talked to Margaret on the phone, I called Dwight, at her suggestion. Dwight had some thoughts on Mark's future, she said, and it was best I discussed it with him. She didn't say what Dwight's thoughts were. "You'll have to talk to him," she said.

It was now June 1964, eleven months after Dwight and Margaret had taken Mark to stay on the farm in Ames. And it was time now to discuss the details of Mark's coming home. Marylyn and I, though we had not set a date, were planning to be married soon. Mark's school term had recently ended; summer vacation would be an excellent time for the transition, and I wanted him here even before the wedding, as soon as possible.

Dwight's words were frightening. God, what did he mean when he said, "Mark's welfare demands that he stay in Iowa, that the state of Iowa might well be the one to make the decision"?

"What's this all about?" I said. "What are you talking about?"

He couldn't tell me, he said—not over the phone. I would have to come see him; he had letters, "letters against me as evidence" . . . "the California situation is dangerous." He couldn't explain; I would have to come to Ames and talk it over—Mark would not be allowed to come to California . . .

"Who the hell do you think you are?" I shouted.

Marylyn, who was standing by the phone and listening, said, "Don't get mad, hold your temper—they'll turn Mark against you!"

God, what was happening?

"What are your intentions about Mark?" I asked Dwight. "I don't understand what you're saying. None of this makes sense—this is the first I've heard of it. What the hell do you mean?"

"You've got to come see me," he said. "We'll have to talk it over. I can't tell you over the phone."

Why was Dwight so adamant? Why was he suddenly telling me that "Mark's welfare demanded he stay in Iowa," that "the state of Iowa" . . . "letters against you" . . . ?

Who the hell was writing letters against me? I wondered. It didn't make sense—none of it.

I was getting nowhere with our telephone conversation. I slammed the phone down. I would write, call again—some way, find out what was happening.

I immediately picked up the phone again and called a lawyer friend, Jim Maguire. I tried to explain what Dwight's intentions were, but I didn't know; some of Dwight's conversation had not made sense. The only thing clear to me was that Dwight did not want Mark to come to California. I immediately wanted to know what my legal rights were.

"How long has Mark been away?" Maguire asked.

"Not quite a year," I said.

"Does he know you?"

"For Godsake, yes, he knows me!"

"They might charge abandonment."

"That's nonsense!"

"You never know what they're liable to do—you've got to protect yourself."

"But how the hell could they charge abandonment? He wasn't abandoned."

"Did you send him support?"

"No. They're well off—none was asked for. I let Dwight claim Mark as a dependent."

"How about gifts, letters . . . ?"

"I sent him birthday presents, Christmas presents, that sort of thing. I didn't write once a week or anything like that. Sometimes I wrote to him, sometimes I called him on the phone."

"Well, they might charge abandonment, but I doubt it would stick. Actually, you have a perfect legal right to go back there and just take him. You might get a California court order, but then it might not carry much weight in Iowa."

"What if they won't let him go?"

"Well, then it gets sticky. You can't break Dwight's door down. If he won't let him go, you'll probably have to get an Iowa court order, a writ of *habeas corpus.*"

"For Godsake, he's *my son!* How in the world can Dwight keep him?"

"I'll research it from this end—but I know from experience the best bet is to get him and take him. Once it gets into court, you submit yourself to the court's jurisdiction. The court will want to know that you have a decent home, don't beat the boy, aren't a dope addict—that sort of thing. Usually, it takes quite a lot to show that a parent is unfit—it has to be pretty bad."

"I don't get it," I said. "By going to the courts, as I understand it, I risk losing Mark. If Dwight refuses to give up my son, I can't by law kick his door in—I can't even call a cop and have him make Dwight give me my son. Instead, I have to go to court and apply for a writ of *habeas corpus,* and by doing that I put myself on trial. In which case it will be up to the court to decide whether Mark will live with his father or his grandparents."

"Not quite," he said. "The grandparents would have to prove abandonment or unfitness. That means you'll have to have witnesses, affidavits—whatever that particular court wants as evidence. It can get costly, especially when you're away from home and have to fly in witnesses."

"But who makes the final decision—the judge? Suppose he doesn't like the way I part my hair? I'm not even a Christian, you know."

His final words were to avoid the courts *if I could*—get Mark out of Iowa. From what I could deduce from my friend's advice, I had a perfect legal right to go and get my son and take him with me—as long as Dwight would let him go. And if Dwight wouldn't let him go, then I had to go to court, and then the court would decide whether I had a legal right to my son, on the basis of evidence presented by Dwight and myself.

It was baffling—and frightening. I wanted no part of it.

If I went into court, how would it stand, my being unmarried? Suppose the judge decided that since I was still unmarried and didn't have a normal home for Mark, Mark would be given to the custody of his grandparents!

None of these questions could be answered, not by me, not by the lawyer—the questions were tied up in endless "ifs"—*if* it could be proved, *if* the court decided, *if* the grandparents wanted to go that far, *if* I had enough money.

If I kicked Dwight's door in, I would likely be arrested for breaking and entering, and this would be used against me if I went into court to get my son: *he is wild, Your Honor, temperamental . . . what kind of parent is it that shows a lack of respect for the law? . . .*

And if I didn't kick the door in, perhaps this would be used against me too: *he didn't care enough, Your Honor . . . why, even my own inclination, as a loving father, would be to . . .*

Who would the judge be—an eighty-year-old sinecurist with an ear trumpet? A wise man? A bad lawyer whose father got him a job? Republican? Democrat? Periodic drunk? Biblequoter? Reasonable young father? Kiwanis president? Any one of them with the doomsday power of God. And the words of only one would be all that would be necessary for the final pronouncement: No, Mark will not be going home. His home now is here, in Iowa, with his grandparents.

I decided the best tack would be for me and Marylyn to get married as soon as possible. This done, there would be no question—if ever the question were put before a court—that Mark would have a father and mother to come home to.

I wrote to Dwight, asking him to explain what he had meant on the telephone, and did he really intend not to let Mark come to California, and, if so, for how long did he intend to keep Mark? It was not Dwight who answered my letter.

Margaret wrote and said I had misunderstood Dwight, that what he really had meant was that I should allow Mark to continue in school the next year, that his teachers and the school psychologist were recommending this. Mark was getting along fine, she said, but his teachers thought another school term would round out, as it were, his sense of security; after all, he'd had some hard knocks and a good deal of adjusting to do.

Margaret's letter made me feel less uneasy, but I couldn't quite reconcile her less adamant suggestion and Dwight's allusion to the courts and "letters of evidence" against me.

Marylyn in turn suggested that perhaps the Bannisters wanted first to be convinced that she would be a good mother for Mark. "After all," she said, "they don't know anything about me, other than what you told Margaret on the phone one day."

This made sense, but I told Marylyn I had doubts.

"I still think Dwight has made up his mind, and there isn't anything we can do about it. I still think the best thing is to get married as soon as possible, and go back to Iowa and get Mark."

Our marriage, however, was not going to be quick and simple. Shortly after my June conversation with Dwight, Marylyn and I broke off our engagement. Suddenly it had seemed to both of us that we had come rushing together much too fast. Perhaps it was only natural that we should go rushing apart, turn about at a sensible distance, and come back together at a contemplative walk. The walk took from June to August, and by the first of September we were thumbing the calendar for wedding dates.

Meantime, I agreed to Margaret's suggestion that since Marylyn's and my wedding plans were uncertain, Mark should complete the school term he began in August. The more my own affairs became clouded by uncertainty, the more I was determined that Mark, when the time came, would have no doubts that his homecoming would be in a straight line, with no contingencies, no uncertainties.

In September, when Marylyn and I had decided we would be married but had not yet set a date, I went to Ames to discuss with Dwight Mark's and my tandem future.

From the time of my telephone conversation with Dwight in June to my boarding the plane for Iowa, Marylyn and I had been under constant tension. Dwight's adamant thoughts on Mark's future, Margaret's reassurances, the fragments of the past, the sudden uncertainty of the future had made me jumpy, explosive, and wanting to piece together the fragments swiftly and forever—and when this wouldn't work, inside I raged and shouted and sought instant and definitive solutions to even minuscule questions of the passing moment. This had not been easy for Marylyn, who was exploring in her own mind the contingencies and meaning of marriage to a man she had known for such a very short time. For both of us, these had been tense months.

I hoped that when I returned from Ames the question of Mark's return would be settled. My hopes rested on Margaret's assurances that I had misunderstood Dwight.

2

I PLANNED TO STAY FOUR DAYS, for I had this much time off from my job. But from the moment I stepped from the airplane in Des Moines, there was a clammy uneasiness in the air, which steadily mounted.

I was disturbed when I found that Margaret and Dwight had come to drive me to Ames and had not brought Mark along to meet me.

"Where is Mark?" I asked, and Margaret said she had not wanted him to miss school. I let it go at that, but wondered. Ames was thirty-five miles away. It was after four in the afternoon. Mark's school was out at three-thirty. Self-consciously and avoiding the obvious, we passed the time of day on the way to Ames.

In about forty-five minutes we were there, and in perhaps ten minutes we were on the road that went by the farmhouse. Margaret passed the house and turned into the neighbor's driveway about a half a mile farther. Suddenly she stopped, and I saw Mark standing by the stump of a tree.

Margaret thrust her head out the car window. "Get in, Mark," she said. "It's time to go home now."

God, didn't Mark know I was in the car?

I jumped out and ran around to the side of the car. I picked up Mark in my arms. "Hi, Bucko!"

He giggled and seemed surprised. I held him on my lap as we drove to the house, but he squirmed and said he'd rather sit next to me.

He had changed a bit since I had seen him last—that day a year and two months ago when he had climbed into my foster parents' station wagon and was taken to the airport and then to Ames by Dwight and Margaret. He seemed tense, not nearly so talkative, not nearly so open. He seemed to have lost that sudden, remarkable impulse for chatty, instant rapport he had had even with strangers. There was a hesitancy now. What was being repressed? What had been forgotten? What had changed?

The Iowa September sky was gray, heavy and moist; the air, thick and sultry. A whitewashed barn, not far from the house, looked green, turgid and thick, as though it had sucked up from the green fields that surrounded it a vegetable essence. From one of the upstairs windows of the house I took a picture of it with a telescopic lens, and I was amazed and pleased when two weeks later I developed the color transparency and saw a remarkable distillation of the same turgid green light I had seen that day. There was something haunting, unnatural and dank —the tiny 35-mm color transparency looked as though it had been taken in a hothouse, or in the indoor tropical conservatory in San Francisco's Golden Gate Park, where the light is forever filtered by thousands of whitish window panes, where the transplanted earth is moist, steamy. Always, when I have been there, Iowa has given me the feeling of being in a glassed, half-open-air museum—a museum not of exotic plants but of dank, insistent green-growing sprung up from the torn pieces of dollar bills.

A fly hanging head down on one of the green walls in Mark's room seemed to be fixed in something sticky and invisible that had pulled with the force of a magnet when the fly had come too close. Suddenly it broke loose, buzzed and flew in a series of erratic, hair-pin, evasive turns, and then was drawn back to the wall, caught by the magnet.

Little was said the night I arrived. The issue was impending but not raised, and it went unspoken while we talked about other things: the weather, the crops, Mark's studies, the farm.

The next day, as usual, Mark went to school, climbing aboard the bus in the morning and returning to the house by late afternoon. When he returned from school, I took him for a walk down the dirt road in front of the house. We must have been out of sight of the house for ten minutes. Dwight must have returned from his office at the university not long after we had left. I hadn't seen Dwight's car pull into the driveway.

Suddenly Dwight came running out of the house. He ran to the road, shouting: "Mark! Mark!" He saw us standing by the side of the road, throwing rocks into a field.

"Oh—there you are," he said. He stopped and smiled embarrassedly. He stayed on the lawn, watching and smiling as Mark and I threw rocks.

There were no busses to catch. The town of Ames was miles away, and I wasn't sure how to get there.

Dwight and I had not yet broached the subject. We would talk about this tonight—and afterward . . .

That night, after Mark had gone to bed, the storm broke. It began with Dwight saying, "I think we ought to sit down and discuss Mark's permanent future." The discussion was simply prefaced: "I would like to adopt Mark," said Dwight, "and we need your agreement on this, of course."

Suddenly I had the sickening feeling there was to be no "discussion"—that Dwight had already made up his mind.

"Why?" I said. "Why do you want to adopt Mark?"

Mine was hardly a question. It was a challenge. I wanted to hear more. And then it broke loose and came pouring down:

He had nothing against me personally, of course . . . I was irresponsible and romantic . . . Mark's welfare demanded that he be with his *own* family . . . I would be an interesting character in Mark's life and I would be able to visit as long as I signed an agreement . . . I wrote poems Mark could not understand . . . I had no money sense . . . I had been indifferent to Jeanne and the children . . . He had written to my former employers, my friends and my relatives and had letters against me . . . I had not worn a necktie to Jeanne's funeral . . .

"Good God," I said, "what *is* it? What is it you're holding against me? Is it Jeanne? Are you blaming me?"

"No," he said, "it isn't that. We just think Mark's welfare demands that he stay here, with his family."

"His family! *I'm* his family—I'm his father!"

Suddenly Margaret joined in. "We don't hold anything against you," she said. "We just don't think you loved Jeanne. You were incompatible. She was unhappy."

"What in the world makes you think that?"

"We have her letters."

"Are you telling me Jeanne said she was unhappy with me?" What was she saying? Why were they telling me this? What didn't I know?

"No," said Margaret.

"But what did Jeanne say that made you think she was unhappy?"

"We just knew she was unhappy. It was in her letters. We read it between the lines. It was obvious."

Suddenly I was being told by Margaret that I had been indifferent to Mark's birth, that I wasn't at the hospital when Mark was born. That I forced the Alaska house on Jeanne and made her life there miserable. That I refused to put in plumbing. That I talked Jeanne out of coming to Ames to have Mark. That I had imposed on Jeanne by letting my foster parents visit us. That I knew nothing about children. That I probably loved Mark but did not understand him. That Mark had been having problems adjusting when he had come to stay on the farm in Ames. That it was a year before he showed them any affection. That they didn't want to lose him now. That the state of Iowa should decide where Mark should stay. That they had letters against me.

Dwight confronted me with a large manila folder full of papers and envelopes. "We have evidence against you," he said.

What the hell was he talking about? I demanded to see the letters, but he said these should wait; they were "for the state of Iowa to see."

"Well, they're from your employers and friends—people who know you."

"What do they say? That I was a bad father? That Jeanne was unhappy with her marriage?"

"No, they don't say that. They tell us things about you

that we think are important, things we feel are important to a small boy's welfare. Letters like that," he said.

The suddenness, the intensity of what the Bannisters were telling me I found amazing, frightening. I had the feeling there was little I could say that would convince them otherwise, though I tried, and resented doing this. Jeanne's, Mark's, Janet's and my life together was ours and ours alone, and I resented this sudden dredging up of the past. And now the past was being used to determine Mark's and my future.

The more we argued, the more Dwight and Margaret insisted that Mark's welfare demanded he stay with them—he would have stability; he should not be moved; I knew nothing about the needs of a boy of seven.

Dwight left the room, and Margaret and I argued on.

"You're turning Mark into another cold Bannister," I said. I knew it was cruel and that it hurt; we were no longer being polite.

Mark lay asleep upstairs, unaware—and yet in the very center of the storm that raged under and above and which would rage on beyond this night, so that he would awaken one morning and find himself engulfed, though the forces that created the storm would be vague, indefinite, incomprehensible. I hoped the moment of awakening would never come, that, in his eyes, time and patience would be all that was necessary to see his world made whole again.

Beneath him, downstairs, in the dining room where he had had breakfast that morning and dinner that evening, the question of his "permanent future," as Dwight had put it, went unanswered.

"Let's leave it open," Dwight suggested, and an uneasy calm overtook the exhausting emotional storm that had gone on for perhaps three hours.

I knew I had to explain to Mark, in a way he would understand, what was happening and what might happen.

The next day Dwight stayed home from the office, and that afternoon when Mark came home from school it was imperative I talk to Mark alone, to explain, to assure him.

Dwight stayed with us as we left the house and went to the front lawn. Dwight watched as I took pictures of Mark and gave Mark my camera and let him take a picture of me. Dwight said little. He held his hands behind his back and smiled as he watched us.

I climbed into one of the big pines in the front yard and pulled Mark up after me. We climbed to the top, and I sat Mark in a branch. Dwight stepped into the house. Now we were alone.

"Mark," I said, "I don't know exactly what's going to happen. I think I've found a new home for both of us, and I've met a very wonderful woman who would like to have you come live with us."

"Did you really find a new home, Hal?" he asked.

"Yes, I'm sure of it, Mark. But your grandfather thinks you ought to stay here. He loves you very much and he wants you to stay with him. Both of us will have to have patience. I'm going to try and work everything out so you can be with me. But it may take a while. I wish I could take you with me now."

"Do you, Hal?" He spoke quietly, introspectively.

"Yes, very much. But it is going to be at least a few months—maybe sooner, I hope so—before Marylyn and I are married and have a home ready. And after that, we'll have to talk it over with your grandfather."

He listened carefully, and I hoped that though he could not understand, he would have faith. There was still hope.

The events of the next day, the third day, ominously foretold the events of the future, as though the third and final happening had taken place in a terrifying fairy tale with an inescapable ending.

The atmosphere was uneasy, explosive, and I felt frustrated, angry. My visit with Mark had been anything but natural and happy. The air was thick with unspoken but self-conscious emotions. At lunch there had been more "discussion," and I became nauseated trying to restrain myself from turning the dining-room table upside down and giving Dwight a very tangible and solid piece of my mind. I wanted to get out of there before I burst. Every ninute was getting worse. I asked to be taken to the bus lepot.

Our "leaving the question open," as Dwight had suggested, was not in fact happening. In my mind there was no question: Dwight could not adopt Mark. When the ime was right, Mark would be coming home with me.

To make this clear, I wrote on Dwight's typewriter a etter of intention, so that there would be no question should we become involved with the courts. On the way out the door I gave Dwight my letter of intent—a letter n which I made it quite plain that Mark was to remain with them only with my permission, that it was my intention that Mark rejoin me as soon as was possible.

Dwight read it through quickly. He had his hat on and was waiting for me to go out the door, to the waiting car. For a moment he said nothing and stared at the paper. Then he tore it into pieces and threw the pieces on the floor.

This was the first time I had seen him angry. During our "discussions" on Mark's future he had never raised his voice, even when he had been the most critical of me. He had been insistent, adamant, but not angry.

He pushed his forefinger between his neck and the collar of his shirt and ran it from the knot of his tie to the back of his neck.

"You, sir," he said, "the only way you can get into this house is to come prepared to sign adoption papers for Mark."

"We'll see about that," I said. "I've already talked to a lawyer. I'll take whatever action is necessary to get a court order."

He ran his finger around the inside of his collar. "When do we get that?" he said.

"The moment I can arrange it." I had no idea what this might entail, or even if it were possible, but I would have told Dwight that I had wired a waiting army of Scots who were coming this instant with drawn claymores if this would have made my intentions clear.

At the bus depot, he suggested I hold off. "I think we

should both think it over," he said. "Let it ride awhile."

Though his suggestion was sensible, I had doubts. Nevertheless, I wanted to avoid the courts; my faith was not in them. I hoped we could talk it out—or, if that didn't work, fight it out. Courts, the law—I had as much faith in these as in the possibility of my turning the bronze figure of Justice into a flesh-and-blood Buddha.

Dwight told Mark to stay in the car, not to come into the depot with me.

I gave Dwight a hard look. I walked over to Mark's open door. "It's all right, Mark. I'm your father. You can come in."

Mark looked at Dwight. Dwight was about to say something.

"It's okay, Mark," I said, "come on."

Margaret said, "Go ahead, Mark."

Dwight was silent. He followed us into the depot.

I said goodbye to Mark and reminded him of our talk in the tree.

How high was that tree! The top of it, where Mark and I had sat, had been in another land, another time.

Have patience . . . all will work out well.

3

BEFORE I had gone to visit Mark in September I had sold the boat and rented a house, a house with little and, in some places, no paint at all on its hundred-year-old exterior.

It came as a rare bargain in these days of exorbitant rents, and came also with a yellow-blooming acacia tree that shaded the second-story master bedroom and softened with green and yellow, the sight of the hard, gray-black parking lot of the huge seven-day-a-week department and hardware store across the street.

The hill on which the house sits is an island out of its own time, in the midst of suburbia's frozen-custard, stucco-and-glass, red-flashing sea of retail sailsmanship—a dreary sea of a million sampans tied to nickel parking meters, of floating cafeterias sinking in hot asphalt, where every day dead bodies are plucked from the water, delivered to the back entrances of the mighty marts, and sold as furniture, clothing, art goods. Only this hundred-year-old house, with its trees and unkempt grass, its crisp, peeling paint and weathered boards—brought here perhaps by a Zen Buddhist monk from an ancient temple in woodland Japan—makes sanity possible here.

I have spent hours photographing its planks, windows and doors, doors that open onto vast regions of the past, or perhaps the future, where trees, running waters, rocks, mountains and stones are sentient, alive and plentiful.

The history of this house is inane, boring. But its flesh is old and weathered; time has sculptured an essence, a smiling Buddha face that is not of the house but knows of it and smiles, even at suburbia, even at death, even at itself.

It was either this house or a boat. Marylyn and I had talked of selling the *Ahab* and buying a larger sailboat. The three of us would go sailing for a summer, to Hawaii perhaps. Perhaps we could find two children Mark's age to take along. What a wonderful way to get acquainted, to rediscover the world.

But then this business with the Bannisters loomed. Suppose—if it comes to this—the judge doesn't like boats: a child living on a boat! A child needs a secure home—four solid walls, three square meals, two approved friends to play with, one well-anchored house—and this only. This is the formula. I'm the judge. Mark stays with his grandparents.

There was too much to risk. I rented the house.

In November, Marylyn and I were married in St. Mary's Catholic Church in Walnut Creek, and Marylyn moved from her tiny cottage to our house of weathered boards and vast, open suburban spaces.

Upstairs, in the bedroom next to ours, we set up the

bunk beds Mark had slept in in Pullman and which had long been in storage. Marylyn sewed curtains and two matching bedspreads, one for the bottom, one for the top bunk. The top bunk—once again—was to be Mark's. We prepared for his homecoming.

It was Kay, Jeanne's sister, who gave us hope. Kay was the only one of Jeanne's three sisters with whom I had contact; I had never heard from Margot and Willa after Jeanne's death.

When I returned from my September visit in Iowa, I telephoned Kay.

No, she said, I had misunderstood Dwight and Margaret. They had been in an emotional state from Jeanne's death, she said, but they had pulled out of it. Yes, she was sure they intended to let us have Mark.

I felt relief. Her surmise, if that's what it was, seemed plausible. I had no doubts Dwight and Margaret were still grieving the loss of Jeanne. I could understand their feelings—Mark was all that was left; he was of their daughter's flesh and blood. If this had been the emotional force behind the terrifying "discussion" of September, then I understood. I could not give my son in offering, but I could understand.

They only wanted assurances, Kay said, that Marylyn would be a proper mother.

Of course, that was it! It was sensible, believable. I wanted to believe.

The effect that a court-custody battle might have on Mark was frightening to contemplate. "We've got to avoid a court fight at any cost, for Mark's sake," Marylyn said. "Let's go slowly, wait. If they want assurances about me, then let's give them assurances. After all, they do have a right to know more about me, I guess. We've just got to try to settle this amicably."

I agreed. And so, during the following months, Marylyn was "certified," as it were, by my mother, by my foster parents, by Ginny, Jeanne's cousin and Margaret's niece, and by Ginny's husband Thornton, now in California and in close touch with Dwight and Margaret. All of their letters went to the Bannisters; each praised, each assured. Frequent reference was made to Marylyn's professional work with children of Mark's age, as a recreation leader and arts-and-crafts teacher; to her training as a hospital recreation worker; to her service in overseas hospitals with the Red Cross.

Nor were her other attributes neglected: her obvious fondness for and instant rapport with children; her genuine hope that Mark would make a smooth and happy transition; her outgoing, affectionate nature.

All of this was planned promotion, as it were, but honest, correct—and imperative. Hopefully, a face-to-face meeting with Marylyn would synthesize the telegraphic fragments to form a complete and acceptable picture. It was difficult to imagine otherwise.

We talked to Mark on the phone almost every week. Both of us talked to him, for I wanted him to become as well acquainted with Marylyn as possible, to know her voice, her laugh. And she wanted to know him. His coming home would be easier this way. There would be no sudden confrontation with a stranger, and the three of our voices spanning half a continent would make the distance between Ames, Iowa, and Walnut Creek, California, between home and home, anything but remote and formidable.

And, gradually, we began to talk about his homecoming. We told him about the room we had prepared, the curtains and bedspreads Marylyn had sewn for his old bunk beds. We told him about the big backyard, the trees, the little boy next door, the school where he would go. And Mark began to talk about the things he wanted to pack and bring with him to California.

Marylyn wrote to Margaret. Several letters were exchanged, and Marylyn asked questions about Mark: what did he eat, what were his hours, his favorite games and books? But Marylyn was disappointed when her questions went unanswered. "It's impossible to describe Mark to anyone who doesn't actually know him," Margaret answered.

Marylyn continued to write, but Margaret's letters got shorter and less frequent as time went on. Then Marylyn began to ask questions about what to pack for Mark, what did he want to bring to California, would he be ready in June? I wrote to Dwight and Margaret and asked if they intended to allow Mark to return with us in June. There were no answers.

A few days before we began our trip to Iowa I phoned Margaret to ask if she would have Mark's things ready to pack. Margaret's conversation was short. Whether it was to the point, I was not sure.

"I don't give a damn whether you come or don't come," she said. "I'm sick and I want to go to bed." She hung up.

Immediately I called Kay. Was all well? Had anything changed?

No, nothing had changed, Kay said.

Marylyn and I were both apprehensive—but hopeful—as we set out for Ames at the end of May. We took our time driving, to have our arrival coincide with Mark's final day in school before the summer vacation.

From Kansas City I called to tell Mark we should be in Ames the following day. My call, in the evening, was person-to-person. I was surprised when Dwight answered and told the operator Mark had gone on a camping trip. I asked to talk to Dwight.

"Where's Mark?" I said.

"He's out camping in the Smoky Hills," he said.

"He's doing what?"

"Camping in the Smoky Hills."

"When will he be back?"

"I don't know," said Dwight. "He went with friends."

"Where are the Smoky Hills?"

"I don't know," said Dwight.

"You don't know! Who's he with? When's he coming back?"

"I can't say when he'll be back," said Dwight.

What was happening? Was Mark out of school already? Why wasn't Dwight telling me where Mark was? Had Mark been taken some place and hidden?

"I'm damned mad about this, Dwight. You'd better have Mark home when I get there."

"I thought you'd be mad," said Dwight.

"If he isn't at the house when I arrive, I'm going to be madder still."

I packed the car with the suitcases and clothes that had been in the motel room and prepared to leave at sunrise. I wanted to waste no time getting to Ames.

The next morning we stopped at a phone booth near the side of the road. I called Mark's school and asked to speak to him. Mark was brought to the phone, and I felt an uneasy sense of relief.

"Where were you last night?" I asked.

Mark seemed puzzled. "I was home in bed," he said.

"Well, I was just wondering," I said. "I called to tell you we'll probably be in Ames tonight. See you then."

I drove faster than ever. Marylyn and I said little on the way.

4

MARYLYN AND I followed Mark around the house, and he showed us the things he wanted to take to California. There was a toy rifle, a tool kit, with a hammer and saw; he said he would help me build a cabinet in my darkroom.

He hadn't changed a great deal since I had seen him last year, in September. He was a little taller, a little heavier. But his large brown eyes—his mother's eyes—were the same. There was the same blondish hair, the button nose, the large, pleasant mouth. But he was less talkative now, a bit tense, uneasy—this had been the change since September.

In the midst of a conversation among the three of us, Mark asked Marylyn if she would like a glass of water and went to the kitchen. When he returned he carried the glass in front of him, like a choir boy carrying a candle, and there was a shy but beamy smile on his face.

He tugged at the sleeve of her dress: he wanted to show her his clubhouse, a small but airy place of a few nailed laths and a great deal of imagination, behind the living-room couch, where a large assortment of wheeled toys had been parked.

He took me upstairs to his room and showed me the clothes in his closet—shirts, coats and pants hanging in a compressed row of wire hangers—and showed me those he wanted me to pack in the car.

Dwight and Margaret waited for us downstairs. They were talking to Marylyn. A few minutes before they had met for the first time, and Margaret had remarked that Marylyn looked much younger than her photograph, that she had expected to see a woman of about forty.

As Mark and I went through the room picking out the toys and the clothes he wanted me to pack, I wondered where the microscope was I had brought him when I had visited here in September. His grandmother, he said, had put it high up in a closet; it had gone mostly unused. I wondered where the pictures were I had taken of the two of us in September, and had mounted on a board, to be hung in his room. They were nowhere in sight.

After Mark went to bed, Margaret, Dwight, Marylyn and I went into the living room. It was time now to find out what Dwight's and Margaret's intentions were.

Why Dwight had called in a third party to our two-way discussion, I didn't know. He was introduced as Mr. Lumpkins, the driver of the bus that each day took Mark to school and a minister of the local Congregational church, where Dwight taught adult Sunday school. He seemed uneasy, a bit uncertain. Dwight prefaced his introduction by saying Mr. Lumpkins knew Mark, had known of his problems in adjusting because he had been a daily witness to Mark's hell-raising on the bus, and would help to fan cool air on what might otherwise be an impassioned exchange.

Perhaps he had come to prevent our snatching and making off; I didn't know. Perhaps he had been ca in as a witness to substantiate Dwight's contention of last September, that Mark's problems in adjusting demanded he stay in Ames. Whatever, the connotation of his sitting in as a third party made me uneasy. I wondered how many other "third parties" there were, waiting to make their entrance, to pass judgment, to make a decision.

As soon as Mr. Lumpkins had arrived and had been introduced he sat down, away from the four of us. Suddenly, swiftly, Dwight sat next to Marylyn, on a faded, narrow settee. He sat on the edge of it, turning so that he faced Marylyn.

"What makes you so selfish as to want Mark?" said Dwight.

Marylyn pulled herself back, pulling her face away from his.

I felt myself rising out of the chair; my left hand was making a fist.

"You don't have to answer anything he says," I said.

Dwight went on. There was a flurry of questions: Why didn't she have a baby of her own—wasn't she able? Did she intend to raise Mark a Roman Catholic? What was her nationality, her ancestry? What did her father do for a living?

Margaret was saying little. Mr. Lumpkins listened, looking from one face to the other. I wondered what would be his part in this. He looked uncomfortable.

Marylyn amazed me. She wasn't cringing, she wasn't intimidated. Calmly, she answered Dwight's questions: No, Mark would not be raised a Catholic. Her father was Danish, her mother Italian. Her father was a retired construction foreman at a gold-and-silver smelter.

What did all this matter? I thought. What did he want—credentials? White Anglo-Saxon Protestant certification? A handed-down relic from the *Mayflower?* An Iowa birth certificate?

"I'm not selfish about Mark," she said. "He's my husband's son—and I want to love him."

Dwight turned, pointed a finger at me. "That little guy

over there is helpless," he said. "You'll find out when it's too late. We know him better than you do."

I was irresponsible, he said, and romantic . . . no money sense . . . I had come from a broken home . . . I didn't love Mark . . . I had been a bad father . . . I didn't want the responsibility of raising Mark . . . I had been a bad husband to Jeanne . . .

We might all of us have been the unwilling characters in a dreary, tedious, inadvertently comic soap opera called *The Alien Corn.*

I played the part of the father who had come to pay his respects to his former in-laws, and to recite, respectfully and logically, his reasons for wanting his son to rejoin him in a home far away in California.

There would be polite nods, and the passing of tea cups.

Marylyn played the part of the former son-in-law's new wife, who had come to pay her respects and to make a favorable impression, to seek approval, the gentle shaking of hands.

Here we were, in the Bannister parlor, with the family minister sitting in and weighing each of our words.

I did nothing to be proud of that night. I should have asked Dwight to step outside with me. We should have settled it there. But no, I tried to reason, to explain, to insist but not assert. I had to get up from my chair every so often and go into the kitchen, to subdue my temper.

Be reasonable, explain, listen to what they have to say, weigh the arguments. Nonsense. But I did it anyway.

At one point I viewed the scene of the five of us sitting there as though I were looking down, through the lens of a camera, from a hovering helicopter; the roof of the house had been taken off for a doll-house effect. There they were, the five of them, having their dreary *discussion.*

This business in the parlor room went on for perhaps three hours. Lumpkins excused himself and left early, before it got really good.

I told Dwight he thought he was God, that someone would have to show him differently. Dwight told me I was irresponsible, had no money sense.

Crumpets and brickbats flew back and forth across the room; but each was carefully aimed at the wall. It was that polite a conversation.

Dwight brought the discussion to an end. "As far as I'm concerned," he said, "Mark will stay here for the next fifty years. There will be no packing."

This is what I had expected, what I had feared.

"Can't we talk it over some more?" said Marylyn. She earnestly hoped to reason.

I agreed. "Why don't we leave it open and talk about it tomorrow?" I said.

"I don't see any harm in it," said Dwight.

The issues were open and shut, all of us knew this; but we left it "open" for further discussion. We were free to tune in again tomorrow.

The camera pulled away for a long shot of the house: Marylyn and I leaving the porch, the house receding, getting smaller; we were two small figures now climbing into the car; the car is going down the dirt road, toward Ames.

The camera pulls farther away, a wide-angle shot: the white houses, the barns, the perfectly square fields of corn, the rectangular dirt roads connecting the fields, the checkerboard greens . . .

Tomorrow, once again . . .

5

THE MOTEL room was hot and sweltry. I had my hand on the telephone.

"There's no point in talking with them," I said. "You heard Dwight. He said no packing; Mark will stay there for the next fifty years. His mind is made up."

"It would be terrible if we had to go to court," said

Marylyn. "Can't we reason with them? Can't we make them understand? He's your son."

"I've had enough *discussion* with them," I said. "Dwight hasn't changed his mind since he made it up last June, if not before."

"It's me," she said. "It's me. They're worried about what kind of mother I'd make. They didn't like me—that's what's wrong."

"It wouldn't make any difference if you were the Virgin Mary. I know what kind of mother you'd make—you'd be wonderful. You and I know. That's what's important. I'm going to call Jim Maguire in California and get his advice. We've got to do more than talk."

"I'm frightened," she said.

"I should just walk into the house and get Mark. I've thought of this. But suppose Dwight panics and makes a lunge at me. Then I get mad and push Dwight, and then there's a scuffle. Here we are, tugging on Mark. Dwight and I can take this sort of thing—but I don't want Mark to see that. And I would have to go through with it and knock Dwight flat if necessary. What a hell of a homecoming.

"One thing we might do," I said, "is take him from school. But I have a hunch the school's waiting for something like this. I'll call Jim."

My lawyer's advice had not changed: simply go and get Mark—this was my right. I explained my fear of having a scuffle in front of Mark and asked about taking him from the school. He wasn't sure about taking Mark out of school—I should check with a local lawyer familiar with local statutes.

"I'll tell you, Hal," he said, "the best thing is just take him. If you submit to the jurisdiction of the court, you have to realize you open yourself to challenge, and you'll be in the old man's home town. You'll be strangers. It might be rough getting witnesses in your behalf, if it comes to this. It'll take time and money. Check with a local lawyer first—be sure. But my best advice is go get the boy."

It was looming again—all the risk, the uncertainty. I

had the terrifying feeling of being a stranger in town, a stranger in Iowa, who had come from California to claim his son and to explain to the local judge, to the school officials, to Dwight and Margaret, to their friends and neighbors why he should have his son, when everyone was telling him—all the strangers, who scarcely knew his name—that Mark was happy here in Iowa; he shouldn't be taken off to California.

"First thing in the morning," I told Marylyn, "I'll find a lawyer in Ames and find out about the legality of taking Mark from school."

We slept fitfully that night. The room seemed terribly small, closing in. The air-conditioner in the window made gurgling noises and blew clammy air at us as we lay in bed, covered with only a sheet. Preferring the already humid air to the noise, I turned it off. Several times in the night I got up and paced the room. It was a long night of hopelessly waiting for a swift dawn.

The sun rose hot and the morning was sultry and stiff; the sky rapidly turned overcast, even before we had dressed, and we dressed rapidly. I wanted to see a lawyer as quickly as possible.

"What do you think about tonight?" said Marylyn. "Should we go out and talk?"

"Okay," I said. "Let's keep that door open. I think it's useless, but I'll call Lumpkins and ask if he'll come."

I caught Lumpkins at home. He was busy, he said, but he could come at 8 P.M. I called Dwight and confirmed the time. He didn't think our talk would do any harm, he said.

Impatience was getting the better of me. We had waited half an hour in the law offices of Payer and Vanderbur, and attorney Donald R. Payer, the sole member of the two-attorney law firm available to us this morning, hadn't arrived. His secretary assured us he was due to report in for the morning at any moment. But as the moments ran on and became the better part of an hour, I left the office, deciding to find another attorney before the morning was out.

We were walking out the front door when I saw a man I supposed was attorney Payer driving into the parking space next to the office. It was the briefcase he carried, as he got out of the car, that caused me to walk over and introduce myself. In this Iowa town of strangers, we had picked the firm of Payer and Vanderbur out of the telephone directory; I hadn't the faintest idea what Donald R. Payer looked like. For all I knew, he might be the Bannister's attorney.

He had heard of Dwight, he told me as we followed him into the office—perhaps in connection with the local Congregational church; he wasn't sure. But he didn't know him. He was both free and willing to represent me, he said.

As we talked on, I was certain that Marylyn and I had done well in taking a chance on telephone-directory roulette. The months ahead would confirm the impressions of the morning.

Payer reminded me of someone I had known in the past—a friend in the Navy perhaps; I couldn't remember who. I guessed him to be thirty-seven, a family man, easygoing, thoughtful. He leaned back in his leather swivel chair, frowned and pinched his lips with the fingers of one hand as I told him the story up to now. He thought awhile, then slowly drew out his advice. His calm was refreshing.

Payer's advice confirmed Maguire's almost verbatim: the best thing to do was to take Mark and avoid the courts, that filing for a writ of *habeas corpus* was apt to get us involved in the sticky business of having to prove, to the satisfaction of the court, my qualifications as a father, over any doubts the Bannisters might cast with a contesting petition.

Despite the refreshing and affable calm of this attorney who had materialized out of a telephone directory, I had no desire to return for further advice; I hoped we had had enough to see us through the day.

It was almost noon. Mark was in his late day of school.

"I think we ought to go to the school right after lunch and get Mark," I told Marylyn.

"What about tonight?" she said. "You told the Bannisters and Mr. Lumpkins you would be there to talk."

"Let them think we're coming," I said. "It will work to our benefit. They might not expect us to go to the school. And if we call and tell them we're not coming, the cat's out."

"That's not honest. Maybe we can still reason with them. They must know in their minds it's not right to keep him."

"I don't think they've been honest with us. They've made up their minds, and we aren't going to change them. I want Mark, and I'm going to get him home."

"It's going to be hard on Mark, taking him from school."

"At this point anything is going to be hard. If I were Mark and my father yanked me out of school, I'd be happy as hell. No—I know it's going to be hard on him. The main thing is to get him home."

There was a look of surprise on Mark's face as Marylyn and I approached.

We were as surprised as he; we hadn't expected to find him in the play yard, which was directly behind the brick-bound classrooms of Gilbert Elementary School. We had driven by the school yard several times without seeing him, and I had figured he was being kept inside.

I was certain the school had been alerted; and from our talks with Dwight and Margaret, I gathered that the school officials were aligned with the Bannisters' contention that Mark should not be taken to California, away from this school. At the last moment I had taken the precaution of renting a car with Iowa license plates. How much influence Dwight had with the school officials I didn't know; he had been a member of the Gilbert School Board and now was active in the Parent-Teachers Association. But I was certain the school officials would not release Mark at my request—not without first calling Dwight.

It would not have surprised me to find Mark tied, with a piece of string, to his teacher's wrist—for his own good, they might have explained.

He stood at the edge of the asphalt playground, against a background of running, clamoring schoolmates, not far from his teacher—and now I had only to pick up my son in my arms.

I had only to untie the string; the car was hardly twenty yards off.

Slowly, gently, I began to undo the knot.

I patted Mark on the shoulder, took him by the hand, and the two of us walked over to his first-grade teacher, Mrs. Sherwood, who was already looking apprehensive. I introduced myself as Mark's father and asked how were Mark's grades, what was his favorite subject, how in general was he doing. He was generally doing quite well, she informed me, though he was sometimes not a good listener. Her answers were vague, nervous—as nervous as my questions.

I picked Mark up in my arms and at the same time handed the teacher the card of the Ames attorney whose advice I had sought.

"I'm taking Mark to California, Mrs. Sherwood. I'm acting within the law, and if you have any questions, please call my attorney."

She looked puzzled, frightened. I turned away from her and started for the car, Mark in my arms. God, it was a good feeling to have my son in my arms, to be walking toward the car.

The teacher lunged for Mark, caught his arm. "I can't let you do this!" she said. "You'll have to see the school superintendent—"

"Take your hand off my son," I said. Not knowing what else to say, I said. "You're breaking the law, madame. Call my attorney, get it from him." I kept walking. She clung to Mark's arm.

Marylyn pulled the teacher's hand away. "Run!" she said.

I patted Mark on the fanny. "Okay, Bucko, let's go—the game's on!"

He half giggled, half cried. I kept talking, patting him as I ran.

"Well, what do you think of this game—just like cowboys and Indians, huh? You're the cowboy, she's the Indian."

Mark's arms were tight around my neck. "Hang on," I said. Marylyn was just behind me, the teacher just behind her.

I made it to the driver's side of the door without interference and put Mark on the front seat. Marylyn was just stepping in. Then she was in, seated, closing the door. I opened my door wide. I was getting in . . .

Someone was shouting at me and running toward the car. Four or five puzzled, confused-looking people converged on the car at once: teachers, high-school boys. A tall, balding man had his hand on the door. "I'm the school superintendent—I can't let you do this. You can't legally take Mark."

I felt an impulse to push him aside, to drive off, to knock them all over if necessary.

"This is not legal," he said. "Come into my office. I can't let you do this."

"What do you mean?" I said. "This is my son. I have a right. Call my lawyer."

He told me it wasn't I who had registered Mark at school. He could release him only to the Bannisters. It made no difference that I was Mark's father. Only the Bannisters could take him. This was the law.

If I had had wings! This horrible snare—Mark was *my son*. Why were these people pulling on him? Let go of him.

Mark was sitting in the front seat of the car next to Marylyn. The door on her side was closed, locked. The school superintendent was holding open the door on my side, his arm locked at the elbow and rigid. Several high-school boys and perhaps two or three teachers were standing in back of the car.

Perhaps they would have parted like sheep had I slowly backed out. Perhaps we could have outrun the police and made it over the Iowa border. Perhaps I could have used my fist on the school superintendent.

I bent over to Mark. He looked frightened and puzzled. "It's okay," I said. "Don't worry about anything. Be patient. I'm going in and talk to the school superintendent. You wait here."

And as he waited, a door was shut, slowly and securely and with the sound of metal against metal, though soft hands pushed it.

6

MRS. LUMPKINS called her husband, Henry Lumpkins, thirty-eight, minister of the Gilbert Congregational Church, school-bus driver and part-time football coach. Mrs. Lumpkins was secretary to the Gilbert School superintendent, in whose office I now sat, Marylyn next to me. She advised her husband to hurry—Mark's father had tried to take the boy from school. Lumpkins hurried from home and arrived moments after I had left the car and stepped into the school office.

Mrs. Lumpkins also called Margaret Bannister at home, and Margaret called Dwight at his office at Iowa State University.

One or two nights before, Margaret had called Mrs. Sherwood, Mark's first-grade teacher, and told her Mark's father was coming to Ames. And Mrs. Sherwood, in the course of their conversation, said she would keep an eye on Mark at the school. Mrs. Sherwood then spoke to the school superintendent, who advised her, yes, keep an eye on Mark.

Now it was my turn to make a call, to the attorney Marylyn and I had consulted that morning in downtown Ames, a little over five miles from the Gilbert School. I hoped he would explain, to the satisfaction of the school superintendent, that I had a right to take Mark from Gilbert School, from any school, and take him to California, out of Iowa—yes, even me, a stranger.

I was relieved when the secretary said Mr. Payer was

available for my call, and the moment he picked up the telephone I asked that he explain my legal rights to the superientendent, Mr. Schwenk—that Schwenk had prevented my taking Mark. I handed the telephone to Mr. Schwenk.

"Hello, Don," he said. "Surely you didn't advise anything like this!"

There was a brief exchange, a mutual request for explanations.

"The father didn't register the boy, Don—I can't let him go."

"Let me talk to him," I said.

He handed me the telephone.

"Is this true, Mr. Payer?" I said. "I can't take Mark out of school without a release from the Bannisters?"

"I'm afraid it is," he said. "I could have told you that, but I didn't know the Bannisters were the ones who had registered the boy there."

"I didn't know this was a factor," I said, "or I would have told you."

I could see no choice now. I had to take the chance.

"File for a writ of *habeas corpus,*" I said.

"Well, if that's what you want. You know, you have a perfect legal right to take the boy after school hours."

"Dwight and Margaret are here," I said. "Somebody from the school called them in. No—there would be a tug of war in front of the school. Mark's had enough for one day."

"If you go to court," he said, "you have to realize it may take time. I know you're not wealthy, and these things can run into quite a bit of money. I can hold down my costs, but even out-of-pocket expenses can run high—filing fees, printing costs, things like that. You might have to fly in character witnesses, and that's expensive too. I'm not trying to discourage you. I want you to know what you're getting into."

"I don't see any choice now," I said. "Go ahead with it."

As I hung up the phone, Lumpkins was half shouting at me.

"You don't know what you're doing to that little boy," he said. "You don't love him. You don't care a whit about that little shaver."

Dwight was standing by one of the two doors to the office, his head down, his lips set and tautly puckered. Marylyn sat next to me, Margaret next to her. Lumpkins was standing by the wall, next to Dwight.

"I know perfectly well what I'm doing!" I shouted.

We flew into an argument.

"Don't raise your voice at me," he said.

"I'll raise it anytime," I said. "If I have to, I'll tear this goddam school apart."

I demanded to talk to Mark. Someone said I couldn't —Mark was in class.

I didn't know who had said it, and I called out to the superintendent, who had left his desk and stood in an anteroom next to his office.

Yes, he said, I could see my son for three minutes.

"I think we should call a cop," said Dwight.

I told them all to leave the room—I wanted privacy with Mark.

Dwight objected. "We can't trust these people," he said.

The superintendent said it would be all right—for three minutes. Then Mark would have to go back to his classroom.

Mark was brought in by a teacher, and I sat him on a chair between Marylyn and myself.

Dwight posted himself at one door, Lumpkins at the other. The doors were closed, and Mark, Marylyn and I were alone.

I told Mark that as a kidnaper I hadn't got to first base. I wondered how to explain to a seven-year-old boy, when I couldn't comprehend it myself, how all of us— Mark, Marylyn, myself—had been engulfed by a kind of grass-root bureaucracy, that judging from the appearance of things I was an interloper, a stranger, a heathen come from California and up to no good.

I wanted to hand Mark a hacksaw blade, tell him to saw his way out of the school, and join us at a secret rendezvous. But no, his teachers would have taken it from him. Or perhaps I should have given Mark a golden trombone.

"Here, take this—just put your lips to it and blow, and it plays its own beautiful music. When the walls and the teachers and the rule books close in, take it and play, blow up a hallelujah chorus, a golden storm and wile the wowsers away!"

No, his teachers would take this away too.

Worse, they were trying to take his father away. They would come marching in chorus into the courtroom: We think that Mark should remain in Iowa. We think that to move Mark would be detrimental. We think that Mark has learned to keep in line. When he first came here, he didn't march in time to the music.

This would come later—but it was written all over the walls of the big brick schoolhouse in Gilbert. It was written in the wet sky, on somber faces; it was written in the fields of corn, in thick-armed semaphore when the moist wind blew. It was written in the mural that so intrigued me in the library at Iowa State University—a subtle cartoon of dead-calm Iowa faces, thick legs and mythical children who heard but did not speak lest they crack the muraled wall and cause $82.47 worth of "unnecessary damage." And under the Grant Wood mural might have been written the motto: Golden trombones, hacksaws, heathen strangers—these aren't wanted here.

As Dwight stood at one door and the minister-football coach at the other, I told Mark that he was a remarkably good boy, that Dwight and Margaret loved him and we loved him, and that now a judge would probably have to decide in which home he was to live.

I pulled on one of his arms and then the other.

"You see," I said, "your grandparents want you and we want you. We pull, and they pull."

I pulled at his arms again, first one, then the other. He laughed.

"That's sort of what it's all about," I said. "It's a real mess, isn't it?"

He nodded. He was too scared, too uncertain to talk much.

I spent most of the allotted three minutes trying to get it across to Mark that we had lost the game on the playground but that maybe we would win the final sweepstakes if we all had patience and if he knew he was loved by me, by Marylyn, by his grandparents.

"Be patient, Mark. It may take a long time. Just know I love you. And Marylyn loves you."

"Yes, Hal," he said. He wasn't saying "yeah" now, and I wondered if he'd been corrected.

He smiled, and it was not an easy smile—a smile I had never seen before this day. It looked brave, scared, puzzled. It flashed on and then off, and it was followed by a nod and a look at the floor. His hands were in his lap, the fingers of one grasping the fingers of the other.

He was not the same boy who had come to me one day in the backyard in Pullman and asked to have something to feed the turtle eggs, nor was he Mark-a-Bean, not the Little Jack Horner in tights with a rip in the seat, nor the boy on the beach with a traveler's bag full of seashells, nor the boy who had sailed with me on San Francisco Bay, in stocking cap and life jacket and dragging his finger in the water as the waves went by.

He was not quite the same boy I had visited in September. No, he was more tense now. He was taller, and he looked a bit like his mother—more so than that day in September when we had climbed into a tree and talked about the past and the future, about his mother and sister, his friends in Pullman and California. Like his mother, he had a remarkable memory for the past; like his father, he could change the subject with rapid dexterity if the subject was painful. Like his sister, and his mother and his father, he had a vast compendium of imaginative words and thoughts and thoughts of words. But now, since September, he was not so inclined to construct palaces of the imagination. Perhaps now there were caves and catacombs, long, dark passageways.

Now the three of us sat here—Marylyn, Mark, and his father, me, Hal, and Papa—in a room with two guarded doors—Dwight, his grandfather, at one; Lumpkins, minister, intermediary, at the other. Three minutes we were given for this visit, and now the three minutes were up.

I had tried to avoid the courts, the intermediary, the great decider, the distant and distantly wise third party—and I had failed. I had tried to pick up Mark in my arms and carry him off as my own, and I had allowed myself to be stopped by the long rigid arm on the door of the car.

Now, one of the doors of the room was opened from the outside, and Mark left quickly, quietly and obediently as someone—it was the voice of a woman, a teacher perhaps—said, "Go back to your class now, Mark."

It was the last time I was to see him without the permission of the court.

7

THE SECOND-FLOOR COURTROOM of the Story County District Court was old, squeaky, and out of plumb; the time, the place, the trial was stern but homey, almost familial, as though all of us—the judge, the Bannisters, the two Bannister attorneys, Marylyn and I, and my own attorney—had assembled, for lack of an official courtroom, in the living room of a 100-year-old Iowa farmhouse, while the owner, a white-haired widow, baked cookies for all of us (had I been on trial for murder, even cannibalism, she would have given me the same share as she served the others), and otherwise kept herself quietly out of sight but within hearing distance of the proceedings.

There was nothing grand, nothing pompous about this courtroom. The bailiff, who sat in the right-hand corner of the room near the door that led to the community rest room (all of us—even the judge, still in his black robes—took turns using it), throughout the trial looked sleepy and bored and sometimes during recesses talked about an imminent vacation fishing trip. The court reporter, a gray-haired woman of perhaps sixty, sat very close to the witness stand (a squeaky swivel chair on an iron ice-cream-parlor stanchion) and recorded the entire proceedings in shorthand with pen and ink; she reminded me of one of my teachers in the fifth grade, who told us stories while she transferred our grades from ledger to report card.

The mid-July heat, the almost visible humid air were next to unbearable, and the apparently broken overhead fan looked like the black propeller of an ancient hand-powered submarine and was hardly more than a make-believe merry-go-round for otherwise bored Iowa flies.

For five days I was on trial here. At stake was my son's future and the future of the two of us as son and father together. And for five days I felt like a stranger, an intruder in the home of an old and respected Iowa family—a heathen father come to reclaim his recently converted son.

Before the trial my lawyer had warned me: my not being a bona-fide subscriber to the Christian faith, my indifference to whether my son went to Sunday School would make my case difficult.

At the outset of the trial I found it difficult to believe that my religious beliefs or my lack of them would have any bearing on the court's decision. Nor did I think it mattered that Marylyn and I lived in a house of unpainted boards and that I liked it this way, and that I had not worn a necktie at Jeanne's funeral.

And at the outset I was amazed that it was I who was on trial, when it seemed to me I should have to do no more than offer simple proof that I was Mark's father and that he was being held against my wishes. But from the moment my attorney, conscientious Don Payer of Ames, filed my petition for a writ of *habeas corpus,* it became frighteningly apparent that I was a stranger in another land, and that I was in danger of losing my son if the

Bannister attorneys could simply demonstrate that my way of life was un-Christian, unconventional, and, apparently, un-Iowan.

Attorney John L. Butler, one of the two hired by the Bannisters, made his case quite clear in his opening statement on the first day of the trial:

"I think our case is presented on the theory of the best interests of the child . . . and I believe that our evidence will show that the child's best interests demand it be left where it is. . . .

"The evidence will further show that the father has contributed practically nothing to the boy's support since he has been with the grandparents; that the father has not been in the habit of maintaining steady employment; that he has shifted about from place to place; that he has characteristics which would not be desirable for the raising of this boy."

Apparently the Bannisters were sparing no expense to make good their case. A few weeks before the trial, my home in Walnut Creek was visited by a private detective who had been on the job at least two days before arriving on my front porch, pretending to be lost.

As far as I could learn, his first visit was to my foster parents' home in Santa Rosa, where he sought information on the pretext of my having applied for a job promotion. Wherever he went, his English accent went with him.

The same man with an English accent visited my former newspaper editor in Walnut Creek and left the editor with the impression that I had applied for a government job that required security clearance; was I a Communist, he wanted to know, and did I have liberal leanings?

It was shortly after leaving the office of my former employer that the chameleonic private detective with the English accent found Marylyn at home; he was lost and looking for the address of an English lady friend, he explained, and stayed just long enough to have a look at the inside of my living room. His visit was either preceded or followed by a photographer who took photographs of virtually every inch of the outside of my house. The photographs showed up in the courtroom and were used as evidence against me.

The two Bannister attorneys, together with their hired court reporter, flew from Iowa in a private plane to my former home in Pullman, where my past bank account and financial transactions were investigated. The two attorneys also took a deposition from the Washington State University editor who had asked my resignation a few months before Jeanne's death, in hopes he would offer damaging evidence. They also cross-examined character witnesses deposed by my Pullman attorney (one of three I had to hire to secure the depositions of witnesses in my behalf; "live" witnesses, at the time of the trial, were preferred, but I could not afford to pay their travel expenses).

From Pullman the two Bannister attorneys flew to Walnut Creek, where they cross-examined character witnesses deposed in my behalf there. With them, all the way from Iowa, they brought along the two poems I had written to Mark, "Yogre the Ogre" and "Sam on the Lam." And though attorney Butler was deadly serious, he provided the only comic relief to occur throughout my entanglement with the Iowa courts when he asked my friend John Lienhard, then visiting San Francisco from Pullman, if he considered the two children's poems suitable fare for a child of seven! John said he liked them, wanted to take them home to read to his own four-year-old. Butler declined; he preferred to enter the poems as evidence against me.

The Bannisters also paid for my examination by a psychiatrist, apparently to document their contention that the poems I had written for Mark, among other things, were indication of an incurable flair for romance and fantasy. My two sessions with the San Francisco psychiatrist, an attractive young woman hired long distance and sight unseen by the Bannisters, were pleasant and chatty, and, ironically, helped my case. Somewhat to my disappointment, she declared me "squarely" within the range of normality, if a bit romantic. Her report was used in evidence in my behalf, over the objections of the Bannister attorneys. The psychiatrist, in her report, said it was evident to her that "there exists a large difference in ways of life and value systems between the Bannisters and Mr. Painter." She was the first to see the emerging conflict of values that would have national repercussions.

How much all this dug into the $100,000 Bannister estate I have no idea. Whatever the amount, I hardly matched them dollar for dollar.

Though our attorney Don Payer worked for a reduced fee and put in remarkably long and compassionate hours of research for not so much as a pittance, court costs and such incidentals has having depositions typed and bound to the court's satisfaction alone came to $729. And this alone cut well into the $1,200 loan I had made, not only in hopes of paying for my entire venture into the realm of jurisprudence, but for Marylyn's and my travel expenses to and from Iowa. Eventually, it would cost me upward of $3,500 to press my claim for my son in the Iowa courts, and the costs are still mounting. My $171-a-week newspaper salary hardly rose to the occasion.

Ironically, even had my wife and I wanted to move into a home more acceptable to Midwestern standards, we couldn't have afforded it. The money I had borrowed was exhausted, and to keep the wheels of justice turning was requiring payments of $100 a month. The $65-a-month rent we paid was our limit, and we sold our unpaid-for car and bought a cheap, used one; the amount of the former car payments we used to keep ourselves above the financial waters.

There was no money left over to hire so much as an armchair psychologist to refute what was apparently the Bannisters' wisest investment: nationally prominent child psychologist Glenn R. Hawkes, then head of Iowa State University's Department of Child Psychology.

As my attorney correctly predicted at the time of the trial, Hawkes's testimony was the most potent we had to deal with—though Marylyn and I were certain, after hearing Hawkes on the witness stand, that his testimony verged on brillig, Alice-in-Wonderland nonsense.

It was Hawkes who pressed home the Bannister contention that Mark's "best interests demand" that he remain in their care.

I think it was on the fourth day of the trial, half an hour after Judge Kelley had dismissed the court, as Marylyn and I and my attorney stood talking by the open door of the clerk's office on the main floor of the courthouse, that Judge Kelley came hop-walking down the last few steps of the stairway that led from the courtroom.

I suppose he thought there was no one present in the otherwise deserted hallway, for he accompanied his rhythmed hop-walk down the steps with a singsong "da-bump, da-bump, da-bump." He passed us with a broad, inner smile that acknowledged but seemed to have nothing to do with us. In his hand swung a large coffee Thermos, and I supposed he was on his way home to his family, and in an especially pleased and happy mood. I liked this man. And would he rule against me, I would like him still. I even liked the way he wore his modish straw hat, more of Panamanian than Midwestern lineage—jauntily, if in a sedate sort of way.

In the courtroom Judge Kelley's demeanor was overtly gruff, laconic, and impatient; he said little, listened a great deal. Surely, in his black robes he suffered more than the rest of us from the outlandish heat and humidity. Only Bannister attorney Butler, in his porous, blue-and-white seersucker jacket, seemed cool and unaffected.

It was the occasional happenstance noises that interfered with the already bad acoustics of the courtroom that were first to elicit a response from Judge Kelley—who once left off in the midst of the trial and went downstairs to impose an immediate injunction upon the unmindful county employee pushing his power lawnmower resolutely back and forth under the courtroom window.

Only once during the trial did Judge Kelley give any indication of what he thought about the proceedings in which he sat in judgment—this on the last day, the last hour of the trial. And there was a pleased, only partially restrained humorous look on his face when Marylyn, close to nervous exhaustion after five tense days in the courtroom (our tiny motel room at the edge of town was itself a trial), was unable to suppress an audible laugh of relief as he said, rather wryly, "I have better things to do than to read the good doctor's book."

The "good doctor" being child psychologist Glenn Hawkes, whose textbook, *Behavior and Development from Five to Twelve,* my attorney had offered as rebuttal to statements the author had made on the witness stand concerning the psychological make-up of seven-year-olds. Judge Kelley had apparently heard enough and had made up his mind about Hawkes's testimony.

Dr. Hawkes, head of the Department of Child Development at Iowa State University, professor of psychology, holder of the degree Doctor of Philosophy from Cornell University; staff member of the 1960 White House Conference on Children and Youth, lecturer, writer for popular magazines and learned journals, co-author of a textbook on child psychology, educational consultant to Project Head Start—his list of credentials, elicited by Bannister attorney Hall as Hawkes took the witness stand, ran long and frighteningly impressive.

If his credentials were in order, his findings on Mark, in my opinion, were not. Nevertheless, I did not take his testimony lightly; his conclusions disturbed me deeply, for he appeared to take lightly my being father to my son.

In a manner both fastidiously academic and blatantly galling, Hawkes told the court, in well-modulated, no-uncertain terms, "Biological fathers are not important. . . . I have spent approximately twenty-five hours in studying Mark," he said. "Mark sees the Bannisters as his parents, and to me this is the only tenable solution . . . in my study of Mark I discovered he is already in a home where he has a mother and a father figure. That to move him from this is not an important alternative because to me this is a rather unthinkable solution. . . .

"The critical thing is the welfare of the child. When a

child has constructed his parents-substitution, I think this is the most critical factor and I think the other [Mark's biological father] is relatively unimportant."

If I understood Hawkes, he was virtually telling the court that in his expert opinion make-believe fathers are more important than real fathers; that Mark, despite having spent the first five years of his life with me—and with his mother—would be a happier child if he were prevented from returning to his father's home.

That Mark looks like me, that he has many of my characteristics, that he thinks a good deal as I do, that he has my genes, that he is loved by me—no, these, according to Hawkes, are not important.

Nor did it matter who or what I was:

"Inasmuch as Mark has already made an adjustment," said Hawkes, "and sees the Bannisters as parental figures in his psychological make-up, to me is the critical factor; a disruption at this point I think would be detrimental to the child even if Mr. Painter—he might very well be a paragon of virtue."

Hawkes had spent twenty-five hours interviewing the Bannisters, Mark's school teachers and Mark himself (for five years Mark's mother and I had been having a remarkable dialogue with Mark that far excelled the *interview*), and from this, and this alone, Hawkes drew the conclusion that Mark's life with me had been one of instability.

I was furious. No, he told the court, he knew nothing about Mark's father—nor was it even helpful to know something about him. His investigation into Mark's past, if it were indeed an investigation, could only have been a verbal excursion led by the Bannisters, who themselves, as Mrs. Bannister later testified, knew little about me.

How could Hawkes possibly make a prediction as to Mark's future if he knew nothing about Mark's father, nothing about Mark's past relationship with his father?

But indeed he thought he could—and did.

It is possible, yes, Hawkes told the court, that Mark might grow up to be a normal child if he lived with his father, but there is a "ninety percent" chance that this would not happen.

With trepidation, wonder and disbelief I listened to this child psychologist spill forth the fruits of his calling. And in his own words did he perhaps reveal that his views came from exclusive and distant provinces:

"I think," he said, "child psychologists are less concerned about natural parents than probably other professional groups are, largely because we feel that—I think we have strong research clinical evidence to back this up, that one earns the father figure, one earns the being of a mother figure, the naturalness of which is less important than what one has earned over a time."

I, then, for reasons known only to Hawkes, had apparently not earned Mark's fatherhood—indeed, I was, as Hawkes put it, "only necessary obviously at the time of conception."

Surely, I thought, Judge Kelley could not take this child psychologist seriously; surely, Judge Kelley, with children of his own, would discount a thesis that took light stock of fathers and sons. Not for an instant, after hearing his testimony, did I think that Hawkes, as my attorney was predicting, would be the Bannisters' most dangerous witness.

For Hawkes not only gave expert credence to the preposterous; converse to his dire predictions for Mark's future with a father Hawkes knew nothing about, Hawkes's testimony pointed out—with the supporting evidence of his own tests—that Mark was a remarkably intelligent and adaptable boy.

If I had correctly pieced together Hawkes's hither-and-yon testimony, Mark's so-called problems had been hardly more than those of a natural hell-raiser who had found his neophyte venture into the confines of schooldom only slightly less a trial than did his teachers.

Mark's grades in school were well above average, but it was his inclination to rough-house his classmates that caused Mark's teachers, Lumpkins, the Bannisters, and now Hawkes to testify that Mark had had difficulty adjusting when he had come to Ames, and that now, after a hell-raising year in kindergarten (his transgressions were considerably less than my own when I was in kindergarten), he was taking to school with acceptably token resistance.

Somewhat vainly, I was proud of my son, as Hawkes confirmed Mark's amazing strength, zest, and adaptability —the same remarkable strengths we had tried to nurture and bring to full bloom and which Mark, though this nurturing had too quickly ended, had brought to bloom on his own—at an age so susceptible to solitary wilting.

But that Mark's strengths and adaptability might have a biological and love-founded link with his father (and his mother), Hawkes did not consider. And, as he said, he knew next to nothing about Mark's father, nor about Mark's past.

That Mark had a father who loved him, and had waiting for him a woman who would mother and love him as her own—these, in the opinion of child psychologist Hawkes, were the "untenable solution" that held for Mark the 90 percent chance of his going bad.

If I had an opinion of Hawkes's incredible pronouncements, Judge Kelley, fortunately, shared it, at least in part:

"The court has given full consideration to the good doctor's testimony," Judge Kelley wrote in his opinion after the trial's end, "but cannot accept it at full face value because of exaggerated statements and the witness' attitude on the stand."

What's more, Judge Kelley wrote, "It is apparent that Mark is a physically well-developed boy seven years of age, considerably above average in mental abilities, pleasant, courteous and well behaved. From the evidence adduced it is apparent . . . that Mark has many of his father's characteristics and exhibits a great deal of the good early training given him by his beloved mother."

Judge Kelley was taking little store in Hawkes's testimony, and this came as a great relief, in light of my attorney's warning that Hawkes was the Bannister witness I had most to fear. But though Judge Kelley, who had heard Hawkes word for word and had observed his manner, gave the child psychologist's testimony little value, others, with appalling awe and naïveté, would. Hawkes's testimony, put into seventy pages of written words, would quietly and ponderously dazzle the Iowa Supreme Court.

Meantime, Judge Kelley had more testimony to hear.

8

HAWKES HAD TRIED to convince Judge Kelley that I should be excluded from sharing my son's life in the manner of other natural fathers on the premise that Mark saw in Dwight and Margaret Bannister the psychological image of a father and mother, and that to remove him from this conditioned sphere of imagery to the home of his real father would be disastrous. Now Margaret Bannister, on the witness stand, found other grounds for exclusion, and made it perfectly clear that she held little in common with her former son-in-law—and with Marylyn, whom she found lacking.

"What do you think of Mrs. Painter?" my attorney asked Margaret in cross-examination, to determine whether Margaret had thoughts on Marylyn's qualifications as a mother to Mark.

"I don't know her," said Margaret. "I didn't know her long enough to form an opinion."

You don't have any criticism of her, do you?

"No."

As far as you know, she is a satisfactory person?

"Not pleasantly," said Margaret. "I am not pleasantly impressed by her."

Why is that?

"She is effusive and intrusive."

Can you tell us why you think that?

"It is a small thing," said Margaret. "She didn't wait for her husband to introduce us, or she didn't wait for me—she introduced herself to me. She didn't wait for me to greet her. She extended her hand, said, 'I am Marylyn.' "

Is that the only reason?

"No."

Can you think of anything else?

"Her letters," said Margaret, "seemed to be in the same tone."

Now, what would you say, Mrs. Bannister, are some of Harold Painter's deficiencies?

"I think his inability to face reality and see things in the light as they really are; his inability to repudiate his fanciful, fantastic schemes, plus his lack of responsibility, his temper, and his erratic behavior."

You didn't want Jeanne to marry Hal, would that be true?

"I didn't know Hal at the time. I had respect for Jeanne's judgment."

Do you think she made a poor choice?

"I do."

You don't really care for him, do you?

"I don't know him, we have nothing in common."

Do you have any doubts he and Jeanne loved each other?

"Yes, I think their natures were incompatible."

Would it be a fair statement, Mrs. Bannister, to say that you are now of this opinion that you would, under no circumstances, want Mark to go back to his father?

"Yes."

And you base this opinion of yours not on the qualifications of the father or where he is going to go, but on your own feelings. Is that true?

"Not just on my feelings, no."

Do you base it at all on having had an opportunity to visit with the father?

"No."

That wouldn't have made any difference?

"No."

It wouldn't have made any difference about who his wife was?

"No."

Really wouldn't make any difference about what anyone wanted, other than this court, would it? You would still want the boy.

"I still think it would be best for the boy."

Regardless of what anyone said?

"Yes."

Can you tell me how this has affected Mark's feelings toward his father? Do you feel this has in any way affected Mark?

"No."

You never said anything bad about Harold Painter to Mark?

"No."

Have you ever said anything good about him?

"Yes."

For instance?

"He and Mark enjoyed the sailing together. I really didn't know too much about him, to recall an instance."

Harold must have some good qualities, doesn't he?

"Yes."

Did you ever tell his boy about this?

"There was no occasion to."

Could you have made an occasion if you had wanted to?

"No."

Would you tell us, Mrs. Bannister, about whatever affection you have for Mark? . . . What are your plans for his education and upbringing?

"I have a great deal of affection for Mark as an individual, as a grandmother and as a grandson. . . . I hope to be able to maintain a stable situation for him, and continue a program of caring for his physical needs and guiding him, disciplining him when necessary. I hope to make him feel a sense of responsibility toward society and see he has a formal education, college education."

Whatever the emotions that drove Margaret, they were perhaps justified, for not easily does a mother lose her daughter; the emotional force of the death of one's daughter—of one's wife—as both Margaret and I well know, is not easily reckoned with. And had Jeanne—Margaret's daughter, my wife, Mark's mother—not been killed one day on the way to work, while I was at home pursuing a compulsive dream of writing and this way making my living for myself and my family, then none of us would this day be confronting one another in the courtroom, claiming rightful possession of Jeanne's remaining child.

Margaret, I thought as I heard her testimony, and though angrily and desperately I wanted to refute and contradict it, was being altogether a mother. Sadly, I could not let her have my son; and I have nothing else in my possession that will relieve her sense of loss.

After Margaret came Dwight, and he had nothing to say about Marylyn and said only of me that he thought I was of little use to my son. He spent little time on the witness stand, and it was about his "desperately" wanting Mark to which he devoted most of his testimony, this being elicited by his own attorney.

Margaret had already established that the Bannister household was in monetary sum and familial substance sufficient for the boyhood-to-college needs of a boy of seven; it remained only for Dwight to give his reasons for wanting Mark.

"I can't say I like this little guy," he said of me. "He is worthless to my—to a child who is young and in need."

For a moment I thought Dwight was going to say I was "worthless to my son," meaning *his* son. He was, he said, desperately desirous of having Mark in his custody.

I did not doubt that Dwight was sincere. Nor did I doubt that his feeling for Mark ran to great depths, depths beyond those to which he was able to give voice in the courtroom, where there were only his slip-of-tongue allusions to go by.

Those acquaintances of the Bannisters—their housekeeper, a distant neighbor woman from whom they bought eggs, Lumpkins, and Hawkes—who had testified in the Bannister behalf drew a telling portrait of a companionship that was indeed like that of father and son: Mark and his grandfather played games together, they made stilts of tin cans, they chased and played ball games, together they rode their bicycles up and down the dirt road in front of the Bannister farmhouse, and it was Dwight who often put Mark to bed and read him stories, took him to Sunday school, who drew him crude but meticulous scenes, with colored crayons, of farmlands idyllically inhabited by horses and cows and chickens.

At times Dwight's words were difficult to follow, and psychologist Hawkes had prefaced Dwight's testimony by saying that Dwight, when in an anxious state and having deep feelings, was sometimes unable to speak coherently; and it was about Mark he felt most deeply.

Mr. Bannister, after Jeanne died did you have any thought about where the best welfare of Mark would lie?

"I . . . had a discussion with Hal Painter in which I said that I would like to have him come with me [to Ames] . . . to discuss what needs and helps Painter needed in his situation and with his one youngster.

"I thought we had an agreement that this was the course he wanted to take . . . he changed his mind. He refused to make any consultation and I had to surrender to the point that the only one who knows our youngster, the only one who knows our remaining living youngster, the only one who knows the background of him, the only one who is able to break loose from what chains and throttles he is bound to have in a floating situation —from that time on I believed that there was no further salvation for that boy's welfare than his opportunity to live in his own family, his own life, with no intervention. . . .

"We wanted to see this child had the opportunities that any good young fellow is going to get. He has to have this with this one family who are not divorced. . . .

"As things have developed it is absolutely impossible to handle him in any other way. . . . I was taking him as best I could in the direction he was supposed to go. That direction requires that he be with his father, a father who can teach him games he wants to play, things he wants to do and to be in Sunday school. . . ."

The day the trial was over, Marylyn and I were allowed to take Mark to the park not far from the Story County courthouse. The judge had given us permission to visit alone with Mark, and the next day we would be going back to California to await the judge's decision; hopefully, we would have it in two weeks.

Dwight followed us to the park and stood by one of the elms, about thirty feet in back of where Mark, Marylyn and I sat on the grass and talked.

Angered by his hovering, I left Mark and Marylyn, went over to Dwight, and told him to leave, that I wanted to be alone with my son.

He nodded and smiled and clasped his hands behind his back; he looked at the ground and made no motion to leave.

"That's mighty interesting what you're doing down there," he said.

I didn't know what he meant.

"Just leave," I said. "I've had enough of this."

He kept nodding, with a broad smile on his face, and then he pulled his tie undone and unbuttoned the collar of his shirt.

I waited for him to leave.

Slowly, looking down at the ground and smiling, he began to walk, with the same slow stride that I remembered of Jeanne; it used to amaze me that Jeanne's walk, though feminine, was so much like her father's.

He walked to the end of the block, and then down a dirt path that cut a thin and arid gash through the center of the lush green park. He was below the slope on which Mark, Marylyn and I were sitting, and he walked slowly, coat under arm, his head down, as though he were deep in thought.

Occasionally he glanced up and seemed to try to catch

a glimpse of the three of us, but his glances would miss us and he walked on and out of the park.

When he had gone, Marylyn and I, with Mark in hand between us, went down to the swings through which the now deserted path passed.

The three of us talked as I pushed Mark in a swing. Mark swung back and forth, in wide, pendulum arcs.

Dwight did not return.

9

BANNISTER ATTORNEY BUTLER had a single purpose in mind when he questioned me on the witness stand: he would show, as he had told the court, that I had "characteristics which would not be desirable for the raising" of my son.

For the first time in my life I was asked to justify myself as a father; I would have to convince those who sat in judgment that what I was, my views, even my hopes and dreams and my personal love for my son conformed to the standards by which I would be judged. And if the standards held by those were alien to my own, then so would I be made alien to my son.

What was the evidence the Bannisters were to offer? I wondered. Already they had offered the two poems I had written for Mark, four pages of manuscript now entitled Court Exhibits #1, #2, #3 and #4.

Next came photographs of my house in Walnut Creek, each so calculatedly unflattering as to make my hundred-year-old house, with its weathered and unpainted boards and its unkempt, windblown yard of grass, seem a bleak, gray monotone of sagging wooden rectangles. Looking at the photographs Butler thrust in my hands and asked me to identify, I myself was surprised not to see a goat ambling about on the front proch.

The Christ child had been born in an unpainted manger, presumably with open-air-front and at a time when such modern and sanitary appointments as indoor plumbing and running hot water were a millennium away. My own house had not only a front door to keep out the worst of weather but indoor toilet, washbasin and bathtub (not shown in the Bannister photographs), and this in itself might have made the humble homestead of all Christianity seem little more than a pauper's lean-to that might at any moment be blown off the face of the Holy Land.

But this, of course, in at least my mind, was not the point; if Christianity had been born in a manger, I supposed that my son, raised in this dilapidated house of mine, might, despite this, grow up to manifest at least a few of the heralded Christian virtues.

Even were my house to fall down about his ears one windy night, he would still have, though the house was gone, his father's love, and upon this rock of his father's love perhaps he might be expected to build his stable house of the future.

But, no, this was not the point either. The point was, as Butler pressed home, that my house was a place of weeds and unpainted dilapidation, unsuitable for the raising of my son.

Another point to be made had to do with the kind of friends I keep:

"About this Alaskan who came to Chinatown," he asked, "who was that?"

I had written a tongue-in-cheek newspaper story about the curious adventure my Alaskan friend Marty Vorys had had one day in Oakland, California, while visiting that city's diminutive Chinatown. Inexplicably hungry for Wisconsin cheddar cheese (apparently this had been notably missing in his Alaskan diet), Marty searched the grocery stores in Chinatown, but was told by an elderly groceryman, "Chinese no eat cheese." Not so much as a slice of cheese of any kind, he was told, was available in Oakland's Chinese markets.

I wanted to take a picture to go with my story, and

posed Marty in front of the largest, most Chinese-like Chinese market in town and had him give a guitar concert while sitting on a lettuce crate and wearing boots, shorts and beret. A little Cantonese boy stopped to gape in wonder.

The thesis of my surrealistic story was that the local Chinese were as puzzled over this beret-and-boot-clad Alaskan's spur-of-the-moment guitar concert as the Alaskan was puzzled over the Chinese disdain for Wisconsin cheddar and apparently all cheese in general.

The Bannister attorney obviously did not share my sense of humor over my Alaskan friend's Chinatown adventure; with an inscrutably Occidental straight face, he entered my story and picture of Marty strumming his guitar in Chinatown as evidence against me, Court Exhibit #20.

Why the Bannister attorneys had selected my friend Marty as evidence of the kind of friends I keep puzzled me; they might have indeed found others who, unlike Marty, had neither graduated from Yale nor come from prominent families. Marty's less tangible assets, such as his extraordinary generosity, sense of humor, and unflagging convictions, would not of course have been of much help to me in the courtroom, since these qualities would be so difficult to prove. "Yale," "prominent family" —these ring more substantial bells for those who judge; the rest, when you are trying to establish a friend's character, is unfortunate clatter.

The friends I have are many and varied; for each my friendship is especial and not attuned to the kind of credentials that would look well in the courtroom. Indeed, the Bannister attorneys might have introduced into evidence any number of my friends, and I would have been hard put to convince the court that the highly individual character of each gave social grace and justification to my friendship and thus substantiated my virtues as a father.

There is, for instance, my friend the professional bum and worker of crossword puzzles, who sleeps in a cardboard box, usually under a bridge, and who begs his bread and the rubber tips for his crutches with the distinct and ethical point of view that this is the *way,* that no other way will give meaning to his life.

There is my friend the alchemist, who has preserved in his head the ancient secrets of making dyes from the most primitive of the earth's flora and fauna—dyes so brilliant, so lasting that one is compelled to believe in the alchemist's magic, to have uncanny faith in a man who cannot abide by bread alone and so distills from the living substances of the earth the guiding chroma of his solitary existence, and yet walks the streets in drab, Chianti-lighted poverty.

And my other friends!

There is the Slavic payroll clerk and self-matriculated student of writing (he disdains *literature*) who is fond of the bright dessert oranges served at a dingy Basque restaurant up a flight of stairs, up an alley in San Francisco, and who was amused when one day he watched a man in a Gurkha battle helmet go down, down to his knees, in a sinking fishing boat that only a fool would have bought sight- and leaks-unseen, a man in a Gurkha battle helmet who was himself amused at his own bizarre and foolish fate.

I have a friend (and mine are Marylyn's friends too) a woman who sews her own dresses; a man who knits afghans and makes his own coats; a little boy with two front teeth missing; a baby with a smile like a blob of chocolate pudding on a Dresden china plate; a singing, wrestling chef; a butcher, a baker, and a man in a straw hat who sells Crackerjacks at Candlestick Park.

And Marylyn and I have for friends a family of five —husband, wife, and three boys—and one night we sat down to their table and before we ate the potatoes, the meat, the bread, and drank the wine, we clasped hands and made a ring around all that was put before us, palm touching palm, fingers touching fingers; we felt the flesh and blood and the pulse, and the warmth of the food was in us before even we had its taste in our mouths, and each of us knew of the other's presence, and of what company he kept in his friendship of hands. None of us asked the other from where have you come? From what school were you graduated? Have you any money? Are you Christian?

Whether *I* was a Christian, whether I was a member of a church, my regard for Sunday school—these matters prompted a good many of the Bannister attorney's questions, as he sought to unveil "characteristics" of mine "not desirable" for the raising of my son.

His questions were sometimes rhetorical and accusatory:

You didn't take Mark to Sunday school . . .

While you were in San Francisco after Jeanne's death, you didn't take him to Sunday school, did you? . . .

No one else took him to Sunday school, did they?. . .

I think you told us you had no church affiliation, did you not, Mr. Painter? . . .

As a matter of fact, you have never believed that Christ was a God. . . . You have never believed that, have you? . . .

I suppose you might define yourself as an agnostic, might you?. . .

Also to be accounted for was my having read a bit of Zen Buddhism, mostly of the Alan Watts variety; for some reason, the Bannister attorney had the notion that Zen Buddhism was a "cult," of which I was a member:

Do you practice or follow a cult known as Zen Buddhism?

How do you spell it, by the way? . . .

It was spelled "Z-e-n," I told him.

He was aware of that, he explained—he wanted to know if I knew. This baffled me.

You have read quite a little of this Zen Buddhism business, haven't you? . . .

Isn't it true you borrow a great deal of philosophy from that cult? . . .

His harping on the word "cult" interested me; I wondered if he meant to conjure a picture of California crackpots who went about in togas or leopard skins, in alarming contrast to Iowan Sunday churchgoers.

There were other characteristics of mine he wished to unveil:

I take it you didn't like the Navy. . . . You didn't like wearing a uniform, did you? . . .

You didn't like the Moses Lake work, did you? . . .

Now, what is your interest in the Civil Liberties Union? . . .

You didn't like the high school work in your senior year . . .

As a matter of fact, your math teacher asked if you wanted to tell stories or study math. You told him you would rather tell stories, didn't you? . . .

You were fired out of school, weren't you? . . .

Jeanne kept the books in your family, didn't she? . . . Name one time when she didn't . . .

What happened to the books you bought while in the Navy? . . . How much did you get back from your investment in books? . . .

Is it true that at the time you picked up your son at the school grounds you said, "Here we go, Bucko, the game is on . . ."? You wanted him to think it was a game, did you? . . .

This sailboat . . . I think you told us you bought it for $3,500, did you? . . . You sold it for $3,200, did you? . . . This is the boat you thought you would make a profit on, wasn't it? . . .

And then he asked me a question I found most difficult, for never before had I been asked this, not by Jeanne, not by Janet, not by Mark—before this moment, not by anyone.

"Mr. Painter," he said, "will you tell us what your concept of yourself is as a father?"

How do I answer this? What is my concept of myself as a father?

"I don't know," I said. "I wish I knew. I would like to think that I am—I am growing; as a child grows, so the father grows . . . it is a sort of mutual experience of two people growing side by side. . . .

"I think that if I had a cardinal principle in my relations with my son it would be one of continual love. That I wanted this boy to know he was loved by his father and his mother. That he was accepted as an equal in the household . . . inculcating an attitude . . . that is one of joy for life . . . of love . . ."

I knew I was botching it and groping. To be called upon, on the witness stand, to try to explain my concept of myself as a father—this was unnerving, and whatever I said might be used against me.

And what *was* my concept of myself as a father?

What was Mark's concept of himself as a son? And the little boy I know who has two front teeth missing and who speaks Turkish more fluently than English—what is his concept of himself as the son of a Turkish father?

What is the Slavic payroll clerk's concept of himself as a Slavic payroll clerk, as a father, a motorist, a pedestrian? What is the bright orange's concept of itself as a bright orange?

Or does one go about his business without asking himself, "What is my concept of myself as what I am doing, what I am?"

But the burden of the question was on me. Please answer the question. The court reporter, the judge, the Bannister's attorney—they are waiting. Who else is waiting? Mark?

Already it's been established by the Bannister attorneys that I don't like neckties; that I'm an agnostic; that I don't go to church on Sunday; that I live in a ramshackle house of unpainted boards in an expanse of wild oats; that I have little regard for money; that I buy books, read them and sell them at a loss; that I spent a sizable portion of my inheritance on a sailboat that I sold for a loss and camera equipment I sold in disgust; that I have quit jobs I didn't like and was fired from others that didn't like me; that I sold Jeanne's and my home in Pullman because I couldn't stand to be in it with Jeanne and Janet gone, and sold it at a financial loss to which I was indifferent.

What is my concept of myself as a father? They're waiting for you to answer!

Mark, I love you.

Come, be by my side, live under my roof, and I shall show you what is my concept of myself as a father. I do not have words for it, and it will be not a concept of words and symbols. It will be a concept I will express over a great length of time, from moment to moment, from day to day, from week to week.

Will it be a concept of continual love?

Yes, but there of course may be moments when I shall be angry at you, when I may, for instance, say, "Get the hell off the living-room couch and stop jumping up and down on it—are you trying to wreck it?"

You want to be a shoe salesman—this is how you want to spend your life? You want to be a poet, a chemist, a virtuoso of bird whistles, a builder of bridges, to be a farmer and grow corn, to be the first man on the moon?

How can I say no? Be what you are, be what you will. Love, hate, whistle, sing, skip, hop, twirl a baton, be your own man, your own boy. Be glad, be sad, be glad and sad when the moment strikes you. Reap, beep and peep—and don't let anything stop you from being what you are—not me, not anyone. Here's my love, do what you can with it, take it for your own, whirl it about your head, paint a mustache on it, hock it if you need the cash, whatever, it's all yours, and *you* are all yours; be glad of it.

Say, stop jumping up and down on the couch—you're wrecking it!

What? You say it's a lousy couch? It ought to be wrecked?

Let's take a look.

Ah, my—you're right. It *is* a lousy couch. One leg's broken already, and this thing's as ugly and useless as a stuffed walrus.

Here, let's both jump up and down on it—we'll wreck it together.

Oh, oh—here comes Marylyn. She looks mad.

Hey, she says, what are you two doing to the couch?

We've decided it's lousy, I tell her—we're wrecking it.

Let me look, she says. She looks a moment.

Ah, yes, she says, you're right. High time we got rid of it.

Now, that's it, all of us together. Jump higher, Mark. Jump higher, Marylyn.

Here it goes—*bang!*

Watch out for the flying springs!

By the way, I tell Marylyn, Mark wants to be the first man on the moon. What do you think about that?

What does Mark think about it? she says.

Yes, that's it—what does Mark think about it? What is his dream, his need? What is the song of himself? I will help him to sing it, to sing it with love.

About my concept of myself as a father—in the courtroom I tried, and I couldn't give the court a concise and definitive answer:

". . . inculcating an attitude . . . that is one of joy for life . . . of love . . ."

But this was botching it, groping, trying to give it words.

"I would like to elaborate," I continued that day in the Iowa courtroom, "I would like to elaborate on this and other things, and I plan to do so extensively, but not in the courtroom . . ."

And here I am, elaborating out of the courtroom, and still I cannot give you a concise and definitive answer.

Mark, I love you.

10

MARK HAD ONE ARM AROUND ME, just barely above my waist. This was as high as he could reach without throwing his shoulder out of joint. My left arm draped across his shoulders as I slowed my pace to his. His new shoes, which he said his grandmother had bought just before Marylyn and I arrived in Iowa, pinched and hurt, but he refused to wear his cowboy boots, which had long had the newness worn out of them. The heel of his right foot was blistered, and neither Band-aid nor talcum powder made the blister go away. But Mark's new shoes were shiny black oxfords, the kind that Mark said the "big kids" wore at the Gilbert School. Blister or no, Mark insisted on wearing the shiny black oxfords. He dragged his right shoe, his bandaged heel rising out of it, leaving a barely perceptible and sporadic wake along the muddy path in back of the Fun House at Arnold's Park.

Arnold's Park—this was Iowa's summer-day Coney Island, on the sealess shore of Lake Okoboji, the lake itself surrounded by a green sea of rattling August corn still dripping yesterday's heavy rain. From out of the cornfields, from out of this passive infantry of victorious green, rose the holiday paraphernalia of Arnold's Amusement Park.

But the Ferris wheels, the merry-go-rounds, the bumper cars were all but deserted and locked up. Perhaps it was too cold, too wet; perhaps, as the proprietor of a hot-dog stand told me, the college kids weren't coming here this summer because the vendors had raised their prices to discourage the small-budget spenders who had rioted last summer in a time of flowing beer and summer heat.

"What do you think about taking a ride on the roller-coaster?" I asked Mark. Mark hesitated.

The roller-coaster was in fact an Iowan miniature, a cautious imitation of the more splendid rides on the East and West coasts. But in Mark's eyes, the eyes of an eight-year-old who still saw adults as giants, the Arnold's Park roller-coaster must have been an awesome, Jack-in-the-Beanstalk challenger of white-planked space high above the surrounding corn fields.

"I think it's scary, Hal," he said. He didn't say no, he didn't want to ride it; he didn't say yes. He would wait and think about it.

It was late August 1966, and this was my first visit with my son since Mark, by order of the Iowa Supreme

Court in February, had been given to the custody of the Bannisters.

Marylyn was at our rented cabin in Vacation Village, on the northwest shore of the lake and about five miles north of the amusement park, preparing a dinner of chicken teriyaki, a dish she had learned to make in Japan and which she now cooked over a double-burner hot plate. This was a pleasant cabin, pine-paneled and with two bedrooms—Mark's and ours—and a reasonably large family room with table and chairs. The cabin was a short walk from the lake and an intriguing selection of boats to rent, including Mark's avowed favorite, a green paddle boat which the three of us had paddled for perhaps a mile before we tired and returned to the dock.

I think it was on the second day of our stay that Mark had looked around the cabin and said, "Aren't we lucky ducks!"

And for eight days, by arrangement of the Bannister attorneys and mine, Mark, Marylyn and I were lucky ducks. We swam, rented boats, took long drives, went to movies (Mark wanted to see *Batman,* the movie counterpart of his television idol), played a host of games, with a Super Ball and tin mop pail (ten balls in the bucket made a winner, and Mark won), and potatoes painted with faces and mounted on a live index finger (Mark's and Marylyn's rainy-day puppet show). There were eight days of banter and quacking as we lucky ducks made the most of our visit.

A month and a year ago I had petitioned the court of Judge Ed J. Kelley to order the Bannisters to release Mark. And indeed it was for more than a mere visit with my son that I asked.

". . . the child, Mark Wendell Painter," wrote Judge Kelley in a decision handed down about two weeks after the conclusion of the 1965 mid-July trial, "shall be delivered unto the permanent custody of his natural father. . . .

". . . the defendants are ordered to deliver the child, Mark Wendell Painter, to his father, Harold W. Painter, forthwith.

". . . the plaintiff, the father of Mark Wendell Painter, is a proper and fit person to have the care and custody of his own . . . son, and . . . it is in the best interests of the son . . . to be reared and educated in his father's home."

But Mark, in the curious language of the courts, was not to be "delivered."

With frightening dispatch, within hours after Judge Kelley issued the written order that the Bannisters release Mark to my custody, the Bannister attorneys appeared before the Iowa Supreme Court, in pursuit of a stay that would prevent my taking Mark from Iowa, pending the Bannister appeal. The stay was promptly granted.

The speed with which the Bannisters moved left me no time in which to fly to Iowa and get Mark, during this brief time when Mark was legally in my custody—the brief and only time in the history of my attempts to remove Mark from the Bannister household that the *law* expressly upheld my right as a father to have possession of my son.

I am certain that in swiftly granting a stay the Iowa Supreme Court well knew—as did the Bannisters—that my bringing Mark to California would play hell with any Iowa claim to jurisdiction. Both the Bannisters and the Iowa Supreme Court appeared determined to keep Mark and the question of his custody well within their own green borders: the place of Mark's possession would have an uncanny influence on my attempts to regain his custody.

I had no choice but to continue my efforts in the Iowa courts, in pursuit of the fast-moving Bannister attorneys, though the court costs and legal fees were taxing my resources to extinction.

What were the chances of the Bannisters winning their appeal in the Iowa Supreme Court?

Don Payer thought their chances minimal—but that there was always the danger that the court would find merit in the Bannister claim that Mark's welfare was exclusively their province.

Once again they took up the hue and cry: Mark's welfare, they argued, demanded he remain with the Bannisters, and underscoring this was the studied implication that Mark's father was a scoundrel who had squandered his deceased wife's estate on a boat and cameras and who did not enjoy wearing his country's uniform—a curious allusion to my disdain for uniforms of any kind. And once again the testimony of Dr. Hawkes was shot to the fore.

It was Dr. Hawkes's testimony that gave my attorney doubts that the Iowa Supreme Court would rule in my favor. He foresaw the possibility that the court would be impressed with the learned perambulations of Hawkes's seventy-some pages of testimony, and foresaw also that the court might use the testimony in support of a growing, new doctrine that put a child's welfare over the presumptive right of a natural parent. Nevertheless, he predicted that our chances of winning were good. His inflections were cautious and tempered with professional pessimism, but his words were optimistic: he would be surprised, he said, if the Iowa Supreme Court found in the record of the trial court grounds to overturn Judge Kelley's decision.

The Iowa Supreme Court's practice of not hearing live witnesses, and only reading from the written record, spared Marylyn and me the added financial strain of having to return to Iowa—but this was perhaps a disadvantage.

The Bannister attorneys, and my own, would appear in our places, in proxy, as it were, and the spoken words of the Bannisters and myself, and the Bannister witnesses, transcribed by the hand of the court reporter, condensed and edited (this is the practice in Iowa), would speak for us. Expressly missing from this expensive printed document submitted to the nine justices were such mannerisms as alluded to by Judge Kelley when in his decision he singled out Dr. Hawkes's "exaggerated statements and the witness' attitude on the stand."

It was Dr. Hawkes's transcribed words that went before the Iowa Supreme Court—cold, learned, with neither inflection nor gesture to temper the doubtful wisdom of them.

The Bannister appeal, and my lawyer's petition asking denial, went before the nine justices in October 1965. Don said he hoped we would have a decision by Christmas. Marylyn and I made plans to build our Christmas celebration about Mark's arrival in California. We delayed sending Mark's Christmas presents until the last minute.

The decision did not come until February, and the bad news came by telephone, from Don. Marylyn was the first to hear it.

She was unable to reach me at work, because I was on my way home, wallowing through the 5 P.M. commuter traffic. It was the second Tuesday of the month, the day when the Iowa Supreme Court regularly handed down its decisions, and all day I had been expecting Marylyn to call. Since it was evening and Marylyn hadn't called, I figured it would be another month before the decision came. I regretted the delay.

When I opened the screen door and went into the house, I knew something was wrong. Marylyn wasn't at the door to meet me, and the house seemed oddly silent. For a moment I thought Marylyn had been called away and the house was vacant. The feeling of dusk was in the house as well as out, as though it were fall rather than February and one month before the first certain signs of spring would begin to take bloom in the trees, flowers and shrubs scattered about the front and backyard.

Marylyn stepped out of the kitchen as I entered the living room. Behind her, the kitchen seemed unusually dark. The bright brass lamp on an accordion extension arm over the sink was not on, as it usually was. Marylyn had been crying. Her eyes were puffed and most of her eye make-up had been blotted away.

"What's wrong?" I said.

"Don called," she said. "Oh, Hal. We lost the case."

I couldn't believe it.

"What did Don say?" I said.

"He said they ruled against you."

"The court ruled against me! Nonsense—what reason did they give?"

"Don hadn't seen the court's opinion—all he knows is that they ruled against you."

For a long while I held Marylyn in my arms and said nothing. It had not yet sunk in. The thought that the decision was preposterous kept repeating itself; the sadness, the meaning of it was yet to come.

A short while later I called Don Payer. I wanted to hear from him what had happened—and what we could do about it. Surely, I thought, the door wasn't closed.

Don said he didn't think there was much I could do to buck the court's decision. "I think we've gone about as far as we can," he said. "There's always the possibility we can ask for a rehearing—but I don't think you should get your hopes up."

He hadn't seen the full text of the court's decision, he said, and would await that before we formulated any plans about carrying the case further. Don was profoundly disappointed.

"All the equities are with you, Hal," he said. "I just don't see how they could come to this decision."

I wanted to know if there was another court to whom I might appeal.

The U.S. Supreme Court, he said, seemed to be the next step. "But I know you folks don't have much money—the cost would be in the thousands of dollars."

I hung up the phone with the understanding I would await Don's reading the text of the court's decision, in hopes they had said something upon which we might hang an appeal. I could not accept the possibility that the Iowa Supreme Court was the end of the road.

Marylyn asked me what I planned to do next. I said I didn't know; we would wait and hear from Don.

"Do you plan to fight the decision in the courts?" she asked.

"I just don't know. We've spent every cent we have now, and we're in debt for years to come. I don't know what we *can* do. I don't know how much we can afford."

Nothing had had time to sink in, to make its mark, when the phone rang. A reporter from United Press International, who had read the decision on the wire, out of Iowa, wanted to know what my reaction was.

I explained to him that I hadn't seen the text of the decision and had little if any idea on what it was based. He read to me that part of the decision that had been picked up by his wire service.

I had been denied my son's custody, it said, because the Iowa Supreme Court considered me "unstable, unconventional, arty, Bohemian, and probably intellectually stimulating,"* that the Bannisters were to have Mark because they were "highly respected members of the community. Mr. Bannister has served on the school board and regularly teaches Sunday school." They would provide Mark, it went on, "a stable, dependable, conventional, middle-class, Middle West background."

What's more, the court had said of me, in deciding that Mark should spend the rest of his natural childhood with the Bannisters, that I was "either an agnostic or atheist," had "read a lot of Zen Buddhism," and was a "political liberal." The court, it seemed, also took exception to the weeds growing in my front yard and the unpainted boards on my Walnut Creek house.

A couple of days later the full text of the court's decision arrived in the mail, and it was even more preposterous than I had imagined after hearing the greatly condensed version read to me by the UPI reporter.

The sum of its findings were contained in words that made me rage:

"We do not believe it is for Mark's best interest to take him out of this stable environment in the face of warnings of dire consequences from an eminent child psychologist and send him to an uncertain future in his father's home."

From what dark age of unreason had this court sprung?

How could this court believe, or profess to believe, that dire consequences awaited Mark should he be allowed

*For complete text of the court's decision, see Appendix.

to live under my roof and share my life—when this warning had come from a psychologist, hired by the Bannisters, who himself said he knew nothing about me and felt it was hardly important whether he did or didn't?

I was convinced that the court's so-called reliance upon the authority of an "eminent psychologist" was hardly more than a half-sophisticated excuse for its own mud-footed conservatism, and that the court's decision was in its full context absurdly blind, cantankerous and stupid.

Had I beaten Mark, been a cannibal who coveted my son for the dinner plate, fed him narcotics or deprived him of food, then I might have cause to stand silent in the face of this court's decision.

But even this court said I was a "fit" parent—whatever in the world this is—but then in the same breath declared my way of life unbefitting *its* own chosen standards. Surely even native Iowans, I thought, must be shocked at this absurd lapse into a caricatured Grant Wood yesteryear.

The more I thought about the court's decision, the more I raged. I was frustrated, baffled.

My rage was tempered with an unspeakable sadness. I didn't know what to do to get my son back, for it seemed that now I was bucking the sovereign state of Iowa, as though the court had stamped the state's seal across Mark's forehead and had taken him away, for safekeeping, to some vault, some locked silo, where I couldn't touch him.

The phone at my Walnut Creek house rang constantly, from morning until night. Sometimes calls came as late as 2 A.M.—when a man who said he was a Catholic priest called from out of state to offer his help and prayers. Most of the calls were coming from the press, from reporters from *Time* and *Life*, the New York *Times*, the Oakland *Tribune*, the San Francisco *Examiner* and the *Chronicle*, the Washington *Post*, the wire services. Calls were coming also from the three major television and radio networks—ABC, NBC and CBS—all wanting interviews and to have my "reaction" to the court's decision.

I was almost as surprised at the press—and the public's—reaction as I was at the Iowa court's decision.

Some of the reporters were curious and suspicious; more than once I was asked, "Come, now—why did the court *really* rule against you?" I was as baffled as they. I could only refer them to the full text of the court's decision—it was all there, and more telling and absurd than the condensed version carried by the wire services.

Others were profoundly puzzled and shocked. One newspaper reporter said, "God, that could have been me they ruled against—or any newspaper man." He referred to his own hopping from newspaper job to newspaper job—a characteristic typical of newsmen, which the Iowa court seemed to think made one unfit to possess his children.

Later, a reporter called from Sioux City, Iowa, just to tell me, he said, that he and his wife were shocked and frightened. "That might have been us," he said. "We're scared stiff that the Iowa court's decision is going to set a precedent, and they'll take our children away too."

Husbands and wives were calling from Maine, New York, Florida, New Jersey—and even Iowa. They expressed sympathy—and fright. They wanted to know what we planned to do. We were urged to "fight." A young professor from the University of Iowa out and out told me I had "an obligation to fight," that every young couple in the country had a stake in our case.

I explained that we couldn't afford to carry the case to the U.S. Supreme Court. And apparently the Bannisters were aware of this, too. When I telephoned Mark, not long after the court's decision, I told him that the only legal recourse now seemed to be the U.S. Supreme Court. Apparently the Bannisters had been discussing this.

"Grandfather," he said, "says you can't go to the U.S. Supreme Court about me. He says it would cost you twelve thousand dollars, and you don't have that kind of money."

Up until now, Marylyn and I had been alone in our ordeal with the Iowa courts, an ordeal that indeed began in Judge Kelley's court, where I had found the line of the Bannister attorneys' questioning unbelievable. Yet it had happened, and no one but us had protested—and then only to ourselves, our friends and our relatives—many of whom thought I was exaggerating when I told how the Bannister attorneys had questioned my religion, my politics, my mode of dress, my school records. I had begun to feel defensive. One morning as Marylyn and I stood outside the Story County courtroom during a short recess, I told her that someday I was going to write a book about this trial—that people would have to read about it to believe it. Even my attorney did not object to the line of questioning but tried, and tried compassionately, to convince the court that I was as Christian, moral and responsible—if unorthodox—as my Iowan opponents. No one knew better than my attorney that I was on trial in Iowa, in an Iowa court, before an Iowa judge, that the history of my life, from the time I was two, would be put to the scrutiny of Iowa standards.

Now it seemed that the Iowa Supreme Court's absurd opinion and the record of the lower-court trial was rising out of the confines of Iowa, plainly visible from across the nation, and just as appalling to those who saw it as it was to me.

It was difficult to accept that my continuing to fight in the courts for possession of my son would fail for the lack of money, because of the high cost of jurisprudence, but this, it seemed, was the truth of it. Not only had Marylyn and I spent all the money we had saved and borrowed, but our future finances, our means to pursue such reasonable creature comforts as clothes and vacations, were wiped out for the duration of the next couple of years—if not disastrously, at least depressingly.

A generous offer from the editor of *McCall's* magazine, in exchange for an interview by Jessica Mitford, held the promise of alleviating at least a few of our financial woes. With the advent of the *McCall's* offer, the skies began to clear.

Also forthcoming was the dollars-and-cents promise of a defense fund raised by little-theater actress and friend

Tish Winkworth, who exhorted on television and radio to make the fund an almost $4,000 success. We could not only pay our lawyer's fees to date but we would have a reserve for further court action. The fund grew quickly, with generous contributions from sympathetic and alarmed persons all over the United States, including a boy Mark's age who sent us, Scotch-taped to the back of a piece of cardboard, the entire fourteen cents he had in his piggybank.

Our blessed gift of riches fell far short of what it might have cost to take our case to the U.S. Supreme Court ($12,000, it turned out, was a few thousand dollars short of being realistic), but along with telephoned and posted offers of financial help, we got offers of legal assistance from lawyers in New York, Chicago and San Francisco and a generous offer from the Yale and Harvard law schools, each offering to research if not prosecute our case.

One telephone call was to be the most helpful. It came from Dave Freeman, a former professor of chemistry at Washington State University, whom I'd befriended in Pullman and who was now living in Maryland. "Hal," he said, "you've got to fight this thing. If those unspeakable Iowa clods get away with this, we're all in trouble. I'll do everything I can to help."

It was a crucial time for Dave and his wife, Linda, for their three-year-old daughter was at the time of Dave's call about to undergo exploratory heart surgery in hopes of correcting a congenital defect. Linda later told me, when the outlook was more encouraging, that the risk involved in their daughter's operation gave poignancy to my failing attempts to get Mark out of Iowa and home. Their desire to help was an expression of both familial empathy and anger—and was typical of the feelings expressed in the more than 500 letters of sympathy Marylyn and I were to receive from couples across the nation.

Dave and Linda sowed telephone calls throughout Washington, D.C., hoping to interest a law firm in taking my case to the U.S. Supreme Court with no mind to fees. Dave succeeded in locating an attorney friend, Anthony

Partridge, who was himself outraged by the Iowa court's decision and who offered to approach the Washington, D.C., law firm of Covington & Burling (with which he had once been associated) by way of former colleague William H. Allen, a partner in the firm.

Marylyn's and my fingers were crossed. Dave, over the phone, had described Covington & Burling as the finest and most respected constitutional-law firm in the country, headed by former Secretary of State Dean Acheson. If Covington & Burling took the case, we knew we would be in expert hands; nothing, it seemed, could offer more hope and promise.

Meantime, as we awaited Covington & Burling's decision, students from the University of Iowa were offering to organize protest marches on the steps of the state capitol. A commercial aviator offered to assist in kidnapping Mark from under the nose of the Iowa Supreme Court. A famous folk singer and composer offered to write a song of protest (and did) under cover of anonymity, to be sung by a professional troubador who would stroll the Midwest.

Unknown to me then, benevolent and powerful compassions were at work in the office of California Attorney General Thomas C. Lynch, who, after reading the Iowa court's decision, was personally and professionally outraged. He took the legal view that since I was a California resident and Mark was my son, Mark's legal domicile was California—to the exclusion of Iowa's jurisdiction. What's more, the Attorney General was deeply concerned that the decision was dangerous to California families who might in time of need turn to potentially hostile relatives out of state for the care of their children.

Also on his mind was concern that the decision was in violation of fundamental rights guaranteed by the U.S. Constitution, in that the Iowa court, though it had declared me a "fit" parent, had blatantly ignored my claim to my son, making its own value judgments as to what kind of home best provided for Mark's well-being.

These views, researched and amplified by Deputy Attorney General Elizabeth Palmer and compiled in a lucid twelve-page brief, were to be submitted to both the Iowa and the U.S. Supreme Courts in Mark's and my behalf.

Meantime, expressions of outrage and deep concern were appearing in *The Saturday Review, The New Yorker, McCall's,* the *Ladies' Home Journal* (its editor used as foil to one writer's "pro" feelings another's attack on my qualifications as a father), *Time* and *Life*. Interestingly, the Des Moines *Tribune* and *Register,* owned by the same firm, were split on the court's decision, the *Register* doggedly supporting the decision and downgrading me, while the *Tribune* assailed the decision as one which gave the state of Iowa an image of classic provincialism.

Columnists, writers and editorialists with the Washington *Post,* the Los Angeles *Times,* the San Francisco *Chronicle* and the New York *Times* were conveying strong feelings of urban outrage.

Marylyn and I were getting an amazing outpouring of support from virtually every major point in the United States, which was both outraged and compassionate. Many of the letters were from young couples, Marylyn's and my age, who expressed fear that the Iowa court had made a blanket indictment of the younger generation. "By the Iowa court's standards, we're Bohemian too," many of them said, in just these and other words, reiterated in letter after letter with amazing consistency. "We too move from job to job, from town to town. We read books, even Zen Buddhism. We have debts, and we're not the best financial managers in the world—God, the Iowa court would take our children too." These were letters from young lawyers, doctors, professors, writers, photographers, electronics technicians, housewives, psychologists and students. And many expressed genuine fright over the court's downgrading "intellectual stimulation" in preference to conventional Midwestern conservatism—this in the "best interests" of a child born to young parents in a modern world.

The miraculous offer came from Covington & Burling. William Allen had talked the matter over with his partners and was given the green light. It remained only for my Ames attorney to make an official request for the firm's assistance. This done, William Allen's answer was yes, Covington & Burling would consider taking the case. He and his associates made a preliminary investigation of the legal proceedings to date, with Don Payer providing long hours of research from his office in Ames.

Indeed, the future was looking brighter. Our hopes were rising.

Soon Bill and Don were hard at work preparing a petition to submit to the Iowa Supreme Court, asking for a rehearing. Their petition was joined by petitions from California Attorney General Lynch and the Iowa branch of the American Civil Liberties Union. Both entered the case as "friends of the court," and all three petitions raised the issue of constitutionality, asserting that the Iowa Supreme Court had violated the First and Fourteenth Amendments, with California introducing the question of state jurisdiction, asserting that the Iowa court had no right to decide Mark's custody.

In May 1966 the Iowa Supreme Court turned us down —refused to grant a rehearing—without comment.

We had exhausted the last legal recourse barring the way to the U.S. Supreme Court. Immediately our attorneys went back to work again, preparing our case for submission to the high court. I couldn't see how the U.S. Supreme Court could possibly overlook the absurd decision rendered by the Iowa Supreme Court.

The U.S. Supreme Court would reconvene in October 1966, after summer recess. At that time they would decide whether to accept my case for hearing or not. It would be a long wait. But Mark, Marylyn and I had waited long already, and waiting a few more months would perhaps settle the matter once and for all.

Perhaps, I thought, I had not lost my son to the Iowa Supreme Court after all. We would know by November.

If Mark hesitated to ride the roller-coaster at this Iowa amusement park, I didn't blame him. I told him as much.

"When I was your age, I was afraid to ride these things

too. It took me a long time to get up nerve. Even Marylyn doesn't like to ride it. Why don't we go ride the bumper cars instead?"

Mark seemed pleased to drop the subject, and he had acquired a fondness—with three or four rides under his seat belt—for these tiny cars that emitted a body-tingling electrical groan as you pressed the throttle all but through the floorboard and sped, with the grace of an arthritic crocodile, toward a hoped-for crackup with whosoever lingered in your path.

Sitting on the edge of the seat, manipulating a steering wheel too big for him—its outrageous bigness like a cowboy hat that fell over his ears—Mark would drive with a fanatical leer of anticipation, bumping here, getting bumped there, leaving behind nary a crumpled fender but an explosion of giggles. He bumped me, bumped Marylyn. I bumped him, Marylyn bumped him. The three of us ganged up on our fellow motorists and bumped them all.

Indeed, Mark preferred this to the awesome uncertainty of the roller-coaster. And I wondered how he felt about all that had been happening in the courts.

We didn't talk much about the case those eight days we visited. For one thing, my visit with Mark was agreed upon by the Bannisters only if I wouldn't bring up the matter of the courts. Yet it had to be talked about. It was on Mark's mind, and certainly it was on Marylyn's and mine.

Mark was amazingly informed about all that had transpired; his grasp of even the complex legal procedures baffling to adults who have never been involved amazed me. He expressed his knowledge matter-of-factly, and made me think of those times in the past, in Pullman and Moses Lake, when he and I had had long, matter-of-fact discussions about things that deeply involved him.

Mark, since birth, had had a mind all his own, but those things that were privately on his mind were more often than not brought up by him for an open and rational forum. But it had been a long while since we had really had a chance to sit down and talk together, freely and out from under the eyes of either the court or the Bannisters.

Somehow, it seemed that our being together for eight days, sleeping in the same cabin and having no other ends to pursue but those that came of our being side by side, had cleared the air and helped to put Mark at ease.

There was no question that at the end of the trial in Judge Kelley's court Mark had been uneasy and uncertain, and some of the uncertainty about his future, generated during the time of the trial for his custody, metamorphosed into hostility and fear. "I'm against you two [Marylyn and me]," he told us once.

I asked why, and his answers were varied.

He explained that Grandfather said I "didn't know how to handle money," that I didn't want him very badly because I hadn't run over the school principal who tried to stop us that day Marylyn and I tried to take him from the school yard.

His grandfather, he said once, had fixed it so that I would "be put in jail" if I tried to take him from Iowa.

Yet he was groping for assurances and feeling for the future. He had wanted to know, when it appeared to him that he might have a say as to where he was to live, during the time of the trial, "What is the sun like in California?" But when his grandmother asked him where he wanted to live, he said, after shutting himself in his room and thinking about it for an hour, that he thought he wanted to stay in Iowa—perhaps knowing that his grandmother would bar his grandfather from carrying through his agreement with me, before we went into the courts, to allow Mark to return to California with Marylyn and me.

Perhaps Mark was getting back at me for the hurt I had caused in sending him to live with his grandparents after his mother's death—and I was almost proud, though hurt myself, that he had the guts and the strength of will to do this.

Our discussions about "the case," as even Mark was calling it, were minimal: Mark knew full well that our next stop was the U.S. Supreme Court; there was no point in going into details or rehashing either the reasons or the nature of my legal efforts. Nor did I put before Mark the question of whether he wanted to come to California.

We had been in the pine-paneled cabin at Vacation Village—a pleasant if very Iowan family resort (one of its advertisements noted that it was "sanitary and morally clean")—for perhaps four days when Mark blurted out words good to hear: "I wish we could all live here!" he said.

Marylyn and I agreed.

"Yeah," I said, "then we'd really be lucky ducks."

And it pleased me, when Mark dressed in the morning, that he wanted to know what I was wearing, whether I was wearing my white jeans so that he might also wear his. He wanted to know what foods I liked, and then said he liked them too.

Was I a city man, or did I like mountains? he wanted to know.

"I like the city, but I really prefer mountains and trees," I said.

"I do too," he said. "I'd like to live in the mountains."

Mark wanted to know when the U.S. Supreme Court would hand down its decision. I told him I didn't know, that it might be next summer before we heard.

"I think you'll win the third time," he said.

"Do you?"

"Yeah, Hal," he said, "I do."

But the U.S. Supreme Court did not so much as raise an eyebrow. On November 15, 1966, Bill Allen, my attorney in Washington, D.C., called me on the phone. It was early in the morning, before Marylyn and I had had the first cup of coffee. I was expecting Bill to call—but not for a couple of weeks yet. His call was not a pleasant surprise.

"I'm afraid I have bad news, Hal. The Supreme Court turned us down flat, without comment. They've declined to hear the case."

For a long while Bill and I said nothing. The faint hum

of the empty receiver gave to our silence a feeling of wordless, contemplative sadness.

"I don't quite know what to say, Bill."

"I know," he said.

"What do we do now?"

"I don't know, Hal. I'll have to think about it. We've gone as far as we can with the Supreme Court."

"Why do you suppose they've declined to hear the case?"

"It's hard to say," he said. "Maybe the constitutional issues were in their eyes not clear enough. Maybe they just didn't want to get involved in this kind of personal litigation. The court didn't comment, and that doesn't give us much to go on."

I was convinced that it was not for lack of expertise that Bill's petition for a writ of *certiorari* had been rejected. I thanked him for all he and his associates had done. They had worked hard.

"I'll keep in touch," I said.

"Fine, Hal. Meantime, I'll be thinking about what's to come next."

I hung up the phone and told Marylyn that I wanted to get out of the house. I didn't want to talk to anyone about the case—I just wanted to sit down and start writing as soon as possible.

Marylyn was crying. I held her in my arms and told her that we really hadn't lost the case. "We haven't lost Mark yet," I said. "We can still go back into the Iowa courts and open the case again in a lower court. I think we should, even if it means more expense, more delay."

Indeed, it would mean more expense, more delay—a dreary excursion through the Iowa courts, with nothing more to look forward to than perhaps another appeal, another encounter with the Iowa Supreme Court.

The Iowa Supreme Court's decision, it seemed, was going to stand—and it would stand for all time. The U.S. Supreme Court had, in effect, witnessed the Iowa court's action in silence. And by its silence it condoned the mind and the works of a court that would deprive a father of his son, and a son of his father, on grounds that had to do with whether he would send his son to Sunday school, whether he wears a necktie to his wife's funeral, whether he is a political liberal, an agnostic who prefers a yard of uncut weeds to a well-kept lawn, has a "Bohemian approach" to life and finance, and is "probably intellectually stimulating."

Whether or not the Iowa Supreme Court's decision violates the basic freedoms guaranteed by the U.S. Constitution, I cannot say—only the U.S. Supreme Court could have decided this, and it would seem to be quite clear that the U.S. Constitution is exactly what the U.S. Supreme Court says it is or is not. The question of whether the Iowa court ignored the precepts of the Constitution is left vague and unanswered by the Supreme Court's silence.

The question of constitutionality was raised, succinctly and compassionately, in the brief authored by William Allen and his Covington & Burling associates, which questioned:

"1. Whether, consistently with the due process clause of the Fourteenth Amendment and other applicable constitutional provisions, a state may deprive a parent of the custody of his child and award such custody to others when it is conceded that the parent is fit and qualified to act as a parent and has not abandoned or otherwise relinquished custody of his child.

"2. If a state in any circumstances may deprive a fit parent who has not abandoned or otherwise relinquished custody of his child of such custody and award such custody to others, whether it may do so, consistently with the due process clause of the Fourteenth Amendment and with the First Amendment, on the ground of the parent's political and religious beliefs and expressions.

"3. Whether, consistently with the due process clause of the Fourteenth Amendment, a state may deprive a parent of the custody of his child on the basis of no evidence other than the testimony of a psychologist, retained by the persons contesting custody with the parent, who had never professionally seen the parent or his household and whose opinions stated in his testimony are not those of other psychologists and are contrary to human experience and to common sense."

That these questions were indeed raised by the Iowa court's decision was perhaps contained in the public outcry, and the deep personal concern, that moved the American Civil Liberties Union, the California Attorney General, and the Board of Christian Social Concerns of the New York Annual Conference of the Methodist Church to entreat the U.S. Supreme Court to make a constitutional appraisal of the human values singularly prescribed by one state's highest court. But even this outcry, couched in the legalese of three *amicus curiae* briefs, was ignored. The U.S. Supreme Court was inscrutably silent, and the Iowa court was left to enforce precepts in violation of common sense and human values common to all who live and breathe.

The values held by the Iowa court are those that affect me as a father and an individual. They are values that negate a father's love for his son, giving love no credence in the bleak ways of the courtroom. They are values that can point only to a void, a mechanistic state of conformity in which an individual, by becoming a father, risks having his children taken from him by a court that reads into his beliefs and aspirations—political, religious and personal—a gross travesty of those aspirations and beliefs sanctioned by the court. They are values that do not implore us to conform, nor point the way to some professed realm of enlightenment; they are values that demand, in the most insidious and ruthless way, that we conform or have our children taken by the state. They are values that negate love and the biological affinity of father for son, and replace love not with anything so ruthlessly sophisticated as computerized predeterminism but with heavy-handed provincialism that mulishly insists it shall have its own way.

The court's decision was the work of nine justices, nine men appointed for a lifetime, and with an average age of over sixty; it is difficult to draw the line between what on the one hand seems to be the nine-fold personal conviction of a tribunal of arch-conservatives speaking as one, or, on the other, the collective voice of a native Iowan consensus expressed by nine appointed shamans of jurisprudence. Whichever, in the text and meaning of their decision, a singularly dangerous precedent has been set, whereby one's political and religious beliefs, and personal beliefs and aspirations, are freely used as grounds to deprive not only a father of his son but deny any parent, father or mother, the possession of his child.

I do not know my own goals, and I find a stable master plan in life a hindrance to day-to-day absorption in the things I find important and meaningful. Meaningful to me is the pursuit of meaning, of discovering, with my camera, with my typewriter, those things that are emotionally genuine and which point to even small enlightenments, that bring zest, beauty, and compassion—whether it is photographing a nude and beautiful woman, a Vietnam protest march, the son of a Solomon Island cannibal who is encountering civilization for the first time, or following a client's children about the house to catch those revealing moments when children bloom forth with naïve inner conviction.

If this is my goal, I have consistently held to it, though I have at times wavered and become disgusted in my attempts to find meaning, though I have been selfishly addicted to these pursuits to the exclusion of more practical things. But if this pursuit of mine is uncommon, I am amazed, and if the Iowa Supreme Court finds it not only uncommon but a negation of a man's love for his son and his claim to have him under his roof, then all of us, with common and uncommon pursuits, are in grave danger.

Last summer, when Mark and I were allowed those eight days together, Mark, on the very last day, as we prowled the amusement park, said, "I think I want to ride the roller-coaster, Hal."

He was obviously frightened. The decision had been on his mind for a couple of days, and during all of the eight days we were together Mark was anxious to win

Marylyn's and my approval, our admiration. And Marylyn and I were anxious to have his approval, his admiration. I also wanted Mark to know that he had my love—and Marylyn's love. And together, in the games we played, the drives we took, the long walks and talks, in those moments before he went to sleep when I lay next to him on the bed and read him comic books, when we held hands together, when we swam for hours in the lake and Mark demonstrated for my benefit his prowess as a neophyte swimmer—together, there was no question of my love, no question of his love. Mark and I knew—and we knew well—the Iowa Supreme Court's uncanny divination was far astray: "Mark has established a father-son relationship with Mr. Bannister, which he apparently had never had with his natural father." Mark and I could snort at this. We knew better, far better than the court and Dr. Hawkes and the Bannisters. Jeanne, Janet, Mark and I—we all of us could laugh and snort.

Mark and I walked to the roller-coaster. We walked together, arm in arm. I was proud of my son. He had made this decision himself, with no coaxing from Marylyn and me. By himself he had been thinking about it.

"Mark, you're a brave boy," I said. I was happy, and I felt like crying. Mark was a brave boy, strong, loving, quick to say what was on his mind, quick to laugh, quick to cry, full of the devil, hell-bent on the completion of his fondest schemes.

Iowa, I thought, won't hold you down. Nothing can hold this boy down.

Even as we bought two tickets and waited for the tiny cars to arrive at the loading platform, Mark had had a roller-coaster ride to top them all. Though he never set foot in the courtroom during the trial for his custody, he was nonetheless firmly centered in the workings of the court, the center upon which the court's decision turned, the hapless pawn of the courts' delays.

How it would haunt me when I would have to say goodbye to Mark and hurry to catch a plane to California—Mark standing by the waiting car and swathed in a paper lei and a Vacation Village sweatshirt, his arms full of paper sacks and suitcase, full of new acquisitions. And he would wave to me as he was driven off, back to the Bannister farm.

We bought our tickets and we were the only two on the roller-coaster. I put my arm around Mark's shoulders as the clacking little train got under way, slowly, easily, down a slight incline, then up a steep mountain of shining track.

We crested the top of the mountain. Mark held the handrail in front of him with both hands, and down we flew, Mark laughing. What a laugh! He might have been Hannibal crossing the winter Alps in an amusement-park bumper car, knocking elephants hither and yon as he went.

Up and down we flew. I kept one arm around Mark; the other I used to keep myself from bouncing out of this little car that flew across the mountaintops.

Mark, I love you.

Nothing will hold you down. Not Iowa, not the Iowa Supreme Court. Nothing shall hold me down.

I'm sorry about the Iowa Supreme Court, and you and I know how stupid they were.

Someday, we'll get the hell off this roller-coaster and walk together, out of Iowa, out of the reach of those who would insist that only in their footsteps can we find right and good, and you and I, and you and I only, will decide what is best for our welfare, what is best for us.

When we climb out of bed in the morning a new world is born, and this is our world. The world of yesterday is not for us.

Yes, Bucko, the game is on. It's been on for a long while.

When we get the hell off this roller-coaster, we'll walk together, with nowhere to go but home and into a new world.

Marylyn will be waiting for us.

EPILOGUE

"Mark is Home to Stay!"

NOT LONG AFTER the first publication of this book, I received a call from a television interviewer who wanted to know if I planned to carry on my fight to regain custody of my son, Mark. I had taken my case to the U.S. Supreme Court—and lost. With what had seemed taciturn disinterest, the one body of men to whom I thought I could turn for help refused to review my appeal. The decision of the Iowa Supreme Court was allowed to stand.

"What more can you possibly do to get your son back?" the interviewer asked me now. "Wasn't the U.S. Supreme Court the last avenue of appeal?"

I was reminded of the large manila folder on my desk, bulging with letters from mothers and housewives and not a few men who had read my story and had followed my case. They expressed great sympathy—and asked the same questions: "Is it over? What can you possibly do now to get your son back?" The moral support I got from these letters was welcome, most welcome, for there were moments when I asked those questions myself; a close friend, trying to console me, advised me to give up my quest for my son and get used to the idea of living without him.

Nevertheless, I now admitted to the T.V. interviewer that I had very definite plans to continue on in the courts; I hadn't given up, not by a long shot. But I refused to tell him what my plans were. My chances of getting Mark back appeared, even to me at the moment, to be slim. The one plan on which I could pin any hope would do me in if it failed. Everything depended on my keeping silent about it.

Since the summer of 1965—nearly four long years ago—I had been engaged in a seemingly endless and certainly fruitless encounter with one court after another, spending thousands of dollars and losing no small amount of my peace of mind, to regain the custody of my own son. It was as though I were involved in a hellishly prolonged court trial that made no sense, and took everything from me, even my sanity as well.

But if my plan for the summer of 1968 succeeded, if Mark decided, during his visit, that he wanted to live in California—this nightmarish encounter with the court would be over, and Mark would be home—for good.

My wife, Marylyn, and I arrived at the San Francisco airport about twenty minutes before Mark's jet was to arrive from Des Moines. We wanted to be sure we were there to greet him when he stepped off the plane, and we didn't want to waste a moment of his visit. Mark's stay was to begin that day, July 15, and end exactly thirty days later, when we were supposed to send him back to the farm in Ames.

It was by court order that I had arranged this visit, and thirty days were all that Dwight and Margaret Bannister would allow. But if all went well, I would not be sending Mark back to Iowa, not ever—he would be staying here, with us, in our home in California. This was the plan I had kept silent about for almost two years.

If I had let it be known that I planned to take action in a California court, Mark's grandparents might easily have prevented his visit. Even now, though I had received a telegram from Iowa telling me that Mark would be on the plane, I was skeptical. So much depended on Mark's setting foot in California, well beyond the jurisdiction of the Iowa courts.

But give or take a minute, the jet from Des Moines was on time. More important, Mark, now ten, was on it, and I spotted him the moment he walked off the ramp and into the waiting room. I worked my way through the crowd of off-going passengers and their friends. Marylyn was right behind me.

"Hi, Bucko," I said. "Good to see you."

"Good to see you, too, Hal," he said.

Neither of us is terribly demonstrative when it comes to revealing our deepest feelings. I hugged him, gave him a pat on the head, and spent a long while looking at him. His shy smile told me so much, and I felt greatly relieved.

Marylyn soon caught up to us, and in an instant she squeezed Mark to her and gave him a kiss that made him beam—a little shyly, but he beamed. Marylyn was as pleased to see Mark as I was, and I was glad that Mark and Marylyn had hit it off so well from the start, when they had first met three years ago. There was no mistaking that Mark and Marylyn were very natural, very warm together, often teasing, hugging, making jokes. At times there was an almost comic poignancy in Mark's attempts to please Marylyn—one more reason I wanted him with us.

Mark beamed all the while it took to get his suitcase from the baggage claim and into our micro-bus. I suppose I am indulging in a father's pride when I say that Mark's smile is my smile, the smile I use when I'm pleased, happy, content. And when I saw that certain smile on Mark, that certain brightness in his eyes, I felt very good.

We went to San Francisco, and spent the better part of an evening hopping on and off cable cars, and then we visited the place where huge, iron wheels, multi-colored like iced Italian pastries, turned the underground cables that pulled the cable cars up and down impossible hills.

Mark was entranced, and his interest lighted with an electronic pop; at the age of ten, he was caught up in the world of turning wheels, rockets, outer space, the ocean's bottom, fish, salamanders, and white rabbits with red eyes that blinked in secret codes that told the wise marvelous tales of genes, irrepressible pigments, and all sorts of astonishing facts about the great mysteries of the universe.

Mark speculated and made scientific observations on the big candy-colored wheels, and I listened with pride, and stood back and watched as he pointed to various whirring contraptions and explained, with considerable authority, how they pulled the cables that pulled the cable cars. I might have corrected some of his knowledge but I was content to bask in the glow of his big-boy's pride of scientific-mindedness. Indeed, he was getting to be a big boy now.

I noticed he hadn't grown much since the last time I had seen him a year before, though certainly he was much taller, much more a boy, than he had been when he was five and I had sent him to stay with his grandparents. His lean frame, a lot like his mother's, made him seem taller than he was. His blond hair was unchanged, bangs an inch or so above the eyebrows, the sides short; his mother's large brown eyes; his features a combination of his mother's and mine. And I don't recall fifteen minutes passing that evening when Mark didn't find something to laugh about, and I was awfully happy, for it is Mark's laugh, his quick and sometimes devilish sense of humor, that has stuck with him since his earliest childhood.

We did a lot of talking, a lot of laughing that evening, and when we went home to our house in Brookdale, we talked and laughed most of the way. What we talked about was of little importance—it was the feeling we had, the feeling the three of us had of being together again: a certain contentment, a certain peace, never pretentious, never strained. I like to think we wear well together as a family. If only the judges of the Iowa Supreme Court could see the three of us together, I thought—they would see what a dreadful mistake they had made.

I didn't say a word to Mark that evening about my hopes of petitioning a California court for his guardianship. For one thing, I wasn't altogether sure it would work. For another, I did not want to turn Mark's visit into an ordeal of waiting and hoping and uncertainty—he had experienced more than enough of this already. We all had.

When we put Mark to bed, in the room we had fixed for him two years before, we were still talking and laughing—and God, I hoped we could keep it this way. Marylyn and I felt so good with Mark in the next room that we didn't talk about the hopes—and the risks—of going to court, although we knew we would have to act soon. Instead, we slept. And we slept well. There was a kind of magic in having Mark in the house.

The day after Mark's arrival I called my attorney, Bob Treuhaft, in Oakland, California, and alerted him to the possibility of my taking action. For the moment, it had to be a *possibility,* for a great deal depended on whether Mark *wanted* to stay in California.

I had a good deal of respect for Bob's legal opinions and ever since the Iowa Supreme Court had ruled against me on grounds he too considered absurd, legally and morally, he had taken a compassionate interest in my case. It had been Bob's suggestion that I take the guardianship action. If I were awarded custody—and there was no assurance at all that this would be done—it would have the effect of voiding the 1965 decision of the Iowa Supreme Court, for the Iowa courts have no jurisdiction in California. Whether this very important legal maneuver would succeed would depend entirely on the opinion of one California judge.

Did Mark *want* to stay in California?

I wasn't sure, and I would have to ask him. Something had happened a year before that gave me pause, and made me wonder if I had best get used to the idea of not having custody of my son.

In the summer of 1967 Mark had come to visit us for thirty days, and that year also I had planned to take action in a California court, to keep Mark here. But when it was time for him to return to Iowa to begin another year of school, he decided he *didn't* want to stay in California, so of course we took no legal action. It was a difficult decision to make, but I felt I had no choice—for Mark's sake. That visit to California was his first since that uncertain and restless time immediately after his mother's death, and the old childhood toys I had saved and stored in my house in Brookdale, the bunk beds he and his late sister had slept in—these gave Mark nightmares and bad dreams.

I shall never forget walking into Mark's room one evening that summer and seeing him sitting on the edge of his bed, staring forlornly at a plastic violin with broken strings. This tiny violin made no music, and never did, even when it had all its strings and had been given new to his sister, Janet. For some reason, this fragile toy violin had survived the zestful ravages of a girl three and a boy four, and I had saved it. When I saw Mark sitting on the edge of the bed and staring at it, I wished I had put the broken violin in the garbage with the other broken toys. All that summer Mark asked to have the light burning in his room when he went to bed, and always I left it burning—but it didn't keep away the bad dreams.

The child psychiatrist I had taken Mark to see put it more succinctly: Mark was having traumatic recall of the past, and he advised me to allow Mark to return to Iowa, to get distance, to have the chance to come to terms with the past, in his own good time.

I agreed, though it was terribly difficult for me to put Mark on the plane and send him back to Iowa, to wait another year, and hope it would be different when he came to visit again. Yet, I was confident there would be a change, one that would amount to Mark's re-birth, partly by the fire of still another court struggle, partly by time and happenstance. Hopefully, his own knowledge that I had given him the freedom to allow these things to happen, in their own good time, would give him confidence in me.

Now, a year later, Mark and I sat down together on the big front porch of our house in Brookdale.

We sat over a map of the Western United States spread over the folding card table, and I roamed the map with my finger, pointing out places where I would like to live.

"If you had a choice of any place in the world," I asked Mark, "what would you pick?"

"I'd like to live here," he said, "where we used to live when I was a baby." Mark pointed out Alaska, and put his finger on the city of Anchorage. Jeanne and I had met and married in Alaska, where we worked on a newspaper. "It gets too hot in Iowa," Mark said. "I like it where it's cold."

It didn't take me long to figure out that he was making a point, however subtle. This was his way of telling me what was on his mind—a kind of telegraphic shorthand. I followed up.

"Do you know what I think?" I asked.

"What?" he said.

"I think a man ought to be able to live any place he wants—and have his son with him. Especially when he loves him and wants him. That's what made me so mad about the Iowa Supreme Court—I just don't think they knew very much about you and me."

"I think so too," said Mark.

Three days before I had told Mark of my plans to petition the court for his guardianship. I had told him my attorney was reasonably sure we could win, but that there was always the risk of losing.

I had told Mark I loved him and that I would do everything I could to keep him here if he decided he wanted to stay—but I would leave that decision up to him. I wanted him to be sure, I said, that there were no more bad dreams of the past, that he was certain he would be happy here.

"I've thought about what you told me, Hal," Mark said now. "And I've made up my mind."

Now, just as Mark was about to reveal his decision, I had the feeling that what he would say would determine —now and forever—whether I would go on fighting.

"What did you decide?" I asked, finally.

"I want to live in California, with you and Marylyn," he said.

Only the laws of gravity kept me from leaping out of my chair and flying over the porch rail and out over the tops of the redwoods, my wings spread and Mark in tow.

I was so happy I didn't know quite what to say, and so I put my arms around Mark and held him close.

"I'm really proud of you," I managed to say. "I think that everything's going to be okay from now on."

"I think so, too," he said.

I hurried into the house to tell Marylyn.

She moved quickly to the porch, ran straight to Mark, and put her arms around him. He was beaming, looking downright proud. There were tears in the eyes of both of them.

"That took a lot of courage," said Marylyn. "You've made your father and me very happy."

"I was hoping maybe I would," Mark said.

Our cat, Fuzzy Fink, jumped up on the map on the table. She looked completely disinterested in what was happening, but I exercised poetic license and said to Mark, "See, you've made Fuzzy Fink happy, too."

Mark giggled. "I don't think she speaks English," he said.

Mark had asked to have one of Fuzzy Fink's expected kittens—and I had told him he could. (God, how I hoped he would be here when Fuzzy Fink had her litter!)

I went right to the telephone, called my attorney, and told him to go ahead as soon as possible with our plans.

This was the moment I had been waiting for since I had had to leave Mark in 1964: Mark had found his own way home. And for all these years I had dreaded the possibility that he would forget me, would decide that his home was in Iowa. This was the reason I had fought in the courts, had written a book, and loudly and insistently proclaimed my love for my son. I did not want him to forget that I am his father, I love him, and my home is his. Now I knew I had not acted in vain.

But there was still one more bridge to cross—one more encounter with the courts. On August 8, 1968, California Superior Court Judge Gilbert Perry, after hearing my petition for my son's guardianship, granted me temporary custody pending a full hearing. The hearing was set for August 28, at which time he would make a final decision. The light seemed to be breaking.

But the question that was on my mind also disturbed Mark.

"Will my grandparents fight?" he asked.

"I don't know," I said. "We'll just have to wait and see. But even if they do, I think we can win—it'll just make it a lot harder." Despite everything, I knew the Bannisters had acted in what *they* thought were Mark's best interest. I could only hope they would now see that I was, too.

My petition now before Judge Perry simply asked that I be appointed Mark's guardian and be allowed to keep Mark in California, and contained an affidavit from the child psychiatrist who had talked to Mark at length that summer and the one before. His affidavit stated he was convinced it would be in Mark's best interests to remain with his father, and it was evident to him that Mark wanted this.

It further stated that Mark showed anxiety over the health of his now sixty-three-year-old grandfather. To my mind—and this I stated in my petition—Mark no longer saw his grandfather as the "father figure" the Iown Supreme Court had found necessary for Mark's welfare, at the behest of an Iowa psychologist. As for back as the summer before last, Mark had made it clear to me that in his mind that "father figure" had lost considerable substance—fortunately, without loss of Mark's affection—to the point that Mark now saw his grandmother as the dominant figure in his home life in Iowa. For a ten-year-old boy on the brink of adolescence, this was hardly desirable, to my mind, though certainly Mark was undergoing neither physical hardship nor lack of affection. But the real issue, I was convinced, was that Mark had decided that my home was his home—and this is what gave me the will to risk another encounter with the courts, regardless of the cost, emotionally and financially.

At the suggestion of my attorney, who shared my hopes this matter might be settled out of the courts, I called Mark's grandmother, Margaret Bannister.

"Mark says he wants to stay here," I told her. "He has made up his own mind. I haven't coerced him. This is what he wants. I just hope we can settle this thing without trouble. It would be the best thing for all of us."

Her voice gave me no clue as to what she thought, but she seemed matter-of-fact, certainly not emotional.

"I don't know what to say about it," she said. "I'll have to think about it."

That was the last I was to talk to her directly. From this time on the talks between us were handled by intermediaries, one an Iowa newspaper reporter, the other the Bannister family minister, whom the Bannisters flew to California, at their expense, to find out whether Mark had really made up his mind to live with me. If the minister, Henry Lumpkins, could provide this assurance, I was told, the Bannisters would not contest my petition for Mark's custody—this would be the end of it.

I had no doubts that Mark would repeat for the minister's benefit his decision to live with me (nor did Mark have doubts)—but I was somehow skeptical that these years of frustration and endless court entanglements would end simply, suddenly—or could end at all.

Marylyn did all she could to keep me calm. But I couldn't relax—not now.

Mark himself was nervous. He kept asking, "Do you think they'll fight, Hal?" And I kept telling him, after Mr.

Lumpkins had reported back to the Bannisters that Mark really wanted to stay, that I thought they wouldn't fight—we had at least the minister's assurances. Privately, I was not convinced.

But on a Sunday morning not long after Mr. Lumpkins had left California, I was awakened by a telephone call from the Iowa newspaper reporter who had been acting as Mrs. Bannister's spokesman. This was the first time I had ever spoken to him; previously, he had been in touch with my attorney. Why Mrs. Bannister had chosen to use the reporter as intermediary, I didn't know. But it didn't matter—at least I was getting some news of what was to happen next—astonishing news! Mrs. Bannister had asked him to tell me that she was satisfied that Mark wanted to live with me: she would *not* contest my petition!

I was stunned. Happy and stunned. After all these years, could this really be the end of it? The reporter assured me it was. It was taking so long for it to sink in. But here it was, a telephone call on a Sunday morning, as simple as that. I could hardly believe it.

I thanked the reporter, profusely, I think—I don't remember. But the truth was, I wanted to get off the phone and run upstairs and tell Mark and Marylyn.

When I finally did, I found Mark awake in his bed. He had heard the telephone ring and wanted to know who had called. He, too, was waiting for news.

When I saw him lying in bed—in *my* house, his head on the pillow, hands behind his neck—I think then the meaning of that phone call came to me with power and conviction and a feeling of peace and joy such as I had never anticipated. Mark was here, in my house, *home*.

I sat on the edge of Mark's bed, and simply said, "Everything's okay. Your grandmother says she won't fight."

As I said before, neither of us is very demonstrative when it comes to revealing our deepest emotions. I sat on his bed looking at him, smiling. He smiled and looked at me. Then he smiled more and said, "I guess now I'm an official resident of California."

"That's about it," I said. And we looked at each other and smiled.

Marylyn is the outgoing one, the demonstrative member of the family. When I called into the bedroom and told her the good news, she leaped out of bed and ran into Mark's room. She hugged him, then me, and then cried. Mark and I kept smiling at each other. Never have I felt so content.

The court "battle" turned out to be a mere formality. It took only a few minutes for Judge Perry, in the hearing of August 28, to award me Mark's guardianship.

"There's nothing very complicated about this, Mr. Painter," he said. "The foundation of our society has always been the family."

I agreed.

Looking back at that ordinary Sunday morning of extraordinary good news, I see Mark, his smile, the gleam in his eyes. And once more, after all these years of separation, I feel like a father, Mark's father. I am very pleased with my son, very proud of him.

He tells me he likes our house in the redwoods, the ocean nearby, and the river just down the road. He has found a friend in Chuck, the boy next door, and other friends nearby who share his interest in salamanders, crawfish and the steering wheel of a vanished car, which Mark brought home and hung on the edge of his bed.

He likes to chop wood for the fireplace, and has made a private room—closed to adults (a rule that Marylyn and I respect)—under the house and invites only his young friends and our cat, Fuzzy Fink, and Fuzzy Fink's new son. And I would like to think that Fuzzy Fink waited until Mark was safely home before having the kitten I had promised to Mark.

No longer does Mark ask to sleep with the light on in his room, and no longer does he have bad dreams of the past.

It's over, and Mark is home, this moment asleep in his bed. He is home, where he wants to be, and I give Mark's grandparents credit for realizing this and not stepping in the way.

Good night, Mark.
Good night, Marylyn.
Be happy in your dreams.
See you in the morning.

APPENDIX:

The Court's Decision

The following is the complete text of the Iowa Supreme Court's decision. Justice William C. Stuart is the author.

WE ARE HERE SETTING THE COURSE for Mark Wendell Painter's future. Our decision on the custody of this seven-year-old boy will have a marked influence on his whole life. The fact that we are called upon many times a year to determine custody matters does not make the exercising of this awesome responsibility any less difficult.

Legal training and experience are of little practical help in solving the complex problems of human relations. However, these problems do arise and under our system of government, the burden of rendering a final decision rests upon us. It is frustrating to know we can only resolve, not solve, these unfortunate situations.

The custody dispute before us in the *habeas corpus* action

is between the father, Harold Painter, and the maternal grandparents, Dwight and Margaret Bannister. Mark's mother and younger sister were killed in an automobile accident December 6, 1962, near Pullman, Washington.

The father, after other arrangements for Mark's care had proved unsatisfactory, asked the Bannisters to take care of Mark. They went to California and brought Mark back to their farm home near Ames in July, 1963.

Mr. Painter remarried in November, 1964, and about that time indicated he wanted to take Mark back. The Bannisters refused to let him leave and this action was filed in June, 1965. Since July, 1965, he has continued to remain in the Bannister home under an order of this court staying execution of the judgment of the trial court awarding custody to the father until the matter could be determined on appeal. For reasons hereinafter stated, we conclude Mark's better interests will be served if he remains with the Bannisters.

Mark's parents came from highly contrasting backgrounds. His mother was born, raised and educated in rural Iowa. Her parents are college graduates. Her father is agricultural information editor for the Iowa State University Extension Service.

The Bannister home is in the Gilbert Community and is well kept, roomy and comfortable. The Bannisters are highly respected members of the community. Mr. Bannister has served on the school board and regularly teaches a Sunday school class at the Gilbert Congregational Church. Mark's mother graduated from Grinnell College. She then went to work for a newspaper in Anchorage, Alaska, where she met Harold Painter.

Mark's father was born in California. When he was 2½ years old, his parents were divorced and he was placed in a foster home. Although he has kept in contact with his natural parents, he considers his foster parents, the McNellys, as his family.

He flunked out of a high school and a trade school because of a lack of interest in academic subjects, rather than any lack of ability. He joined the Navy at 17. He did not like it. After receiving an honorable discharge, he took examinations and obtained his high school diploma.

He lived with the McNellys and went to college for 2½

years under the G.I. bill. He quit college to take a job on a small newspaper in Ephrata, Washington, in November, 1955. In May, 1956, he went to work for the newspaper in Anchorage which employed Jeanne Bannister.

Harold and Jeanne were married in April, 1957. Although there is a conflict in the evidence on the point, we are convinced the marriage over-all was a happy one, with many ups and downs as could be expected in the uniting of two such opposites.

We are not confronted with a situation where one of the contesting parties is not a fit or proper person. There is no criticism of either the Bannisters or their home. There is no suggestion in the record that Mr. Painter is morally unfit.

It is obvious the Bannisters did not approve of their daughter's marriage to Harold Painter and do not want their grandchild raised under his guidance. The philosophies of life are entirely different. As stated by the psychiatrist who examined Mr. Painter at the request of Bannisters' attorneys: "It is evident that there exists a large difference in ways of life and value systems between the Bannisters and Mr. Painter, but in this case, there is no evidence that psychiatric instability is involved. Rather, these divergent life patterns seem to represent alternative normal adaptations."

It is not our prerogative to determine custody upon our choice of one of two ways of life within normal and proper limits and we will not do so. However, the philosophies are important as they relate to Mark and his particular needs.

The Bannister home provides Mark with a stable, dependable, conventional, middle-class, middlewest background and an opportunity for a college education and profession, if he desires it. It provides a solid foundation and secure atmosphere.

In the Painter home, Mark would have more freedom of conduct and thought with an opportunity to develop his individual talents. It would be more exciting and challenging in many respects, but romantic, impractical and unstable.

Little additional recitation of evidence is necessary to support our evaluation of the Bannister home. It might be pointed out, however, that Jeanne's three sisters also received college educations and seem to be happily married to college graduates.

Our conclusion as to the type of home Mr. Painter would offer is based upon his Bohemian approach to finances and life in general. We feel there is much evidence which supports this conclusion. His main ambition is to be a free lance writer and photographer. He has had some articles and picture stories published, but the income from these efforts has been negligible. At the time of the accident, Jeanne was willingly working to support the family so Harold could devote more time to his writing and photography. In the ten years since he left college, he has changed jobs seven times. He was asked to leave two of them: two he quit because he didn't like the work; two because he wanted to devote more time to writing and the rest for better pay. He was contemplating a move to Berkeley at the time of the trial. His attitude toward his career is typified by his own comments concerning a job offer.

"About the Portland news job, I hope you understand when I say it took guts not to take it. I had to get behind myself and push. It was very, very tempting to accept a good salary and settle down to a steady, easy routine. As I approached Portland, with the intention of taking the job, I began to ask what, in the long run, would be the good of this job: one, it was not really what I wanted; two, Portland is just another big farm town, with none of the stimulation it takes to get my mind sparking. Anyway, I decided Mark and myself would be better off if I went ahead with what I've started and the hell with the rest, sink, swim, or starve." There is general agreement that Mr. Painter needs help with his finances. Both Jeanne and Marylyn, his present wife, handled most of them. Purchases and sales of books, boats, photographic equipment and houses indicate poor financial judgment and an easy-come easy-go attitude. He dissipated his wife's estate of about $4,300, most of which was a gift from her parents and which she had hoped would be used for the children's education.

The psychiatrist classifies him as "a romantic and somewhat of a dreamer." An apt example are the plans he related for himself and Mark in February, 1963: "My thought now is to settle Mark and myself in Sausalito, near San Francisco; this is a retreat for wealthy artists, writers and such aspiring artists and writers as can fork up the rent money.

My plan is to do expensive portraits ($150 and up), sell prints ($15 and up) to the tourists who flock in from all over the world. . . ."

The house in which Mr. Painter and his present wife live, compared with the well-kept Bannister home, exemplifies the contrasting ways of life. In his words "it is a very old and beat up and lovely . . ." They live in the rear part.

The interior is inexpensively but tastefully decorated. The large yard on a hill in the business district of Walnut Creek, California, is of uncut weeds and wild oats. The house "is not painted on the outside because I do not want it painted. I am very fond of the wood on the outside of the house."

The present Mrs. Painter has her master's degree in cinema design and apparently likes and has had considerable contact with children. She is anxious to have Mark in her home. Everything indicates she would provide a leveling influence on Mr. Painter and could ably care for Mark.

Mr. Painter is either an agnostic or atheist and has no concern for formal religious training. He has read a lot of Zen Buddhism and "has been very much influenced by it." Mrs. Painter is Roman Catholic. They plan to send Mark to a Congregational Church near the Catholic Church, on an irregular schedule.

He is a political liberal and got into difficulty in a job at the University of Washington for his support of the activities of the American Civil Liberties Union in the university news bulletin.

There were "two funerals" for his wife. One in the basement of his home in which he alone was present. He conducted the service and wrote her a long letter. The second at a church in Pullman was for the gratification of her friends. He attended in a sport shirt and sweater.

These matters are not related as a criticism of Mr. Painter's conduct, way of life or sense of values. An individual is free to choose his own values, within bounds, which are not exceeded here. They do serve, however, to support our conclusion as to the kind of life Mark would be exposed to in the Painter household. We believe it would be unstable, unconventional, arty, Bohemian, and probably intellectually stimulating.

Were the question simply which household would be the

most suitable in which to raise a child, we would have un
hesitatingly chosen the Bannister home. We believe securit
and stability in the home are more important than in
tellectual stimulation in the proper development of a child
There are, however, several factors which have made u
pause.

First, there is the presumption of parental preference
which though weakened in the past several years, exists b
statute.

We have a great deal of sympathy for a father, who in th
difficult period of adjustment following his wife's death, turn
to the maternal grandparents for their help and then find
them unwilling to return the child. There is no merit in th
Bannister claim that Mr. Painter permanently relinquishe
custody. It was intended to be a temporary arrangement.

A father should be encouraged to look for help with th
children from those who love them without the risk of there
by losing the custody of the children permanently. This fac
must receive consideration in cases of this kind.

However, as always, the primary consideration is the bes
interest of the child and if the return of custody to the fathe
is likely to have a seriously disrupting and disturbing effec
upon the child's development, this fact must prevail.

Second, Jeanne's will named her husband guardian of he
children and if he failed to qualify or ceased to act, name
her mother. The parent's wishes are entitled to consideration

Third, the Bannisters are 60 years old. By the time Mar
graduates from high school they will be over 70 years old
Care of young children is a strain on grandparents and Mrs
Bannister's letters indicate as much.

We have considered all of these factors and have con
cluded that Mark's best interest demands that his custod
remain with the Bannisters.

Mark was five when he came to their home. The evidenc
clearly shows he was not well adjusted at that time. He di
not distinguish fact from fiction and was inclined to tell "ta
tales" emphasizing the big "I." He was very aggressive to
ward smaller children, cruel to animals, not liked by his class
mates and did not seem to know what was acceptable con
duct.

As stated by one witness: "Mark knew where his freedon

was and he didn't know where his boundaries were." In two years he made a great deal of improvement. He now appears to be well-disciplined, happy, relatively secure and popular with his classmates, although still subject to more than normal anxiety.

We place a great deal of reliance on the testimony of Dr. Glenn R. Hawkes, a child psychologist. The trial court, in effect, disregarded Dr. Hawkes' opinions stating: "The court has given full consideration to the good doctor's testimony, but cannot accept it at full face value because of exaggerated statements and the witness' attitude on the stand."

We, of course, do not have the advantage of viewing the witness' conduct on the stand, but we have carefully reviewed his testimony and find nothing in the written record to justify such a summary dismissal of the opinions of this eminent child psychologist.

Dr. Hawkes is head of the Department of Child Development at Iowa State University. However, there is nothing in the record which suggests that his relationship with the Bannisters is such that his professional opinion would be influenced thereby. Child development is his specialty and he has written many articles and a textbook on the subject.

He is recognized nationally, having served on the staff of the 1960 White House Conference on Children and Youth and as consultant on a Ford Foundation program concerning youth in India. He is now education consultant on the project "Headstart." He has taught and lectured at many universities and belongs to many professional associations. He works with the Iowa Children's Home Society in placement problems. Further detailing of his qualifications is unnecessary.

Between June 15 and the time of trial, he spent approximately 25 hours acquiring information about Mark and the Bannisters, including appropriate testing of and "depth interviews" with Mark. Dr. Hawkes' testimony covers 70 pages of the record and it is difficult to pinpoint any bit of testimony which precisely summarizes his opinion.

He places great emphasis on the "father figure" and discounts the importance of the "biological father." "The father figure is a figure that the child sees as an authority figure, as a helper, he is a nutrient figure, and one who typifies maleness as far as the child is concerned."

His investigation revealed: ". . . the strength of the father figure before Mark came to the Bannisters is very unclear. Mark is confused about the father figure prior to his contact with Mr. Bannister." Now, "Mark used Mr. Bannister as his father figure. This is very evident. It shows up in the depth interview, and it shows up in the description of Mark's life given by Mark. He has a very warm feeling for Mr. Bannister."

Dr. Hawkes concluded that it was not for Mark's best interest to be removed from the Bannister home. He is criticized for reaching this conclusion without investigating the Painter home or finding out more about Mr. Painter's character. He answered:

"I was most concerned about the welfare of the child, not the welfare of Mr. Painter, not about the welfare of the Bannisters. Inasmuch as Mark has already made an adjustment and sees the Bannisters as his parental figures in his psychological makeup, to me this is the most critical factor.

"Disruption at this point, I think, would be detrimental to the child even though Mr. Painter might well be a paragon of virtue. I think this would be a kind of thing which would not be in the best interest of the child. I think knowing something about where the child is at the present time is vital. I think something about where he might go, in my way of thinking is essentially untenable to me, and relatively unimportant. It isn't even helpful.

"The thing I was most concerned about was Mark's view of his own reality in which he presently lives. If this is destroyed I think it will have rather bad effects on Mark. I think then if one were to make a determination whether it would be to the parents' household, or the McNelly household, or X-household, then I think the further study would be appropriate."

Dr. Hawkes stated: "I am appalled at the tremendous task Mr. Painter would have if Mark were to return to him because he has got to build the relationship from scratch. There is essentially nothing on which to build at the present time. Mark is aware Mr. Painter is his father, but he is not very clear about what this means. In his own mind the father figure is Mr. Bannister. I think it would take a very strong person with everything in his favor in order to build a relationship as Mr. Painter would have to build at this point with Mark."

It was Dr. Hawkes' opinion "the chances are very high [Mark] will go wrong if he is returned to his father." This is based on adoption studies which "establish that the majority of adoptions in children who are changed, from ages six to eight, will go bad, if they have had a prior history of instability, some history of prior movement. When I refer to instability I am referring to where there has been no attempt to establish a strong relationship."

Although this is not an adoption, the analogy seems appropriate, for Mark who had a history of instability would be removed from the only home in which he has a clearly established "father figure" and placed with his natural father about whom his feelings are unclear.

We know more of Mr. Painter's way of life than Dr. Hawkes. We have concluded that it does not offer as great a stability or security as the Bannister home. Throughout his testimony he emphasized Mark's need at this critical time is stability. He has it in the Bannister home.

Other items of Dr. Hawkes' testimony which have a bearing on our decision follow. He did not consider the Bannisters' age anyway disqualifying. He was of the opinion that Mark could adjust to a change more easily later on, if one became necessary, when he would have better control over his environment.

He believes the presence of other children in the home would have a detrimental effect upon Mark's adjustment whether this occurred in the Bannister home or the Painter home.

The trial court does not say which of Dr. Hawkes' statements he felt were exaggerated. We were most surprised at the inconsequential position to which he relegated the "biological father."

He concedes "child psychologists are less concerned about natural parents than probably other groups are." We are not inclined to so lightly value the role of the natural father, but find much reason for his evaluation of this particular case.

Mark has established a father-son relationship with Mr. Bannister, which he apparently had never had with his natural father. He is happy, well adjusted and progressing nicely in his development. We do not believe it is for Mark's best interests to take him out of this stable atmosphere in the face of warnings of dire consequences from an eminent child psychologist and send him to an uncertain future in his father's home.

Regardless of our appreciation of the father's love for his child and his desire to have him with him, we do not believe we have the moral right to gamble with this child's future. He should be encouraged in every way possible to know his father. We are sure there are many ways in which Mr. Painter can enrich Mark's life.

For the reasons stated, we reverse the trial court and remand the case for judgment in accordance herewith.

REVERSED AND REMANDED